Not Weary of Well Doing

Not Weary of Well Doing

Essays in Honor of Cecil W. Stalnaker

EDITED BY
Thomas J. Marinello and
H. H. Drake Williams III

WIPF & STOCK · Eugene, Oregon

NOT WEARY OF WELL DOING
Essays in Honor of Cecil W. Stalnaker

Copyright © 2013 Thomas J. Marinello and H. H. Drake Williams III. All rights reserved. Except for brief quotations in critical publications or reviews, no part of this book may be reproduced in any manner without prior written permission from the publisher. Write: Permissions, Wipf and Stock Publishers, 199 W. 8th Ave., Suite 3, Eugene, OR 97401.

Wipf & Stock
An Imprint of Wipf and Stock Publishers
199 W. 8th Ave., Suite 3
Eugene, OR 97401
www.wipfandstock.com

ISBN 13: 978-1-62032-363-2
Manufactured in the U.S.A.

Unless otherwise indicated, all Scripture quotations are from The Holy Bible, English Standard Version® (ESV®), copyright © 2001 by Crossway, a publishing ministry of Good News Publishers. Used by permission. All rights reserved.

Scripture quotations in chapter 5 are from the New Revised Standard Version Bible, copyright © 1989 National Council of the Churches of Christ in the United States of America. Used by permission. All rights reserved.

Contents

DEDICATION vii
    Jeffrey J. Seume
FOREWORD ix
    Thomas J. Marinello
    H. H. Drake Williams III
CHAPTERS
    Ellis R. Brotzman   1
        The Need for Missions and Evangelism:
        An Exegetical and Theological Study of Genesis 3
    Peter J. Hays   22
        When is the Task of Gospel Ministry Complete?
    H. H. Drake Williams III   43
        Obstacles for a Church Planter:
        Paul's Greatest Struggles in Planting the Church at Corinth
    Edward M. Curtis   63
        God's Word and Life as it was Meant to Be
    Jordan M. Scheetz   77
        Christian Preaching and the Old Testament
    Gerald C. Ericson   100
        Recognizing and Affirming the Personhood of
        the Senior Adult in the Church
    Thomas J. Marinello   124
        Development of the *Evangelische Christengemeenten Vlaanderen*:
        Its Characterization, Rapid Growth, and Relationship with the
        Flemish Roman Catholic Church
    Philip A. Gottschalk   148
        Can a Christian Defend the Death Penalty Rationally?
CONTRIBUTORS   189

Dedication

It is my privilege to write the dedication for this *festschrift*, written in honor of my friend and former colleague, Dr. Cecil W. Stalnaker. Throughout the nearly fifteen years that I served with him at Tyndale Theological Seminary, Cecil proved himself to be one of the most committed, hard-working, dependable, humble-spirited, and godly men I have had the opportunity to work alongside. He has been an excellent teacher, appreciated by his students and fellow faculty members alike. His commitment to the Lord, His Church, and to the mission of the Church has been exemplary. He will be greatly missed by all at Tyndale as he ends his decades of fulltime service in Europe and returns to the U.S.

Cecil is also a very wise man, one whose balanced perspectives and contributions as a member of the seminary's leadership team were much appreciated. I valued his counsel, time and time again, on issues that we faced at the school through the years.

Finally, I loved Cecil's dry wit and sense of humor. Few people I've known have made me laugh like Cecil.

As you read the essays which follow, I pray that you will be moved to deeper commitment to the great work of world missions, the work to which Cecil has given his life. I know that would please him, and His Lord, very much.

Jeffrey J. Seume, DMin
Past President, Tyndale Theological Seminary, The Netherlands

Foreword

William Tyndale was an English Reformer in the sixteenth century. He was an outstanding scholar of the original languages. For him as well as other Reformers, the entire Bible was the first and only authority for faith and practice. For this reason, William Tyndale labored to put the Scripture in the language of the people so that every man, woman, and child could have access to it in the English language.

He was determined with this desire to make the Scriptures accessible. On one occasion in the early sixteenth century, Tyndale found himself responding to a learned clergyman. This man claimed that people were better with the Pope than with the Scriptures. To this, Tyndale replied famously, "I defy the Pope and all his laws. If God spare my life ere many years, I will cause a boy that driveth the plough shall know more of the scripture than thou dost."

This determination for making the Scripture accessible continues at a school that bears this Reformer's name, Tyndale Theological Seminary in Badhoevedorp, The Netherlands. Founded in 1985 by Dr. Arthur Johnston and encouraged by Billy Graham, Tyndale Theological Seminary has been equipping international Christian leaders so that the Scriptures can be understood better worldwide. Since 1985, Tyndale has graduated over 250 students who have gone to serve the Lord in over 70 different countries.

One of the main contributors on the faculty over the years has been Dr. Cecil W. Stalnaker, Department Chair and Senior Professor of Intercultural Studies and Practical Ministry. At the age of 19, Cecil came to know Christ as Lord and Savior. After two years of university, he entered active military service with the U.S. Navy. During this time, he was discipled in Christ through Campus Crusade for Christ. Upon completion of his military active duty, he enrolled at Biola University, where he sensed

Foreword

God calling him to vocational Christian work. Marrying Kathleen Browning and starting seminary brought new opportunities for ministry—an internship at Bethany Baptist Church in California. Upon completion of this two-year training, he became part of the staff ministering to young adults while in seminary. They joined Greater Europe Mission in 1976. Cecil, Kathy, and their eight-month old daughter eventually ended up in French-speaking Belgium, where they served the Lord from 1978 to 1996. Cecil gave the majority of his ministry time to training church leaders at the *Institut Biblique Belge* and in church planting. In 1997, the Stalnakers moved to the ministry at Tyndale Theological Seminary. During his tenure, Cecil was the Chairman of the Department of Intercultural Studies and Practical Ministries. In this role, he designed and oversaw both the student internship program and the spiritual formation program. While both were first-rate, the outstanding caliber of the spiritual formation program was such that the Dutch governmental accreditation agency noted it for special recognition. Besides teaching at Tyndale, Cecil taught periodically at the *Teoloska Biblijsika Akademiha* in Croatia, and has taught courses at The Master's College and Seminary in California.

Since moving to the Netherlands, Cecil also has been active in the leadership of and preaching at Trinity International Church in Leidschendam, a city next to The Hague. Further, he has made time to compose a number of well-written, practical articles which have appeared in such journals as *Le Messager Evangelique, The Master's Journal*, and the *Evangelical Missions Quarterly*, in addition to contributing chapters of books dealing with missions and evangelism.

It is in honor of this beloved colleague's return to the U.S. after decades of ministry in Europe that the volume is named *Not Weary of Well Doing*. This was a phrase coined by William Tyndale in his translation of the New Testament in Galatians 6:9: "Let us not be wery of well doynge. For when the tyme is come we shall repe with out werines." And indeed Cecil has served faithfully and tirelessly, leaving the results of his work to the Lord. It speaks volumes of his efforts that Tyndale will look for two faculty members to do his work after his return to the U.S. The essays which follow are a collection which draws from all the academic departments of Tyndale. Some are quite practical, some are more academic, and one is a historical case study. All, however, are focused in some manner on missions or local church ministry.

Foreword

Perhaps a fitting end to this foreword is to quote one of the contributors to this volume:

> It is a pleasure to offer something for inclusion in a volume honoring Cecil Stalnaker for his contributions to ministry over these thirty-plus years. As I considered a topic for such an article, I could not imagine anything more appropriate than to reflect on the benefits of Scripture—something that has been the driving force behind this work and ministry. Cecil and Kathy Stalnaker exemplify the truth of these principles, as do many of those into whose life they have poured themselves in ministry.

Thomas J. Marinello, PhD
H. H. Drake Williams III, PhD

The Need for Missions and Evangelism: An Exegetical and Theological Study of Genesis 3

ELLIS R. BROTZMAN

The average believer might associate the mandate for missionary activity and evangelism with the Great Commission that is clearly found in Matthew 28:16–20, and that passage is certainly one of the most well-known biblical anchor points for the task that has been assigned to Christ's church. But when we ask why that endeavor is necessary, the answer is found in the earliest pages of Scripture. The thesis of this chapter is that both the need for God's redemptive work and the initial promise of that work are found clearly portrayed in the text of Genesis 3.

Structure and Content of Genesis

The main organizing scheme for the book of Genesis seems to be the repeated use of the *toledoth* formula.[1] This formula is found in eleven passages in Genesis, but the double use in Genesis 36 should probably be taken to indicate a single section rather than two separate sections.[2] The use of

---

1. *Toledoth* is an approximate transliteration of the Hebrew term תּוֹלְדֹת. The word is spelled in a variety of ways in the Hebrew text of Genesis. The italicized term will be used throughout this chapter, but perhaps a word is in order about how it should be translated. English versions usually opt for generations, account, or story. But a paraphrase may be more helpful, because the term introduces the subsequent developments in the course of a particular genealogical line. Thus, the *toledoth* of Adam (Gen 5:1) tells the genealogical development of Adam's line; i.e., what happened to his descendants.

2. The formula is found in Genesis 2:4; 5:1; 6:9; 10:1; 11:10, 27; 25:12, 19; 36:1, 9; 37:2. The word *toledoth* is also found in Genesis 10:32 and 25:13, but it is not the formulaic use.

this formula yields the following global structure for Genesis: a prologue (Gen 1:1–2:3), which contains the account of creation, followed by ten sections that are all introduced by closely similar versions of the formula. The sections, references, titles, and main contents are shown in Table 1.

Table 1

Sections	References	Titles	Main Contents
Prologue	Gen 1:1–2:3	Creation Account	Creation of the Cosmos
Section 1	Gen 2:4–4:26	*Toledoth* of the heavens and the earth	Mainly narrative with short genealogy
Section 2	Gen 5:1–6:8	*Toledoth* of Adam	Mainly genealogy with short narrative
Section 3	Gen 6:9–9:29	*Toledoth* of Noah	Flood narrative
Section 4	Gen 10:1–11:9	*Toledoth* of the sons of Noah	Short narrative and extensive genealogy
Section 5	Gen 11:10–26	*Toledoth* of Shem	Genealogy
Section 6	Gen 11:27–25:11	*Toledoth* of Terah	Narrative (Abraham)
Section 7	Gen 25:12–18	*Toledoth* of Ishmael	Genealogy
Section 8	Gen 25:19–35:29	*Toledoth* of Isaac	Narrative (Jacob)
Section 9	Gen 36:1–37:1	*Toledoth* of Esau[3]	Expanded Genealogy
Section 10	Gen 37:2–50:26	*Toledoth* of Jacob	Narrative (Joseph)

Implications of the Global Structure of Genesis

The use of the *Toledoth* formula throughout Genesis clearly indicates that the book has a unified outlook. Students of this first book of Scripture often title the first eleven chapters as "primeval history" and chapters 12 through 50 as "patriarchal history."[4] For the purposes of this chapter, we will refer

---

3. This Toledoth is actually given in two parts. The Toledoth formula is found in both 36:1 and 9, but both parts have to do with Esau and his descendants.

4. See Tremper Longman III, *How to Read Genesis* (Downers Grove, IL: InterVarsity Press, 2003), 64, although he divides 12 through 50 into two sections: Patriarchal Narratives (12–36) and the Joseph Story (37–50).

The Need for Missions and Evangelism

to chapters 1 through 11 as "The Early History of the Human Race," and chapters 12 through 50 as "The Early History of the Nation of Israel." The scope of chapters 1–11 includes all nations, but the focus narrows in chapters 12–50 to Abraham and his descendants. But the two sections are to be seen as parts of a whole, unequal in length, that serves as a kind of introduction to the biblical corpus. Genesis and Revelation share a certain kind of canonical uniqueness; Genesis opens the biblical canon, and Revelation closes it.

Theological Reflections on the Creation Account (Gen 1:1–2:3)

Much has been written about the meaning and the implications of the creation account that is given in Genesis 1:1–2:3. The interest here is not to enter into the controversy of precisely how the creation was accomplished. Rather, it is to trace the theological emphases that are apparent in the passage. The passage mentions God (אֱלֹהִים) thirty-five times, something which may indicate that the theology of the chapter has more to do with revealing the nature of the Creator and less to do with the detailed mechanics of creation. The portrait of God as Creator in Genesis 1 emphasizes his speech. Each of the six days of creation features God speaking.[5] This divine speech brings various parts of the created order into existence.[6] The speech in relation to the creation of man and woman is especially noteworthy. In Genesis 1:26, we read that "God said, 'Let us make man in our image, after our likeness.'"[7] This passage presents a dialogue or a deliberation within the godhead that prefaces the creation of man and woman, and this feature serves to highlight the greater importance that humans would play within the created order on earth.

A second feature of God as Creator that is emphasized in this passage is his evaluative capacity. At various stages in his creative work, we read

---

5. God blesses the seventh day, and earlier occasions of blessing were associated with the verb אמר, "to say." On the seventh day, however, the verb "to bless" is used alone.

6. This creation by divine word (*fiat* creation) serves as an important distinction between the Old Testament account of creation and the corresponding accounts of creation now known that originated in the cultural context in which ancient Israel may be situated. Many of those accounts featured creation by combat between various gods. See, for example, the treatment of Alexander Heidel, *The Babylonian Genesis*, 2nd ed. (Chicago: University of Chicago Press, 1951).

7. All citations of Scripture in this chapter are from the ESV, unless otherwise indicated.

that "God saw that it [some feature of the created order] was good." And in Genesis 1:31, we read that ". . . God saw all that He had made, and behold, it was very good." All parts of the created order, including mankind, were functioning as God had intended. Here already is a hint regarding the need for redemption, for our world as it now operates is anything but "very good." Paul's comment in Romans 8:23 that "the whole creation has been groaning together in the pains of childbirth" highlights the horrific change between the creation as it came from the hand of God and creation as it came to be subsequently.

A final feature that is stressed in the creation account is how God communicates with his human creatures and what he communicates to them. When God created the sea creatures and birds, he blessed them. In other words, he conveyed to them the ability to be fruitful and multiply (Gen 1:22). He spoke a similar blessing to the first humans, but the manner in which he did so was much more emphatic and personal. He simply made a general pronouncement of blessing to the sea creatures and birds (Gen 1:22). In the case of the first humans, however, he said to them (spoke to them directly, communicated with them; cf. the precise wording of Gen 1:28), "Be fruitful and multiply, and fill the earth." This fact of God's desire to communicate with his human creatures and their ability to receive that communication from him testifies eloquently to the importance of the first man and woman about God's plans for His creation.

So the major emphases of the theology of Genesis 1:1—2:3 are that God simply spoke the created order into being. He evaluated that initial creation and pronounced its various stages good, and he even pronounced it all very good at its conclusion. He was involved in direct and personal communication with his human creatures, those who were made in his image and likeness, so that they could enjoy fellowship with him and serve him in the created order.

The *Toledoth* of the Heavens and the Earth (Gen 2:4–4:26)

This *toledoth* section is unique in Genesis because it is the only one that does not use a person's name following the word *toledoth* in the construct state. The "heavens and the earth" are not viewed literally as somehow engendering the early history of the human race. The term must clearly be seen as used metaphorically in this passage. The reader of this portion of Scripture is immediately struck by an intriguing change in the form of reference to the deity. In Genesis 1:1–2:3, the deity was exclusively referred to as God (אֱלֹהִים) a total of thirty-five times. Beginning in Genesis 2:4, however, the deity is referred to as the Lord God (יהוה אֱלֹהִים).[8] This compound name for God is not used frequently in the Old Testament, but there are twenty uses of the name in Genesis 2 and 3.[9] Students of the Old Testament used to consider that the different names of God used in Genesis were a signal of different documents that had been combined to form the book as we know it today.[10] But more recent study has recognized that each of the names usually carries a specific theological meaning or emphasis. The Hebrew word אֱלֹהִים, which is used for God, is found in passages where God's majesty, greatness, and power are emphasized. This name is obviously very appropriate in Genesis 1:1–2:3 where it is used without exception in the account of the creation of the entire universe. The name YHWH, whose significance was explained to Moses in Exodus 3:12–14, is the personal name of Israel's God, and it is used in contexts where his intimate and personal ways are being stressed. In his own mouth, the name is *I AM*, but in the mouths of his people, it becomes *HE IS*. This conveys not just an idea of static existence; it stresses his active presence. *HE IS*, and *HE IS WITH* Moses and even with Moses' mouth (Exod. 3:12 and 4:12). This name is surely more suitable in the portion of Genesis that speaks of the details of YHWH God's creation of the man and woman and his personal interaction with them.[11] The attentive reader will have noticed that the name used 20 times in Genesis 3–4 is not just יהוה (Lord), but יהוה אֱלֹהִים (the Lord God). The reason for its use in these chapters is doubtless that the writer wants to clarify that the Creator of the universe is none other than the God who had revealed himself to the nation of Israel as their personal Lord (יהוה).[12]

8. The divine name יהוה is written without vowel signs, since the name was pronounced אֲדֹנָי, *Adonay*, by religious Jews throughout the ages. The form given in the Masoretic text actually represents a *qere perpetuum*, a perpetual *qere*; that is, an alternate reading tradition. There is some question as to the name's original pronunciation, but YaHWeH is most likely correct.

9. The name is used only 38 times in the OT. The statistics are: Genesis (20); Exodus (1); 2 Samuel (1); 2 Kings (1); 1 Chronicles (4); 2 Chronicles (5); Psalms (6); Jeremiah (1); Jonah (1).

10. Thus, portions using אֱלֹהִים were supposed to represent a document E, while portions using יהוה were thought to represent a document J.

11. A similar change of divine name is observed in Psalm 19. Verse 1 says that the heavens declare the glory of God (Heb. אֵל, a singular form similar to אֱלֹהִים in usage). Verse 8, however, speaks of the law (תּוֹרָה, teaching) of the Lord (יהוה).

12. Umberto Cassuto, *From Adam to Noah*, trans. I. Abrams (Jerusalem: Magnes

This portion of Genesis, the Toledoth of the Heavens and the Earth, is made up of at least three units. Genesis 2:4–25, though often seen as a "second" creation account, is actually a more in-depth treatment of additional details of the creation of man and woman on the sixth day of the week of God's creating. In terms of a modern analogy, this passage is like a slow-motion replay of an important play in a televised sporting event. The passage highlights even more the Lord God's gracious provision for the first man and woman. He created them so that they might complement each other, and that together they might serve him as his viceregents in the world that he had created for them to inhabit. The passage closes with the statement that the man and woman "were both naked and were not ashamed" (Gen 2:25)." The statement seems to underscore and even extend the "very good" evaluation of creation from the previous chapter (Gen 1:31).

The second unit of this *Toledoth* is Genesis 3:1–24. It has been traditionally called "The Fall," and it is without doubt one of the most tragic and strategic chapters of Scripture. In the following section, this chapter will be studied in detail. Cassuto and Wenham each offers a more detailed view of the structure of this portion of Scripture. Both see a development in sevens: seven paragraphs (Cassuto) or seven scenes (Wenham).[13] Although their sets of seven do not fully coincide, both ways of representing the structure of the section have merit. The final unit of the *Toledoth* of the Heavens and the Earth is 4:1–26, although the chapter contains at least three distinct sub-units: (1) The Life of Cain and Abel (4:1–16); (2) The Life of Cain and His Descendants (4:17–24); and (3) The Line of Seth (4:25–26). For the purposes of giving the context for Genesis 3, however, the less detailed three-part structure suggested above will suffice. Genesis 2:4–25 gives the additional details that are necessary to flesh out the fuller understanding of how God created the first humans. Chapter 3 then focuses on what initially took place in the garden where the Lord God had placed the man and woman that he had created. Then, chapter 4 shows the further development of sin and its consequences in the earliest stages of the growth of the human race.

Press, 1961), 86–88.

13. Cassuto, *From Adam to Noah*, 96–172. His seven paragraphs cover Genesis 2:4–3:24. G. Wenham, *Genesis 1–15* (Waco: Word Books, 1987), 50. His seven scenes cover the same part of the *toledoth* of the heavens and the earth (2:4–3:24).

An Exegetical and Theological Study of Genesis 3

Structural Analysis. If we focus on the difference between "pure" narrative (description of events) and narrative that includes reported speech (dialogue), the chapter may conveniently be broken down into a series of main scenes: (1) the serpent tempts the woman and the man (vv. 1–5); (2) the woman and man partake of the fruit and experience the consequences of that act (vv. 6–8); (3) YHWH God interrogates the man and the woman (vv. 9–13); (3) YHWH God pronounces judgment on the serpent, the woman, and the man (vv. 14–19); (4) the man names his wife, and YHWH God provides clothing for the man and the woman (vv. 20–21); and (5) YHWH God expels man and woman from the garden (vv. 22–24).[14]

The Temptation of the Woman and the Man (Gen 3:1–5). The chapter begins with a disjunctive clause, "Now (or but), the serpent . . . ."[15] This creature was not previously mentioned in the account of creation, but here he enters the scene in a very striking manner and begins a dialogue with the woman. The identity of this creature is certainly one of the cruxes of the passage. The use of the definite article with this first mention of the Serpent[16] is an unusual feature at this point in the Genesis account. In chapter 1, the pattern was regularly that the first mention of an entity was made without the article, and subsequent mentions had the definite article.[17] But here at the beginning of Genesis 3, the Serpent is directly introduced into the account with the definite article. Such usage serves to emphasize the importance of this creature to the development of the narrative account. In trying to pin down an identity for the Serpent, it will be convenient to consider first the immediate context, and then the rest of Scripture.

The identity of the Serpent in the immediate context is cloaked in mystery. He is said to be "more crafty" than any of the animals of the field that YHWH God had made.[18] And he manifests the ability, not just to speak,

---

14. Wenham, *Genesis 1–15*, 50, suggests a similar structure, although he combines vv. 14–19 and 20–21 as a single section. The titles he assigns to the sections are much briefer than the ones listed above.

15. Heb. וְהַנָּחָשׁ. Wenham, *Genesis 1–15*, 47, calls it an "episode-initial circumstantial clause."

16. I capitalize Serpent because I take the creature to be more than a simple snake. See discussion to follow.

17. This practice can be observed with light (vv. 3–4), atmosphere [ESV translates "expanse"] (vv. 6–7), light-bearers (vv. 14–16), and even mankind (vv. 26–27).

18. The Hebrew is עָרוּם. BDB, 791, offers possible meanings of "crafty, shrewd,

but to initiate a reasoned dialogue with the woman. His discussion with the woman speaks of what God had said to the man (and, by implication, to the woman as well) at an earlier moment in the account. The combination of these aspects of his nature suggests strongly that the Serpent is more than just a snake.[19] In Genesis 2, it was clearly shown that there was no "suitable helper" to be found for the man among the animals of the field. This must have to do, at a minimum, with the animals not having the ability to speak, that is, to enter into communication with the man. The further development of the passage clarifies that the Serpent is an enemy of both YHWH God and the man and woman. His aim in the encounter in the garden was to drive a wedge between YHWH God and his human creatures and, in this way, to attempt to frustrate God's sovereign purposes.

Does the rest of Scripture help narrow down the issue of the identity of the Serpent? A look at two key passages seems to yield additional information. Paul writes in Romans 16:20 that "the God of peace will soon crush Satan under your feet." This passage seems to be making an allusion to the wording of Genesis 3:15 (to be further discussed below), and the allusion points to the identification of the Serpent of Genesis 3 as Satan. The language of Revelation 12:9 seems to move in the same direction when it refers to ". . . the great dragon . . . , the serpent of old who is called the devil and Satan." So it would seem clear that the Serpent of Genesis 3 is none other than the being referred to in other portions of Scripture as the devil or Satan. As to mechanism, he was either using (possessing) a physical serpent as a means of appearing to the woman and man, or he may have simply appeared to them in the form of a physical serpent (snake), just as he is able to appear as "an angel of light" (2 Cor 11:14). The latter option makes it easier to understand the curse pronounced later in the chapter as falling exclusively on the Serpent—i.e., Satan. The other option requires

---

sensible." The word occurs a total of 11 times in the OT. It is used with a positive sense in Proverbs, but with a negative sense in Job. It is not used of an animal in any of its occurrences outside of this one text in Genesis. Here in Genesis 3, the rest of the chapter will make clear that the negative sense is appropriate.

19. Some English versions seem to imply a mere snake; cf. ESV's rendering "more crafty than any *other* beast" (emphasis added). NIV renders "more crafty than any of the wild animals," which at least leaves open the possibility that the serpent is no ordinary snake. Cassuto, *From Adam to Noah*, 140, citing ancient Talmudic sources, sees the serpent as "just a species of animal," although he notes the difficulty that this view encounters with the mention of speech along with the knowledge that the creature has of the Lord God's purposes. But later on, he confuses the picture even more by suggesting that the serpent's speech is in reality the woman's own internal speech in her heart.

a parceling out of the words of the curse to physical serpents as well as to Satan.

The Serpent enters into a dialogue with the woman in the form of a question: "Did God actually say, 'You shall not eat from any tree in the garden?'"[20] The verb here ("you shall not eat") is plural. Even though the serpent directed his question to the woman, it appears that Adam was included in the Serpent's overall focus. Now the Serpent's dialogue is anything but innocent. He is guilty of introducing a number of elements of distortion into his question. Genesis 2:16 records that YHWH God "commanded" the man not to eat of the tree of the knowledge of good and evil, but the Serpent's question asks whether God had *said* something. The Serpent diluted the force of YHWH God's command by not using the verb that the narrator had used in Genesis 2:16. In addition, YHWH God's prohibition of the eating of the fruit of one tree was given in the context of a very generous provision for man and woman to eat from the fruit of any and all other trees. The Serpent, however, was silent regarding this divine provision. In addition, the Serpent refers to the divine being as God, not as YHWH God. It is certainly appropriate for the Serpent to use this designation for the deity since he obviously had no intimate relation with YHWH, but his use of this generic way of referring to God was a clear distortion of the warm relationship that the man and woman enjoyed with the Lord God.

A final element of distortion can be seen in the Serpent's question. It is focused only on the prohibition that YHWH God had expressed, and yet it gives the prohibition an exaggerated extent when it applies the prohibition to "all trees" rather than the one tree whose fruit YHWH God had prohibited. So the Serpent weakened the sense of the command; he ignored the rich provision that had been made; he sought to portray the Lord God as a distant and uncaring deity; and he exaggerated the original prohibition. The result of it all was to encourage the woman and the man to question and doubt what the Lord God had said. In passing, this passage has great practical importance for every believer living today. We can be sure that whenever we face the temptations of the enemy of our souls, we will encounter his crafty distortions that are aimed at leading us to doubting what the Lord God has said to us in his Word.

---

20. What the Serpent said is not explicitly marked as a question in the Hebrew text, but most English and Spanish versions treat it as a question. The LXX understands it as a question and renders τί ὅτι εἶπεν ὁ θεός, "Why did God say . . . ?"

Not Weary of Well Doing

The woman's initial response to the Serpent's dialogue did not accurately represent her relationship to God, for she adopted one of the Serpent's distortions when she referred to the deity as God instead of YHWH God. She also misconstrued what the Lord God had said, for she carelessly reported what God had said, and she even added to what God had said. In her response to the Serpent's temptation, she said that she and her husband could eat from the fruit of the trees. She failed to specify that they were able to eat from *all* the trees of the garden, and she also failed to mention that they were able to eat *freely* from all of those trees. Furthermore, she accepted what the Serpent had said when she spoke of God's *saying* instead of *commanding* them not to eat of the fruit of one specific tree. In the way she spoke of God, she was ignoring his nature as a loving God who sought to intimately enter into the lives of his people and to provide for their needs. Finally, the woman failed to report accurately what God had said in regard to death. The Lord God had specified that they would "surely die" if they ate of the fruit of the prohibited tree. The woman did not express the sense that they would surely die; she simply said that they were not to eat *lest* they should happen to die. In addition to these failures of accuracy, the woman added something that the Lord God had not said when she said that they were not to *touch* the fruit of the prohibited tree. While we might think the woman's words were a logical extension of the divine prohibition, she still added a stipulation that the Lord God had not commanded. Sadly, the woman is an example of the seriously flawed approach to the words of God that is described in several places in Scripture: she both took away from and added to what God had said (Deut 4:2; 12:32 [MT 13:1]; Prov 30:6; Rev 22:18–19).

The Serpent's response to the woman's wavering stance on what God had said was to be even more severe. Where he initially questioned what God had said, now he categorically denied what God had said. Eve left out the "surely" of God's command, and the serpent put it back in—while simultaneously denying its truth—and thus he expressed an outright denial of what God had spoken: "You will not surely die." In addition, he attacked the very character of God by introducing doubt in relation to the nature of God. He essentially said to the woman that God was stingy and self-serving when he suggested that God was seeking to keep the woman and the man from experiencing something that sounded very positive and could have added something of value to their existence. The serpent's words also represented a mixture of truth and falsehood, and that mixture proved to be deceptive and deadly. The man and woman would indeed have their eyes opened, but the result would not be what the Serpent promised. Indeed, how could the creature's disobedience to the Creator's command result in their becoming like God the Creator?

Eating the Fruit and its Consequences (Gen 3:6–8). In verses 6 to 8, the narrator describes in economical but very forceful language how the woman was brought to eat of the forbidden fruit. This portion of the chapter features only "pure narrative;" there is no reported speech of any of the participants.[21] The narrator first describes how the woman perceived the fruit. She "saw" the fruit; that is, she observed the fruit and reached certain conclusions about its nature. Her first conclusion was that the fruit was "good for food." This conclusion was very likely true. There is no indication in the text that the fruit of the forbidden tree was poisonous or would produce even the slightest physical harm to one who ate it. Second, she concluded that the tree was "desireable to the eyes;" that is, it was pleasant to look at. Again, the woman was very probably correct. The trees that God had created were certainly not ugly trees, trees that would have produced revulsion in the observer. While the woman was correct in her reasoning in these first two areas, she was sadly and completely mistaken in her third conclusion, that the tree was "desired to make one wise." The language of this phrase is difficult to render accurately in an English translation. This is true, first, because the word translated "desirable" is likely much stronger. The same Hebrew word is related to the verb used in the tenth commandment, "You must not *covet* your neighbor's house . . ." (Exod 20:17, emphasis added).[22] Since "covetable" is not ordinarily used in an adjectival form in English, perhaps the best that can be done is to translate it as "extraordinarily or inordinately or dangerously desirable."

In addition, the word translated above as "wise" reflects a single Hebrew word. The semantic range of this Hebrew term is wider than any single English equivalent can represent, so a doubled English rendering, "prudently wise," might be more appropriate. Prudent wisdom, or the wisdom that leads to a prudent lifestyle, can never be attained when the creature goes against the teaching given by the Lord God, the Creator. Because her reasoning was flawed in this third area, the woman's overall judgment of the situation with the fruit of the tree was completely erroneous.

---

21. Cf. Wenham, *Genesis 1–15*, 50.

22. The word is וְנֶחְמָד, a niphal participle. The form used in the tenth commandment is לֹא תַחְמֹד, "you must not covet."

The latter half of verse 6 reports the woman's actions that were based on her faulty reasoning. First, "she took and ate of its fruit." With unbelievable economy, the narrator reports her actions. Derek Kidner's comment on these words is still one of the most helpful: "So simple the act, so hard its undoing. God will taste poverty and death before 'take and eat' become words of salvation."[23] After she ate the fruit, the woman "also gave some to her husband, who was with her, and he ate." This statement reads almost like an afterthought to the reasoned analysis of the woman that led to her eating of the fruit, but the deed was done. The reader is then left with the question of what would happen to the Lord God's purposes for creation and for his human creatures.

The consequences of their eating of the forbidden fruit were immediate and multiple. First, the narrator tells us that their eyes were opened. To a degree, then, the words of the Serpent were correct, but the further consequence of their eyes being opened was not what the Serpent had promised. The Serpent had promised that they would become "like God," but the result of their eyes being opened led to their knowing that they were naked. Before eating, they had been "naked and not ashamed" (Gen 2:25). Now, their eyes were opened and they knew that they were naked. The implication of the text seems to be that they were also ashamed. The further consequence of their eating was that they sewed fig leaves into some sort of aprons that they used in an attempt to cover their newly perceived nakedness.

The additional consequence described in verse 8 is perhaps the most significant. They heard the sound of YHWH God walking in the garden in the "cool of the day." As traditionally understood, this phrase refers to a particular time of the day during which the Lord God would make Himself available to his human creatures for interaction. As a result of their eating of the forbidden fruit, the man and woman no longer looked forward to interaction with their Creator. As the text adds, "the man and his wife hid themselves from the presence of the Lord God among the trees of the garden." As the man would later explain, they attempted to hide because of their fear.

There may be more involved in the wording of this verse than what the traditional interpretation leads the reader to understand. The Hebrew wording of verse 8 that has given rise to the traditional translation "in the cool of the day" is לְרוּחַ הַיּוֹם. Jeffrey Niehaus has argued that the word יוֹם in

---

23. Derek Kidner, *Genesis* (Chicago: InterVarsity Press, 1967), 68.

The Need for Missions and Evangelism

this verse should not be translated "day," but rather "storm."[24] This translation is based on the fact that there are two different Akkadian words that are cognate to Hebrew יוֹם: first, the most common, yielding the translation "day," and a second, yielding the translation "storm."[25] If this alternate understanding of the word יוֹם is adopted, then the passage may be rendered as follows: they heard the sound of YHWH God walking in the garden in the "wind of the storm." Niehaus suggests that the "the storm wind is the advancing of Yahweh" as "He advances . . . in judgment . . . ."[26] Such a rendering may more accurately portray the setting in the garden as the man and woman try to hide from the Lord God who is coming in judgment.

YHWH God's Interrogation of the Man and the Woman (Gen 3:9–13). This section again features the dialogue of the participants within the narrative. The Lord God first initiated an interrogation of the man. The text says that "the Lord God called to the man and said to him, 'Where are you?'" We should not view this passage as describing some sort of cosmic game of hide and seek. Nor is the deity asking the man for information. The question is surely rhetorical and seeks to elicit from the man an acknowledgement of his guilt due to having eaten of the forbidden fruit. The man's reply, however, is anything but a recognition of his own responsibility. He does not answer the Lord God's question directly. His answer does mention the fear that he felt when he heard sound of the Lord God in the garden, a fear that was motivated by his awareness that he was naked and a fear that moved him to attempt to hide himself from the deity.

This initial response by the man elicits a further question from the Lord God. "Who told you that you were naked? Have you eaten from the tree of which I commanded you not to eat?" The second of these questions is very emphatic, but the emphasis is difficult to express in English. A literal rendering of the question might be, "From the tree of which I commanded you not to eat—have you eaten *of it?*" The placing of the prepositional phrase in the forward position of the sentence strongly emphasizes the nature of the tree and the fact that the Lord God had commanded the man not to eat from it. The issue was not just eating from a tree; it was eating from a *forbidden* tree. The deity in his interrogation was trying to lead the man to

24. J. Niehaus, *God at Sinai* (Grand Rapids: Zondervan, 1995), 155–9.

25. Niehaus indicates that the Akkadian word cognate to יוֹם is ūmu*(m)*. This word in Akkadian actually has two different meanings: 1) ūmu*(m)* = "day;" and ūmu*(m)* = "storm." This second meaning for יוֹם may be observed in Zepheniah 2:2b. Cf. Niehaus, *God at Sinai*, 156–7.

26. Niehaus, *God at Sinai*, 156–7.

acknowledge his guilt. To this further question, the man responds by trying to blame both the woman and the Lord God who had given the woman to the man! He does say that he had eaten of the fruit, but his confession is as empty of personal responsibility as he can make it, since he tries to shift the blame to the woman and to God.

At this point, the Lord God begins to interrogate the woman. As represented in most English versions, he asks, "What is this that you have done?" Again, there may be more emphasis in the question than these English renderings indicate. The *New Living Translation*, though a paraphrase, captures this emphasis when it renders this question, "How could you do such a thing?"[27] The woman's response, like the man's, tries to shift responsibility to someone else rather than to shoulder it herself. She replies that "the Serpent deceived me and I ate." The words are so simple and direct, and yet they mark a tremendous watershed moment in the history of the human race (cf. Rom 5).

YHWH God's Pronouncement of Judgment (Gen 3:14–19). At this point, the interrogation is finished. The Lord God next speaks to the Serpent, but not to interrogate him as he did the man and the woman. He speaks only words of judgment. Verse 14 speaks of personal judgment that the Serpent would experience. The content of the judgment is, in a word, that the Serpent is cursed. Should we understand this curse to be somehow related to physical serpents and to normal snakes? It seems better to understand that the words apply to the Serpent himself, the being that we know from other parts of Scripture as the devil and Satan. There is no clear teaching in Scripture that serpents were able to move about in an erect manner prior to the pronouncement of this curse. Moreover, the diet of actual serpents is not literally to eat dust. If we understand that the words relate directly to Satan, then we can understand that the mode of locomotion that physical serpents still demonstrate can be considered as a reminder of Satan's judgment and resulting humiliation.

What do the words "eat dust" mean in relation to Satan? Eating dust would be descriptive of the ultimate defeat of the Serpent. It might be similar to the later Old Testament custom of victorious kings placing their feet on the necks of defeated kings (Josh 10:24). Those kings would be "eating dust" as their necks and heads were held down on the ground by

---

27. B. Waltke and M. O'Connor, *An Introduction to Biblical Hebrew Syntax* (Winona Lake, IN: Eisenbrauns, 1990), 312–3 classifies this as the emphatic use of the demonstrative pronoun in exclamatory questions. They suggest a rendering such as, "What *in the world* have you done?" (italics their emphasis).

The Need for Missions and Evangelism

their conquerors.[28] So the teaching of Genesis 3:14 is that the Serpent who tempted the first man and woman would be cursed with suffering ultimate defeat.[29] Even though the Serpent had won a battle against YHWH God's first human creatures, that triumph would not be the last word in regard to the Serpent's destiny.

Before examining the details of verse 15, it will be important to highlight something of the structure of the verse and its relation to the preceding verse. Since it begins with the conjunction *waw*, meaning "and," verse 15 must be somehow a continuation of verse 14. That verse (Gen 3:14) states both a fact (the Serpent is cursed) and a result (the Serpent will suffer defeat). It would appear that verse 15 is intended to give additional detail in regard to how the Serpent will experience the curse of defeat. The first clause of verse 15, then, expresses the Lord God's intended action that will affect both the Serpent and the woman; the deity's action will affect two individuals. The second line of the verse is a phrase, not a clause, but it extends the action of the deity in the first line/clause to the seed/descendants of both the Serpent and the woman. The deity's action also would affect two groups that would come progressively onto the stage of history, one group from the Serpent and another from the woman. Finally, the third line speaks of what he (seed or descendants) would do to the Serpent, and what the Serpent would do to him (seed or descendants). Note that the reference is clearly to the Serpent in this final clause, and not to the seed of the Serpent. So the focus has clearly returned, as regards the Serpent, to him as an individual. The question will be if the reference in this third part of the verse is to the seed of the woman as an individual or as a collective (note Table 2).

---

28. A similar idea may be present in the promise included in Psalm 110:2 that YHWH would one day make the enemies of the Messiah "the footstool of his feet."

29. Victor Hamilton, *The Book of Genesis: Chapters 1–17* (Grand Rapids: Eerdmans, 1990), 196–7, sees these two actions as indicating humiliation and subjugation. J. Walton, *NIV Application Commentary: Genesis* (Grand Rapids: Zondervan, 2001), 235–6, holds that "Gen 3:15 describes only the ongoing struggle between evil (represented by the serpent and all representatives of evil that succeed it) and humanity generation through generation." This view, however, does not recognize the force of the statements of Genesis 3:14 that refer to the defeat that the Serpent would experience.

Table 2

A Serpent	B Woman	Individual Focus
A' Serpent's Seed	B' Woman's Seed	Group Focus
B" Seed of Woman	A" Serpent	Group or Individual?

The statement of judgment spoken to the Serpent continues in verse 15 with additional details that would relate to how the curse of defeat would happen. In particular, Genesis 3:15 concerns what would be the subsequent relation between the Serpent and the woman and their respective seeds, and who would be involved in the defeat of the Serpent. In some sense, at least, the defeat would not be immediate. The defeat of the Serpent would be played out over the passage of a certain amount of time that is implied in the reference to the seed of both the Serpent and the woman. Verse 15 has been traditionally known as the *Protoevangelium*, the first gospel.

What exactly does Genesis 3:15 communicate? There seem to be three things that are described in the verse. The first is a reversal of the state of cooperation that had developed between the Serpent and the woman, for the verse speaks of the Lord God's putting "enmity between you (the Serpent) and the woman." The word order conveys an emphasis here that is due to the presence of the direct object (enmity) being placed in the first position in the Hebrew clause. It is important to note that the development of this enmity is the work of the Lord God himself. Even though the Serpent and the woman had entered into a working and cooperative relationship, the deity would establish a condition of enmity in the future.

The reversal of the state of allegiance between the Serpent and the woman also implies the reestablishment of a positive bond between the woman (and the man) and the Lord God. This can be appreciated if we consider the relationships between the man and the woman and the Lord God and the Serpent as they change within the confines of the account of what happened in the garden. When the Lord God created the man and woman, they existed in a positive and healthy relationship with him. He had assigned them tasks to do and a commandment to keep, and they were able to enjoy fellowship with him as the bearers of his image. Then, the Serpent enticed them to rebel against the Lord God in the matter of eating the forbidden fruit, and when they rebelled, they entered into a working relationship with the Serpent. At this point, they were no longer capable of enjoying a relationship with the Lord God. They demonstrated this when

The Need for Missions and Evangelism

they tried to flee and hide when they heard him in the garden. So when the deity states that he will establish enmity between the Serpent and the woman, those words must also contain an implied promise that he will also once again establish a healthy relationship between them and himself.

The second part of Genesis 3:15 indicates that the enmity that the Lord God would create between the Serpent and the woman would continue to be maintained between the seed (descendants) of the Serpent and the seed (descendants) of the woman. The work of reversing the impact of the woman's entering into league with the Serpent would continue through the passing of time. It would not be something that would immediately occur in its fullest and most complete sense.

It is in the third part of verse 15 where the text begins to speak of the agent (or agents?) who would be involved in the defeat of the Serpent. The word "seed" in the Old Testament can be used in both a concrete singular sense and in a collective sense.[30] It is clearly used in the singular sense in Genesis 4:25 where Eve remarks at the birth of Seth that ". . . God has appointed for me another offspring (seed) instead of Abel, for Cain killed him." It is clearly used in the collective sense in the many expressions of God's covenant with Abraham when he promised that he would grant him seed, meaning descendants (Gen 12:7 and other passages). The question in regard to Genesis 3:15 is whether the word should be taken as referring to an individual or to a collective group of descendants. Though it is impossible to decide the answer to this question in the immediate context, the structure of the verse that is shown in Table 2 above may help to move the exegete toward an answer. The focus in relation to the Serpent and his seed in verse 15 is clearly individual (the Serpent) in the first and third parts of the verse, and collective (his seed) in the middle part (Serpent-seed of the Serpent-Serpent). The structure in regard to the woman is clearly individual in the first part of the verse, and clearly collective in the second part (woman-seed of the woman). If the focus in the third part were also individual, then there would be a match between the two spheres that are presented in balanced opposition in the verse (woman-seed of the woman-seed as individual would match the structure Serpent-seed of the Serpent-Serpent). Whether the individual or the group is in view, what is clear in this third panel of the verse is that it is not the woman, but one or several of the woman's descendants who is or are viewed as being in combat with the

---

30. Heb. זֶרַע.

Serpent, a combat that will ultimately bring about the Serpent's defeat that was mentioned in verse 14.

The question is often asked whether Genesis 3:15 is a Messianic prophecy. Two issues need to be discussed in relation to this question. The first has to do with the previously mentioned key word "seed," זֶרַע. Hamilton argues that the word seed can be used of an individual descendant in the near future, but that it is not used to indicate an individual descendant when the time frame is distant.[31] While the Messiah is clearly a distant single descendant of Eve from our modern perspective, there is nothing in the immediate context of Genesis 3 that would require that only a distant descendant was in view. The promise of some descendant of Eve who would be involved in the defeat of the Serpent was a prophecy that was renewable as each human generation would appear. Perhaps it is best within the immediate context of Genesis 3:15 to leave the reference ambiguous. What the verse promises is that a descendant/descendants of the woman would come who would somehow be involved in the defeat of the Serpent. We should not rule out, however, the possibility that an individual descendant is in view in the passage.

A second issue has to do with the word Messiah itself. This word is derived from the Hebrew term מָשִׁיחַ "anointed one." Prophets, priests, and kings were all "anointed ones" in Old Testament times. The word came to be especially associated with David and the descendants who were promised to him who would arise to sit on his throne (2 Sam 7). The New Testament writers assigned this word to Jesus of Nazareth when they called him Christ (Χριστός, the Greek equivalent of Hebrew מָשִׁיחַ). So the term has come torefer to Old Testament prophecies that are understood to refer to Jesus as the Messiah. Since the text of Genesis 3:15 does not refer to an anointed one, perhaps the direct designation of it as "Messianic" can do more harm than good. It might be better to say that the New Testament writers see Jesus as the one who fulfills this prophecy of the one/ones who would be involved in the defeat of the Serpent. The words of Genesis 3:15 are the first mention of what the Lord God would do to reverse the Serpent's initial victory. There are certain parts of what the verse promises that are perplexing to the reader who seeks to place himself in the situation of Adam and Eve as they first heard the words spoken. In a way, all the rest of Scripture can be viewed as a commentary on Genesis 3:15. The life and work of Jesus the

---

31. See, for example, the extended discussion in Hamilton, *The Book of Genesis: Chapters 1–17*, 198–200.

Messiah can be ultimately traced back to this initial promise of the defeat of the Serpent and the concomitant redemption of fallen humans.

The message of judgment for the Serpent can be summed up by noting that, while the Serpent might have won a battle in the garden, he was destined to be defeated. That defeat would be worked out through time as the Lord God would establish enmity where once there was cooperation. That enmity would be experienced between the Serpent and the woman, and it would also be experienced between the descendants of the Serpent and the descendants of the woman. The decisive blow against the Serpent would be delivered by one of the descendants of the woman who would strike the head of the Serpent even as the Serpent would strike the heel of the woman's descendant.

Once the Lord God's judgment against the Serpent had been voiced, judgment was also passed on both the woman and the man. Briefly, the judgment of the woman included the experience of heightened pain in childbirth and a lack of marital harmony that would be marked by a mutual attempt of the man and woman to exercise control over their marriage partner. The man's judgment involved the cursing of the ground and the resulting frustration of trying to stay alive by growing crops from a ground that would produce thorns and thistles far more readily than it would produce edible crops.[32] Death also entered into the experience of the human race from this point.

The Naming of Eve and the Provision of Clothing for the Man and the Woman (Gen 3:20–21). According to verse 20, the man named his wife "Eve,"[33] and the narrator sees in this the man's recognition that life would go on and descendants would be born who would carry on the history of the human race. His naming his wife Eve seems to be an indication that he had heard and believed what the Lord God had said in his words of judgment to the Serpent. Verse 21 records the deity's gracious and merciful action whereby he crafted garments made of animal skins for their clothing. Such clothing would be a much more long-lasting remedy for their perception that they were naked and needed clothing than their own misguided efforts. This action of the Lord God may give a hint of how redemption would be obtained in the future, for the obtaining of the animal skins implies the

---

32. Much more could, and should, be said about these verses. For the aims of this essay, however, that discussion must be postponed to another occasion.

33. Heb. חַוָּה. There is a word play between the name Eve and the Hebrew word for living, which is חַי.

death of those animals. Later revelation would develop this hint, as the Israelite sacrificial system was graciously given to God's people (Lev 1–7). The ultimate sacrifice for sin, Jesus, would also later be described as "the Lamb of God who takes away the sin of the world" (John 1:29).

The Expulsion of the Man and the Woman from the Garden (Gen 3:22–24). These verses contain yet another demonstration of the Lord God's mercy to the first man and woman. The passage is marked by another example of divine deliberation that is much like the dialogue within the godhead that was reported in Genesis 1 when God first created man and woman. These words are not addressed to the man and woman, but are simply expressed as deliberation within the godhead. The words are elliptical, and what is elliptical must be supplied for full understanding of what is said. The following is the author's personal translation of the words of the Lord God, with what must be supplied shown in italics.

> And YHWH God said, "See here, the man *and his wife*[34] have become like one of us in respect to knowing good and evil. Now then, *we must remove them from the garden* lest they stretch out their hands and take also from the tree of life and eat and live forever." So YHWH God expelled *them* from the Garden of Eden to till the ground from which they had been taken.

The man and woman were removed from the Garden of Eden for their own protection. Had they remained in the garden, they presumably would have been tempted to eat of the tree of life, and that eating would have doomed them to continue in their sinful state without any chance for redemption.

Conclusion

Genesis 3 gives us the explanation for the radical difference between the nature of God's world as it came from his creative hand and how it exists today. God himself described the creation once it was complete as "very good" (Gen 1:23). That condition included the ability for man and woman to enjoy fellowship with their Creator without difficulty. With reason, Paul describes the current state of the world as "groaning . . . in the pains of childbirth until now" (Rom 8:22). The change was brought about by Adam and Eve's disobedience in relation to God's first command regarding the

---

34. Man is grammatically singular, as are the corresponding pronouns and verb forms. The words *and his wife* are added, and the other forms are translated as plurals because both the man and woman were banished from the garden.

forbidden tree. That disobedience opened the door for death to enter the cosmos (Rom 5:12).

Happily, Genesis 3 did not leave the first man and woman without hope. In the words of judgment addressed to the Serpent, there was the first glimpse of what God would do to redeem his sinful creatures and their descendants. That redemption involved judgment on the Serpent, as well as the restoration of fellowship between God and his human creatures. The words are enigmatic and do not offer sufficient detail for full understanding, but to the listening ear these words provided a message of hope. God would not turn his back on his sinful creatures. He would wage war to undo the effects of their sin. In a sense, the rest of Scripture can be seen as a fleshing out of the first brief and puzzling words of the gospel message. The *Protoevangelium* does indeed contain the truth of the gospel in its most condensed and earliest form.

When is the Task of Gospel Ministry Complete?

PETER J. HAYS

"I have fulfilled the ministry of the gospel of Christ. . . I no longer have any room for work in these regions " (Romans 15:19, 23)[1]

When is the task of gospel ministry complete? How can one determine that the commission that has been given to preach the gospel has been fulfilled? What exactly needs to be done or communicated in order to consider people "reached" and the evangelistic work of ministering the gospel complete? An answer to these questions can serve as a strategic guide for missions, as well as giving insight into responsibilities in personal evangelism.

The Lausanne Movement has addressed the topic of "finishing the task" of world evangelization. The question, "When is the job complete?" is central to this matter.[2] In a pilot version of the Lausanne Global Analysis of issues facing the church and worldwide evangelization, 639 Unengaged, Unreached People Groups (UUPG) with populations of 100,000 or more were identified. These 639 UUPGs total over 500 million people.[3]

A "people group" was defined as "the largest group through which the gospel can flow without encountering significant barriers of understanding and acceptance." "Unreached" meant that "less than 2% of the population

---

1. This and all subsequent Scripture quotations are from *The Holy Bible: English Standard Version* (Wheaton: Crossway Bibles, 2001).

2. The Lausanne Movement is a worldwide movement that mobilizes evangelical leaders to collaborate for world evangelization and sponsors the Lausanne Global Conversation, an online forum helping the global church to cooperate on issues related to world evangelization.

3. Albert W. Hickman, "Finishing the Task," Lausanne Global Conversation, http://conversation.lausanne.org/en/resources/detail/11974# (accessed February 29, 2012).

are Evangelical Christians," with "Evangelical Christian" defined as "a person who believes that Jesus Christ is the sole source of salvation through faith in Him, has personal faith and conversion with regeneration by the Holy Spirit, recognizes the inspired word of God as the only basis for faith and Christian living, and is committed to Biblical preaching and evangelism that brings others to faith in Jesus Christ." Finally, "unengaged" meant "as far as could be ascertained, no one was even trying to reach them."[4]

By this definition, the task of reaching a UUPG is considered finished when at least two percent of the population is evangelically converted and conveying the gospel unhindered by significant barriers.[5] International organizations are declaring that the Great Commission, when understood this way, can be completed in this generation.[6] But is there a biblical basis for the idea that Christians can fulfill the task of preaching the gospel without communicating it personally to every one of the seven billion persons living on the planet?

Completing the Gospel Ministry

In Romans 15:19, Paul says that he has "fulfilled the ministry of the gospel of Christ." He uses this phrase to explain that he has completed his God-given task of ministering the gospel to the Gentiles in Asia. In fact, he adds in verse 22, "I no longer have any room for work in these regions." When one considers the fact that there were still millions in Asia who had not responded—either by faith or by rejection—to his gospel ministry, Paul's understanding of having completed the task becomes significant. What factors made it clear

---

4. Hickman, "Finishing the Task.

5. Two percent is also the figure used by the Joshua Project editorial committee. The committee acknowledges that these percentage figures are somewhat arbitrary. However, they believe that "the quality of a whole culture may be changed when two percent of its people have a new vision." Robert Belair, Institute for Advanced Study at Princeton University, quoted in *Christianity Today*, Oct 2011, 42. Joshua Project, "Definitions," http://www.joshuaproject.net/definitions.php (accessed February 29, 2012).

6. Call2All has assembled a sizeable number of Christian leaders who believe that the Great Commission can be fulfilled in this generation. Cf. Call2All, "Endorsements," http://call2all.org/Groups/1000020717/Call2All/About_Us/Endorsements/Endorsements.aspx (accessed February 29, 2012). The organization called "Finish the Task" acknowledges that accomplishing the Great Commission can be understood in many ways, but emphasizes, "What is most important is that we start to finish the task." Finishing the Task, "About Finishing the Task," http://finishingthetask.com/about.html (accessed February 29, 2012).

to Paul that he had completed the gospel ministry? And what guidelines are present in Paul's writing that can guide strategic ministry decisions today, both in personal evangelism and church and parachurch ministry?

Knowing this answer would be of value to all who are involved in bringing the gospel of Jesus Christ. It would be of great benefit for strategic planning for churches as well as for mission boards and other parachurch organizations such as Evangelical Alliances, as well as for individuals doing evangelism. Knowing when the task is finished would enable a more strategic ministry engagement. For example, knowing whether the task is complete or not would help determine whether ministries in a given community should be emphasizing discipleship over evangelism, or should still be maintaining a priority of evangelism over discipleship. This would concretely affect the available human and financial resources, as well as the allotment of time given to these endeavors. And at the level of personal evangelism, one also often wonders if there is a moment when it can be concluded that the ministry of the gospel of Jesus Christ has been fulfilled with a friend, acquaintance, or family member.

Paul's Ministry of the Gospel of Christ (Romans 15:14–19a)

In Romans 15:14–19a, Paul returns to the theme with which he opened the letter: his ministry and his vision to expand the gospel.

> I myself am satisfied about you, my brothers, that you yourselves are full of goodness, filled with all knowledge and able to instruct one another. But on some points I have written to you very boldly by way of reminder, because of the grace given me by God to be a minister of Christ Jesus to the Gentiles in the priestly service of the gospel of God, so that the offering of the Gentiles may be acceptable, sanctified by the Holy Spirit. In Christ Jesus, then, I have reason to be proud of my work for God. For I will not venture to speak of anything except what Christ has accomplished through me to bring the Gentiles to obedience—by word and deed, by the power of signs and wonders, by the power of the Spirit of God.

There are a number of reasons that this text can serve to give insight into the issue of completion in the gospel ministry. First, Paul understood that his responsibility was to bring the gospel of Jesus Christ to the Gentiles (Gal. 2:7–8, etc.). He had a clearly defined target group. He describes this as a "grace given me by God to be a minister of Christ Jesus to the Gentiles"

(vv. 15–16). This call constituted a responsibility for Paul, a kind of "job description." As such, it determined his freedom or lack of freedom in what he did and where he went (cf. vv. 22–23).

Second, the description that Paul gives to the Romans of his ministry uses the language of the cult. His is a "priestly service" to result in the "sanctified offering" of the Gentiles which was "acceptable" (v. 16). This description makes clear that Paul's work was not only intentional and holy, but also had a clearly defined goal (a sanctified offering). There was also a standard of measure by which he worked, to make the offering "acceptable."[7]

In his commentary on Romans, Hultgren sees in Paul's words here the idea that the Gentiles receive the Word of salvation as a fulfillment of God's prophetic promise that they would be eschatologically gathered in. In this context, the offering seems to be best understood as a "first fruits" offering, where the first part represents the whole.

Third, Paul claims to "have reason to be proud" of his "work for God" and what Christ "has accomplished" (vv. 17–18). The use of the aorist "has accomplished" places the work in the past—it is "done." The work, since it has been finished, has reached a point where there is reason to be proud. This is not a dream or a vision for the future that Paul has. It is something already "accomplished" in the past.

A fourth reason that Paul's pattern of ministry qualifies as a model is because of its designation and affirmation as a work of God. Paul declares in no uncertain terms that it is "Christ [who] has accomplished" the work (v. 19). God has done this "by word and deed, by the power of signs and wonders, by the power of the Spirit of God" (vv. 18–19).[8] This is a recurring pattern of the Scripture when explaining the work of God.[9] Men who brought God's

---

7. This is true whether one interprets "acceptable offering" as referring to a financial offering made by the Gentile believers which is accepted by the Jewish believers in Jerusalem, or as meaning an offering of Gentiles reached with the gospel which is accepted by God. Arland J. Hultgren. *Paul's Letter to the Romans: A Commentary* (Grand Rapid: Eerdmans, 2011), 542–3.

8. There is a textual issue in this verse. B has simply πνεύματος, while P[46], et al. add θεοῦ. A, D*, G and a smaller number of the miniscules and fathers add ἁγίου. While this is a difficult issue to resolve based on the manuscripts, none of the readings significantly alters the meaning of the text in its context. Schreiner says, "B is notoriously unreliable in these verses, and should not be followed, since it stands alone. The variant ἁγίου is probably a correction, and thus θεοῦ should be preferred as the harder reading, which also has good manuscript evidence." Thomas Schreiner, *Romans* (Grand Rapids: Baker Academic, 1998), 772.

9. Hultgren cites Sir. 3:8; 4 Macc. 16:14; Luk. 24:2; Col. 3:17, p. 243.

message at key times in redemptive history had that message confirmed by miraculous signs and wonders. This can be seen in Moses at the Exodus, as well as in the prophetic ministries of Elijah, Elisha, and Daniel. This same confirmation pattern recurs in Jesus' own ministry and that of the apostles. God unmistakably confirms that it is His message that is being revealed by giving miraculous signs to accompany the message. Acts 14:3[10] and 15:12 specifically record these confirmations in Paul's ministry, and his reference to this pattern demonstrates that his ministry takes place as a direct extension and continuation of God's redemptive plan.[11] This makes it clear that Paul's ministry was occurring specifically as part of a larger, ongoing work of God. The fact that Paul sees his work in this context enables him to determine its "completion." The consistency that has been achieved between Paul's message preached ("word") and works ("deed") that are done (v. 18) functions as a measure that the gospel ministry has been fulfilled.

In light of these considerations, the description of Paul's ministry will provide valid, helpful insight into intentional, strategic gospel ministry, and particularly to the issue of "completeness" in the gospel ministry. What, then, are the qualities of gospel ministry that is fulfilled?

The Gospel Ministry Fulfilled from Jerusalem to Illyricum (Romans 15:19b–21)

> So that from Jerusalem and all the way around to Illyricum I have fulfilled the ministry of the gospel of Christ; and thus I make it my ambition to preach the gospel, not where Christ has already been named, lest I build on someone else's foundation, but as it is written, "Those who have never been told of him will see, and those who have never heard will understand."

Having laid the foundation by giving the background of his work, Paul now transitions with "so that" (ὥστε) and describes the result. The work that Christ has accomplished through Paul has had specific, concrete, and

---

10. "So they remained for a long time, speaking boldly for the Lord, who bore witness to the word of his grace, granting signs and wonders to be done by their hands" (Acts 14:3).

11. "And all the assembly fell silent, and they listened to Barnabas and Paul as they related what signs and wonders God had done through them among the Gentiles" (Acts 15:12).

When is the Task of Gospel Ministry Complete?

astonishing outcome: "from Jerusalem and all the way around to Illyricum I have fulfilled the ministry of the gospel of Christ" (v. 19).

By the designation "from Jerusalem and all the way around to Illyricum," Paul is describing a large geographic region extending from Jerusalem as far the Adriatic Sea. His mention of Jerusalem is likely a reference to OT prophecies (Isa. 2:2–3, Mic. 4:1–14) concerning the Word of the Lord going out from Jerusalem to the Gentiles. Indeed, despite the doubts of some, Paul did preach in Jerusalem (cf. Acts 9:29), even if he was not further personally active in Judea (cf. Gal. 1:22).

Illyricum refers to the western Balkan peninsula, an area also referred to as Dalmatia (cf. 2 Tim. 4:10). If Paul means to include all of Illyricum, then he is indicating an area as far north as Croatia and southern Albania. If he means only "to the border of Illyricum," then the reference is to the southern part of Illyricum, today called Macedonia.[12]

The Scriptures nowhere specifically record that Paul entered Illyricum; nor do they deny it. Paul's own phrase is "all the way around to Illyricum." Paul's journeys, his ministry from Jerusalem to Illyricum, are recorded in Acts 9:28–29; 13:4–5, 14, 51; 14:6, 10, 20, 25; 15:12; 16:6–12; 17:10, 15; 18:1, 19; 19:1; 20:1–2, 6.[13]

---

12. Cf. Gustav Droysen, *Allgemeiner historischer Handatlas in 96 Karten mit erläuterndem Text* (Bielefeld: Velhagen & Klasing, 1886), S. 16. Accessed via Wikipedia Commons, "File:Roman provinces of Illyricum, Macedonia, Dacia, Moesia, Pannonia and Thracia.jpg," http://commons.wikimedia.org/wiki/File:Roman_provinces_of_Illyricum,_Macedonia,_Dacia,_Moesia,_Pannonia_and_Thracia.jpg (accessed April 2, 2012), public domain. Bible interpreters differ in their understanding of what Paul meant by his reference to Illyricum. Some believe that Paul extends the impact of his ministry quite far into Eastern Europe. Matthew Henry wrote, "We have in the book of the Acts an account of Paul's travels. There we find him, after he was sent forth to preach to the Gentiles (Acts 13:1–52), labouring in that blessed work in Seleucia, Cyprus, Pamphylia, Pisidia, and Lycaonia (Acts 13:1–14:28), afterwards travelling through Syria and Cilicia, Phrygia, Galatia, Mysia, Troas, and thence called over to Macedonia, and so into Europe, Acts 15:1–16:40. Then we find him very busy at Thessalonica, Berea, Athens, Corinth, Ephesus, and the parts adjacent. Those that know the extent and distance of these countries will conclude Paul an active man, rejoicing as a strong man to run a race. Illyricum is the area now called Slavonia in eastern Croatia which borders on Hungary. Some take it for the same with Bulgaria; others for the lower Pannonia: however, it was a great way from Jerusalem." Matthew Henry, *Matthew Henry Complete Commentary on the Whole Bible*, http://www.studylight.org/com/mhc-com/view.cgi?book=ro&chapter=015 (accessed February 16, 2012). Henry's view seems overly enthusiastic, however, considering the fact that the locations actually named in the Scripture are quite distant from Bulgaria and that no towns or cities that far north are ever mentioned in the Scripture.

13. Cf. map of Paul's journeys at Bible Survey, "Paul's Missionary Journeys," http://

27

Acts 20.1–2 provide the most likely opportunity for Paul to have personally visited Illyricum, since his travels in Macedonia would have brought him to the border with Illyricum. "After the uproar ceased, Paul sent for the disciples, and after encouraging them, he said farewell and departed for Macedonia. When he had gone through those regions and had given them much encouragement, he came to Greece" (Acts 20:1–2). "Those regions" may well have included Illyricum.

The distance from Jerusalem to Illyricum is between 3,600 km (southern border) and 4,700 km (northern border). But Paul uses κύκλῳ, meaning "in a circle, round about." This expression widens the impact of Paul's words significantly. He was not simply claiming to have reached the particular towns and cities he had visited but was including a larger area. It is not entirely clear whether Paul is attempting to describe an arc extending from Jerusalem to Spain (Cranfield, Dunn), or a circle from which Jerusalem forms the center (Knox, Scott).[14] However, by either interpretation, Paul is specifically including an entire sweep of the region, rather than only specific population centers.

There are indeed many towns and villages between Jerusalem and Illyricum that Paul is never mentioned to have visited. Nevertheless, as the discussion above indicates, Paul included these as places where he had "fulfilled the ministry of the gospel" even when he had not been personally present there.[15]

The population of the Roman Empire during Paul's ministry is estimated at 50 to 65 million. However, the population of just Asia Minor, the area referred to by Paul, was likely around 14 to 20 million, plus perhaps another 10 million for Macedonia and Achaia.[16] Therefore, Paul is making the astonishing claim to have brought the Gentiles to obedience along

---

hiwaay.net/~wgann/survey/bs-map08.gif (accessed April 14, 2012).

14. Schreiner, *Romans*, 769.

15. This may be because, through his ministry in a given area, he had established churches from which the gospel ministry was sufficiently able to penetrate into the surrounding area. On the other hand, perhaps Paul perceived the gospel ministry as being fulfilled without every individual or town hearing the gospel personally. In any case, fulfilling the gospel did not mean that he needed to personally go to every man, woman, and child, nor to every geographical location, town, and village.

16. John D. Durand, "Historical Estimates of World Population: An Evaluation," *Population and Development* 3, no. 3 (1977): 253–96, as cited at Wikipedia, "Classical Demography," http://en.wikipedia.org/wiki/Classical_demography#cite_note-4 (accessed February 17, 2012).

an arc extending thousands of kilometers and including a population of around 25 million people in a span of 14 to 22 years.[17]

The Meaning of the Phrase, "I have fulfilled the ministry of the gospel of Christ"

Interpreters have struggled greatly with Paul's words, "I have fulfilled the ministry of the gospel of Christ." Käsemann says that Paul's statement here is "an enormous exaggeration when measured by geographical reality," and concludes: "it is understandable only on the basic premise that the apostle views his work as preparatory for the imminent *parousia*."[18]

Schreiner calls Paul's claim "surprising," and states, "This does not mean the gospel was proclaimed to every single individual in this area."[19] Barrett understands Paul to be saying that, "when Paul says that in this region he has completed the gospel of Christ, he does not mean that he (or anyone else) has preached the gospel to everyone in it, but that it has been covered in a representative way. The gospel has been heard; more could not be expected before the *parousia*.[20] Barrett understands that Paul's idea of completion is related to the "fulfillment of the eschatological programme entrusted to him."[21]

There seems to be a predilection in the Western mind that gospel ministry can only be complete when each and every person has been personally presented the gospel and been given an opportunity to personally respond in faith. But Paul clearly demonstrates here a different idea of completion. To resolve this tension, Lenski considers this phrase to mean that Paul fulfilled the gospel ministry by preaching the Word rightly, in its fullness

---

17. Fourteen years would just include the years of his missionary journeys, from the start of his first journey around A.D. 44, until the ending of his third journey in Jerusalem around A.D. 58, including respites. Twenty-two years would include all the years from his conversion and subsequent preaching in Jerusalem around A.D. 33. Paul wrote Romans in A.D. 56–57, a year or so before the end of his third missionary journey. So it might be possible to reduce by one more year the amount of time involved in fulfilling the ministry of the gospel of Christ.

18. Ernst Käsemann, *Commentary on Romans*, trans. Geoffrey William Bromiley (Grand Rapids: Eerdmans, 1980), 395.

19. Schreiner, *Romans*, 769.

20. C. K. Barrett, *The Epistle to the Romans*, 2nd ed., rev. ed. (London: Hendrickson, 1991), 253.

21. Barrett, *Romans*, 253.

without any omissions.²² However, the context leads strongly to the conclusion that the fulfillment refers to the completion of a task, and particularly verses 20–23 of Romans 15 and the parallel with verse 23, where Paul says, "I no longer have any room for work.."

Cranfield agrees, dismissing other interpretations as "unlikely." Interpretations of "fulfilling" as meaning the fullness or completeness with which Paul has preached the gospel message, or as meaning the powerful effect of the gospel preaching (Lenski, Schlatter), or as meaning that Asia had been saturated with the gospel message—such interpretations are all are in conflict with the context between verse 19 and verses 20–23. Cranfield also rejects Munck, Barrett, and Käsemann's idea that Paul had completed all the gospel ministry needed to make the *Parousia* possible, for the same reason.²³ Instead, Cranfield concludes, "we understand his claim to have completed the gospel of Christ to be a claim to have completed that trail-blazing, pioneer preaching of it, which he believed was his own apostolic mission to accomplish."²⁴ What help is there to find an answer among these conflicting views offered by the interpreters?

πεπληρωκέναι

Input can be gleaned from the grammar that will aid in a right understanding of Paul's phrase "πεπληρωκέναι τὸ εὐαγγέλιον τοῦ χριστοῦ." "πληρόω" has, according to Strong's, the lexical meanings of fulfill (51), fill (19), be full (7), complete (2), end (2), and miscellaneous (9). TDNT asserts that the usage in Romans 15:19 is "to complete" or "to execute fully."²⁵ The word picture is that of filling a net with a catch of fish. The force Paul seems to be giving to the word here is "to carry through to the end, to accomplish, carry out, (some undertaking)." In other words, he accomplished, or carried through to the end, the ministry of the gospel. Therefore, the semantic idea is one of completion. Paul's ministry filled up what was lacking in the

22. R. C. H. Lenski, *The Interpretation of St. Paul's Epistle to the Romans* (Columbus, OH: Wartburg Press, 1945), 884–885.

23. Charles Ernest Burland Cranfield and William Sanday, *A Critical and Exegetical Commentary on the Epistle to the Romans*, Vol. II. 6th ed. (Edinburgh: T & T Clark, 1979), 762. "As the world is permeated by the gospel, the gospel itself comes to fulfillment." Käsemann, *Romans*, 394.

24. Cranfield, *Romans*, 762.

25. Gerhard Kittel, Geoffrey William Bromiley, and Gerhard Friedrich, *Theological Dictionary of the New Testament*, Vol. VI (Grand Rapids: Eerdmans, 1968), 297.

preaching of the gospel, where others have not been in this geographical area until it was completely full.[26]

The form of the verb πεπληρωκέναι ("I have fulfilled"), the perfect active infinitive, also emphasizes the idea of completion. The perfect tense refers to an action completed in the past with continuing result. By stepping away here from the aorist, Paul goes out of his way to emphasize that the work he had done was lacking nothing to make it a perfect work. There was no more to be added. It is not merely true that Paul has "worked at" the gospel ministry, doing part of the job. He has truly brought the task to completion. This also means that there is an ongoing sense of completion to what Paul has accomplished. While it likely goes too far to conclude that there will never again be any need for gospel ministry, still there comes a point (and for Paul, this point has arrived) when one can say, "The work of gospel ministry is complete." As evidence of this, Paul makes a definite change in his ministry plans as a result, deciding to leave and pursue plans to go to Spain via Rome (v. 24).

πεπληρωκέναι is also active, likely with causative force. The active voice brings the emphasis that the work which Paul has done is what has resulted in the task being complete. In other words, Paul did not simply work until he noticed that God was finished. Rather, he acknowledges that God used his efforts and gave fruit to his ministry so that he was able to accomplish this goal.

So both the context and the grammar of Romans 15:19 argue for the idea that Paul's claim that he had "fulfilled the ministry of the gospel of Christ" meant that he had "completed" the ministry of the gospel of Christ.

How did Paul Practically Fulfill the Ministry of the Gospel?

A survey of the ministry of Paul gives insight into his fulfillment, or completion, of the ministry of the gospel. Paul's major ministry patterns are well established: he traveled from place to place and engaged in public (marketplace) preaching; he discipled and organized believers into churches; and he followed up on the churches with visits and letters.[27]

---

26. Fritz Rienecker and Cleon L. Rogers, "Romans 15:19," in *A Linguistic Key to the Greek New Testament* (Grand Rapids: Zondervan, 1976), 382.

27. Paul does not spell out specifically which activities fulfill the ministry of the gospel of Christ and which may have been actually ancillary. However, a sense of the character and patterns of Paul's ministry provides a clear framework within which he

Not Weary of Well Doing

Paul himself has already characterized his ministry as "what Christ has accomplished through me to bring the Gentiles to obedience—by word and deed, by the power of signs and wonders, by the power of the Spirit of God" (Rom. 15:18b–19a). The following texts from elsewhere in Scripture give an overview of how this took place and demonstrate Paul's "commitment" or "stated goal" for the work (emphases added):

> how I did not shrink from *declaring* to you *anything that was profitable*, and *teaching you in public and from house to house* (Acts 20:20)

> But the Lord said to him, "Go, for he is a chosen instrument of mine to *carry my name before the Gentiles* and kings and the children of Israel. (Acts 9:15)

> And Paul and Barnabas *spoke out boldly*, saying, "It was necessary that the *word of God be spoken* first to you. Since you thrust it aside and judge yourselves unworthy of eternal life, behold, we are turning to the Gentiles. For so the Lord has commanded us, saying, "'I have made you *a light for the Gentiles, that you may bring salvation to the ends of the earth.*'" (Acts 13:46–47)

> delivering you from your people and from the Gentiles—to whom I am sending you *to open their eyes, so that they may turn from darkness to light* and from the power of Satan to God, that *they may receive forgiveness of sins and a place* among those who are sanctified by faith in me.' (Acts 26:17–18)

> through whom we have received *grace and apostleship to bring about the obedience of faith for the sake of his name among all the nations,* (Romans 1:5 ; cf. Rom. 16:26)

> But when he who had set me apart before I was born, and who called me by his grace, was pleased to reveal his Son to me, in order that I might *preach him among the Gentiles*, I did not immediately consult with anyone; (Galatians 1:15–16)

> of which I became a minister according to the stewardship from God that was given to me for you, to *make the word of God fully known,* (Colossians 1:25)

Scripture provides consistent testimony that Paul's ministry did indeed focus on bringing the gospel of Jesus Christ to Asia, and in particular to the Gentiles. Paul does not speak of his ministry as "church planting" or "evangelism campaigning," let alone as "justice ministry." Rather, it was

---

completed his task and therefore gives valuable insight.

centered around bold proclamation and teaching of the gospel with the goal of making Christ known and people responding in faith.

Paul's words in Romans 15:20, "thus I make it my ambition to preach the gospel," give further significant insight into the enterprise of gospel ministry. He has an "ambition," a specific and serious goal for which he strives. Paul conceived of the gospel ministry as striving for glory. Preaching the gospel was a matter of honor for Paul, certainly not because he sought honor for himself: he boasted not of what he himself did, but of what Christ did through him.[28] Preaching the gospel, especially but not only in pioneer situations, is more often a source of dishonor than of honor for the preacher (1 Cor. 4:9–13, but cf. Jer. 20:8). The honor of which Paul speaks, his ambition, is that the purposes of God be accomplished through the ministry of the gospel, the salvation of the lost. Paul is conceiving of his gospel ministry as vitally related to God's sovereign, eschatological plan. This connection of the gospel ministry to the greater, sovereign plan of God yields important insight into what Paul means when he says that he has "fulfilled the ministry of the gospel of Christ."

Paul's further explanation in Romans 15:20 that he has preached the gospel "not where Christ has already been named" reveals a fundamental understanding of Paul's calling. Paul has made it clear in this passage that he is not motivated by selfish gain or fame, so he is not ministering in new areas for his own purposes. Rather, he understands that inherent to his task of fulfilling the gospel ministry is seeking to take the gospel to places where it has not been heard.

This expression is the key interpretive phrase for Schreiner, who says,

> Paul's apostolic goal is to plant churches where Christ has not yet been confessed, for he does not want to "build on another man's foundation." That is, he does not want to preach the gospel where another person has already planted a church. A claim to have fully preached the gospel of Christ is understandable in this sense, for Paul's point is that he has finished planting churches where Christ has not been named in the area extending from Jerusalem to Illyricum. This hardly means that every village or town had heard the gospel. Paul's strategy was apparently to plant churches in key cities, and from there coworkers would fan out and evangelize smaller towns (cf. Epaphras in Colossians).[29]

---

28. Martin Luther, *Lectures on Romans*, ed. Wilhelm Pauck (Philadelphia: Westminster Press, 1961), 416–419.

29. Schreiner, *Romans*, 770.

Lenski, however, rejects the notion that Paul's ministry should be limited to only the major cities. Lenski reads Acts to tell that Paul, together with his regular coworkers, was successful at penetrating with the gospel deeply and effectively, not only into the key cities, but also into the provinces surrounding these cities.[30] The specific leading of the Holy Spirit, directing Paul where to go and how long to stay, enabled Paul to fulfill the ministry, and established a foundation for ongoing work.[31]

It is tempting to speak of Paul's ministry being extended to those yet unreached in the same breath when reading that he has "fulfilled the ministry of the gospel of Christ." Many millions simply had not yet heard the gospel. Even Lenski's confidence in Paul's zealous hard work cannot change that reality. Yet, despite the fact that there were still people who had not heard, and despite the fact that the believers and churches would certainly carry on the work of ministry, Paul still claimed that he had *already* fulfilled the ministry of the gospel of Christ. The completion of his gospel ministry simply did not depend on every individual being reached, nor did the completion of his gospel ministry depend on further work yet to be done by local churches and believers. Paul declared the ministry fulfilled as is.

Paul certainly did not consider the task of the gospel ministry "finished" in the sense that there were no more people to become followers of Christ in Asia. He states clearly that God wants "all" to come to a saving knowledge of the truth (1 Tim. 2:4), yet by no means did everyone in Asia believe. The churches that Paul established were charged with carrying on the testimony from a foundation which was made by Paul's completed work.[32] One must be careful in making too much of this, however, as the fact is that the foundation in local churches was not large. Paul did not have time to bring these churches toward a great deal of maturity or even to a large size. Paul actually says nothing about the churches that he is leaving behind. He never says that they will "complete" the task he has "begun." Rather, he claims to have "fulfilled" the gospel ministry himself. He even

---

30. Lenski, *Romans*, 885.

31. "He kindled thousands of fires, so many that the wind spread the conflagration until fire merged into fire." Lenski, *Romans*, 886.

32 Moo even suggests that Paul's example may indicate that "our missions work should have as its goal the planting of self-reproducing churches." Douglas J. Moo, *The NIV Application Commentary: Romans* (Grand Rapids: Zondervan, 2000), 498. Interestingly, Moo adds the comment: "Sometimes we do not stay long enough in a given area for a church to reach this critical mass." Might this thought be relevant to the current interest in, and practice of, the North American church to short-term missions?

When is the Task of Gospel Ministry Complete?

asserts that there is nowhere left for him to preach. While it is certainly correct to assume that gospel ministry will be carried on by these churches (see Paul's instructions in Acts and the Epistles), Paul simply does not hinge the completeness of his work on what others will do. Paul's work was finished, regardless of what the new churches would or would not do.

Thus, it is beginning to become evident that Paul had an understanding of what completion means that was not determined by an absolute numerical or geographical standard. Paul's idea of fulfillment was determined by another factor, one which has begun to be revealed already, but in the following verses becomes quite clear.

Paul now cites Isaiah 52:15, "Those who have never been told of him will see, and those who have never heard will understand" (Romans 15:20). There are two points that can be understood from Paul's quotation. The first relates to the description of what Paul has accomplished in fulfilling the gospel ministry, and the second relates to understanding the prophetic promise that Paul's ministry fulfills.

Paul considers his work done once there is "seeing" and "understanding." The seeing is done by those who have never had a report of Christ. The "understanding" is done by those who have never heard of Christ. Paul uses this chiasm to describe the fulfillment of the gospel ministry as that moment when Christ had been presented in a fashion such that those who had never heard of Him could understand the gospel message and be struck to the heart ("shut their mouths," cf. Isa. 52:15) by it.

But the quotation from Isaiah (in wording nearly identical to the LXX, which has there a greater Gentile orientation than other versions) indicates that he conceived of his work as part of the fulfillment of the prophecy whereby the message of the Suffering Servant goes to "nations" and "kings" (Isaiah 52:15). As such, his ministry, which does not build on another man's foundations, represents the fulfillment of this prophetic Scripture.[33] Paul is unmistakably describing his work as "fulfilling the gospel ministry" by being part of the execution of a greater, eschatological plan.[34]

---

33. For Schreiner's compilation of the various positions on this, cf. Schreiner, *Romans*, 770.

34. Schreiner sees further evidence in this passage of Paul's concept of his ministry fitting into God's sovereign plan, arguing that the collection made by the Gentiles to support the poor Jewish believers in Jerusalem is a demonstration of the solidarity of Gentile and Jew and therefore was evidence of God's fulfillment of His promise, made to Abraham, to save the nations (Gen. 12.3). Schreiner, *Romans*, 761.

Paul sees his ministry as fulfilling the promises made concerning the Suffering Servant. Specifically, it was prophesied that the message of the Suffering Servant would go out to the Gentiles. This is in fulfillment of the covenant made with Abraham, whereby all the families of the earth would be blessed (Gen. 12–17). In other words, Paul "fulfilled the ministry of the gospel of Christ" by bringing the gospel message to the Gentiles as promised in the Old Testament. It is in this sense that Paul completes the task, because now it is really true that Gentiles have been brought in and are blessed in Abraham through faith.

Paul and his contemporaries knew that Jesus had taught that the gospel must be proclaimed to all the nations (Mark 13:10; Matt. 28:19) and that Jesus even conditioned His *parousia* on the nations hearing the gospel (Matt. 24:14). The real, effective presence of Gentile believers, grafted into the plan of God, served as Paul's standard by which he could determine that he had "fulfilled the ministry of the gospel." While Israel had "eyes that would not see and ears that would not hear" (Rom. 11:8; Deut. 29:4), God's plan was to graft in the Gentiles (Rom. 11:17) according to Paul's ministry (Rom. 11:13). This plan involved the partial hardening of Israel "until the fullness of the Gentiles has come in. And in this way all Israel will be saved" (Rom. 11.25–26) in the culmination of God's eschatological plan.

The Proof and Consequence of Paul's Fulfilling the Gospel Ministry: Next Steps (Romans 15:22–24)

> This is the reason why I have so often been hindered from coming to you. But now, since I no longer have any room for work in these regions, and since I have longed for many years to come to you, I hope to see you in passing as I go to Spain, and to be helped on my journey there by you, once I have enjoyed your company for a while.

With the words of Romans 15:22–25, Paul makes clear that he is "now" free to minister elsewhere.[35] Up till now, Paul was not free ("hindered") to go to Rome, because his task of gospel ministry was not yet fulfilled. Paul makes crystal clear that he has indeed fulfilled the gospel ministry by his claim that he no longer has "any room for work in these regions" (Rom. 15:23).

---

35. Paul obviously saw that there was more work to be done among peoples who hadn't heard in Spain, so he was nowhere saying that the work of gospel ministry should cease.

When is the Task of Gospel Ministry Complete?

There was a period of "many years" in the past when the work was not yet complete. Even though Paul "longed for many years to come," the fact that the task was not done took priority over his consistent, steadfast personal longing! Now, however, there is completion, and Paul is free to move on.

Käsemann stumbles over these words, stating categorically, "No matter how far Paul went on his journeys the statement can hardly be correct historically, and is psychologically impossible apart from his basic apocalyptic conception."[36] Käsemann is confounded as to how Paul could have meant these words literally. Yet he insightfully asserts that these words are key to understanding Paul and his mission, and that exegetical efforts to skip over Paul's assertions "irresponsibly ignore Paul's theology as a whole."[37]

Käsemann is entirely correct when he says that to misunderstand or ignore these words is to misunderstand a great deal of Paul's theology. What Paul meant by no longer having any room for work points to the genuine fulfillment of the gospel ministry of verse 19. It is not Paul, but a Western interpretive grid that has erected the absolute, numerical and geographical standard of completion for gospel ministry. Paul saw his work as complete even when each and every individual had not had a gospel presentation.

Paul claimed to have fulfilled the ministry of the gospel of Christ because he saw his ministry in Asia as the outworking of God's plan of blessing the families of the earth. From the covenant with Abraham (Gen. 12–17), and all through the Old Testament,[38] God's plan was to bring blessing and salvation to all mankind (cf. 1 Tim. 2:4). This covenant was fulfilled in Christ (Gal. 3:14, 16) who reconciled God to man (Eph. 2:11–22) and commissioned His followers to preach this message to all the nations (Luke 24:27). Paul conceived of and explained his ministry in just these terms:

> And Paul and Barnabas spoke out boldly, saying, "It was necessary that the word of God be spoken first to you. Since you thrust it aside and judge yourselves unworthy of eternal life, behold, we are turning to the Gentiles. For so the Lord has commanded us, saying, "'I have made you a light for the Gentiles, that you may bring salvation to the ends of the earth.'" (Acts 13:46–47)

---

36. Käsemann, *Romans*, 397.

37. Käsemann, *Romans*, 397.

38. For example, Ps. 22:27–29; 67:2–7; 98.2; Isa. 42:6; 43:12; 49:6; Jer. 16:19; Mic. 4:2–3; Zeph. 3:9; Zech. 2:11; Mal. 1:11, etc.

Fulfilling the ministry of the gospel of Christ, according to Paul, involves the direct, intentional carrying out of God's redemptive, eschatological plan to bless all the peoples of the earth through the seed of Abraham.

Conclusion

Many cannot conceive of the gospel ministry being fulfilled if not every individual has been given the gospel message. Based on Paul's teaching, however, we must release ourselves from the captivity of this kind of individualistic thinking. We must do so, not because it is unkind or unfair, but because it is not biblical.

The decision of the Lausanne Committee to consider a people group no longer unreached when it has two percent believers would seem to have biblical credibility. The exact number of Christians in the first century is difficult to determine. Estimates range from ten thousand[39] to one million.[40] Using the conservative estimate of fifteen million people in the arc spoken of by Paul, this would represent between .07 percent and 7 percent of the total population.

Certainly Paul knew that there were individuals and towns that had not yet received the gospel message located within the arc he described.

---

39. For a survey of the scholarship of Rodney Stark (sociologist) and Keith Hopkins, who are behind the low-end numbers, cf. Richard Carrier, "Was Christianity Too Improbable to be False?" The Secular Web, http://www.infidels.org/library/modern/richard_carrier/improbable/luck.html#18.2 (accessed April 1, 2012).

40. "Christianity began in Jerusalem when disciples of Jesus of Nazareth proclaimed that he was the expected Messiah. The movement spread slowly while Jesus was alive, but after Jesus' death it spread more rapidly. The diffusion was greatly assisted by Christian preachers and missionaries. It spread first to Samaria (in northern ancient Palestine), then to Phoenicia to the north-west, and south to Gaza and Egypt. Afterwards it was adopted in the Syrian cities of Antioch and Damascus, then subsequently in Cyprus, modern Turkey, modern Greece, Malta and Rome. It spread fast, and numbers quickly grew. Within the first century there were an estimated million Christians, comprising less than one per cent of the total world population. But within 400 years over 40 million people, nearly a quarter of the total population, had adopted Christianity. Imperial sponsorship of Christianity in the fourth century accounted for its rapid increase in influence and membership. The early spread of Christianity through the Roman Empire was achieved mainly by relocation diffusion aided by the well-developed system of imperial roads. Christian missionaries like Paul travelled from town to town spreading the gospel message." Chris Park, "Religion and Geography," in *Routledge Companion to the Study of Religion* (ed. John Hinnells; London: Routledge, 2004), as seen at p. 15 of Chris Parks, "Religion and Geography," Lancaster University, http://www.lancs.ac.uk/staff/gyaccp/geography%20and%20religion.pdf (accessed April 1, 2012).

When is the Task of Gospel Ministry Complete?

But this did not trouble him. He had fulfilled the ministry of the gospel of Christ, preaching the gospel where Christ has not already been named. The result of this work was that there was a real sense in which no one could claim, "Paul, there is room for you to work here or there." It seems likely from Paul's strategic geographic and demographic choices that, no matter where one went in the arc, it would be true that there was now some access to the gospel as a result of Paul's work. However, this does not form any part of Paul's argument. Never in Romans does he mention the cities he has been to, or the locations of the churches that have been started.

In light of this study, a number of conclusions can be drawn and applications can be made.

- There is such a thing as having fully preached the gospel. Paul did not conceive of the Great Commission as requiring an endless stream of preaching and convincing.
- Until the task of the ministry of the gospel is done, there is work to do and an obligation to do it. Paul was not free to leave the task and pursue something else until the ministry of the gospel was complete.
- Fully preaching the gospel in an area does not entail a personal presentation made to every individual.
- Fully preaching the gospel in an area does entail a degree of preaching the gospel in geographic proximity. (Paul had no more place left in Asia, but needed to go to Spain.)
- Fully preaching the gospel entails bringing the gospel into the public marketplace where it can be seen and understood and responded to.
- Fully preaching the gospel is driven primarily by God's redemptive, eschatological plan, and not by absolute numbers or geography.
- Practical applications of this understanding of fully preaching the gospel arise from what Paul says in this passage of Romans.

Paul has given four measuring sticks in verses 14–19a: his task of ministering the gospel to the Gentiles; the liturgical concept of his ministry accomplishing an acceptable offering; it is a work that can be spoken of in the aorist; and a point has been reached where there is a consistency between the word preached and the deeds done.

The task of fully preaching the gospel must be conceived of in light of God's greater plan, and particularly in light of the fulfillment of His divine plan already promised in Abraham. The peoples must be reached in this eschatological sense in every generation. Ambassadors of the gospel of Christ must strategically answer the question whether the peoples of their world have received the ministry of the gospel in their day as God wills. They must demonstrate the same intentionality that Paul did. This is not just "big picture" thinking, such as prioritizing the so-called "10–40 Window" over Europe as mission fields. Every ministry and minister should be asking what is "unfinished" about the gospel ministry in their own context. This is what Paul did.

Ministries should be seeking to answer questions such as these: Are there any groups of people that have not seen or heard the gospel? Is there an unreached age group within the population? An unreached social or economic class? An unreached language group? An unreached sub-culture? Is there any ministry of the gospel to these people? When and how can these unreached people be reached? But an important corollary, one that enables these new outreach initiatives, are these questions: Are there any people groups that *have* been reached by the gospel ministry? and, if so, what resources (manpower, finances) can we re-allocate from that group to an unreached group?

Fully ministering the gospel of Christ to a people does not necessarily mean that every single individual will have the gospel presented to him. However, sufficient work must be done that an acceptable "firstfruit" offering can be made. In doing this, it is both legitimate and important to strategically penetrate "centers" for the gospel ministry. Just as Paul targeted the geographic and commercial centers of Ephesus, Corinth, and Thessalonica, we can target political centers, social centers, economic centers, educational centers, business centers, linguistic centers, media centers, and so on with the hope and express purpose of fulfilling the gospel ministry in a given place. And a "firstfruits" focus will prevent us from becoming discouraged or overwhelmed at the large numbers who haven't heard, or the small numbers who respond.

The work needs to have a definable end-point, a moment when it is completed and does not require the further gospel ministry of the churches in order to be considered fulfilled. There should be a moment when it can truly be said that the task is complete. The idea of working toward a goal of completion and fulfillment of the ministry should shape the ministry from the very start. Fulfilling the gospel ministry is not simply an endless series of evangelistic thrusts, but rather a specific, definable task to

When is the Task of Gospel Ministry Complete?

be accomplished.[41] Ministries and ministers should design their ministry commitments in light of specific goals and even time frames. Paul's own ministry desire, to preach the gospel in Spain, was dependent on his first accomplishing his goal, bringing it to completion. He would not allow himself to proceed until he had fully accomplished the task before him. He did not assume that God would raise up someone else, but understood that he had a specific responsibility before God.

The ministry of the Holy Spirit should confirm the word that is preached in demonstrations of God's power. The work of the Holy Spirit should be evident in the miracles of salvation and sanctification, along with any other works that the Spirit wills to accomplish.

Each of these four standards can be held up to the gospel ministry. They are concrete gauges whereby God's ongoing eschatological plan can be seen of bringing blessing to all the families of the earth.

Paul's "seeing" and "understanding" (Romans 15:20) concept of gospel ministry has a parallel in what Paul has already said in verse 18, that the Gentiles have been brought "to obedience." Together these phrases make it clear that the gospel ministry is complete when there is a *response* to the message. This idea is vital and delegitimizes proclamation-centered ministry which is not geared toward response. Such, by Paul's standard, does not "fulfill the ministry of the gospel." Ministries that claim to have reached a people group by *impersonal* tract distribution or media broadcasting, for example, would need to incorporate response mechanisms in order to meet the qualification that Paul sets for fulfilling the gospel ministry.

With the words of Romans 15:22–25, Paul makes clear that he is now free to minister elsewhere. Up till now, Paul was not free to go to Rome because his task of gospel ministry was not yet fulfilled. The implications of this for strategic ministry planning include a responsibility to completely fulfill the gospel ministry before we are "free" to work on other ministries. Paul was actually hindered (presumably by the Lord), prevented from moving on to other things, until he fulfilled the ministry of the gospel to the peoples of Asia. Once a people group has been reached, Paul's model of moving on to the next people group is equally compelling.

---

41. This is nascent in Jesus' own commission to His followers to make disciples "of all the nations" and be His witnesses "in Jerusalem and in all Judea and Samaria, and to the end of the earth." These commands, to be obeyed, require a systematic, intentional approach. They are specific. They give clear information concerning who the target group is and the extent to which the gospel should be preached.

Not Weary of Well Doing

Often evangelistic or gospel ministry is motivated by the vague idea that "we should be sharing the gospel." Gospel ministry can even be guilt-motivated. It can be a mechanical, perfunctory involvement in an evangelistic method or campaign because we "should" be doing evangelism. This concept of gospel ministry is wrong and will not result in fulfilling the gospel ministry truly.

Paul shows us that the correct understanding of gospel ministry comes from a profound grasp of God's great redemptive plan as revealed in His Word. We should and must be committed to ministering the gospel because we understand that this work of spreading God's salvation is most central to God's heart and plan for the world today. We evangelize, not simply to obey a command, but to enact the fulfillment of the divine purpose throughout the ages. When we conceive of our gospel ministry in these terms, it should focus our efforts, just as it focused Paul's efforts. It should cause us to be more strategic. It should cause us to consider the field before us. It should cause us to prioritize certain mission efforts over others. It should cause us to conceive of gospel ministry in terms of measurable goals, geography, demographics, and time frames. And, finally, it should encourage us to seek God for what the next step of ministry is, as well as to resist moving on to that next step until the present step is completed.

Paul was guided, even strongly constrained, in his ministry by an understanding that the gospel ministry is not some "general principle," but rather a specific, central plan of God that is being carried out in the world. Paul understood God's plan and saw his own ministry in the light of that plan. By connecting to this plan, Paul knew both what he should do and when he was (and was not) finished with the ministry of the gospel. May the Spirit of the Lord so guide us.

Obstacles for a Church Planter: Paul's Greatest Struggles in Planting the Church at Corinth

H. H. DRAKE WILLIAMS III

Church planting can be one of the most important ways to evangelize. Many who do not understand the Christian faith are brought into a loving community. They hear the good news of Jesus Christ taught weekly, and experience Christian life with others. As a result, those who do not know Jesus are attracted to the Savior. Many new converts come to the faith as a result of church planting.[1]

Starting new churches, however, is difficult work. Great church planters have dealt with many challenges, encountering many obstacles in their quest to establish a community of faith. What can begin as a noble vision often faces unforeseen opposition. Changing leaders, conditions, internal problems, and funding are some of the many barriers that church planters face.

One of the great church planters of early Christianity was the Apostle Paul. Despite his outstanding education, dramatic conversion, and extensive support, he experienced many barriers in his church planting work in cities such as Thessalonica, Philippi, and Ephesus. While there are records of this work, the lengthiest communication that we have about his church planting work is with the church in Corinth. At this city, he experienced extensive opposition.

---

1. I thank my friend and colleague Cecil Stalnaker for drawing this to my attention.

Paul arrived in Corinth in A.D. 50, planted a church, and then left. He corresponded with this young church through A.D. 57, and visited them several times. Through most of these years, the church was in danger of not continuing. Even as late as writing 2 Corinthians, Paul was wondering if the work had been in vain (cf. 2 Cor 5:20; 6:1).

The following will explore the most significant obstacles to establishing the church at Corinth. The facts will be derived largely from information within Acts 18 and the letters of 1 and 2 Corinthians. Some details about Paul's visit can also be found from Acts 20:2–4 and Romans 16:21–23. These passages will be considered for the background to the significant opposition that Paul faced in planting the church at Corinth.

Paul's First Opponents: Those from Outside the Church

Paul first visited Corinth during his second missionary journey. Upon his arrival, he attached himself quickly to Aquila and Priscilla. He lived with them and worked with them as tentmakers, and then preached in the synagogue (Acts 18:1–6). The first part of Paul's ministry in Corinth was to those who were Jewish, but he also ministered to Gentiles who feared God. He was opposed by the Jews in the synagogue and then expelled. Despite this poor reception, however, there was fruit from this activity. Titius Justus and Crispus, the synagogue ruler, believed the message (Acts 18:8). The first church meeting may even have met in Titius Justus' house, as he also is known as Gaius (Rom 16:23; 1 Cor 1:14).[2] Paul's first opposition to his church planting work thus came from non-believers, particularly Jewish leaders.

His mission work in many other cities faced this type of resistance. After Paul was sent out from the church in Antioch, he faced opponents from outside the church frequently and from the very beginning of his missionary journeys. In the first extended narrative of his missionary journeys, Luke records Paul's confrontation with the Jewish prophet Bar-Jesus, also known as Elymas in Acts 13:6–8. This leads to Paul calling him a "son of the devil," and then calling down blindness upon him (Acts 13:6–11).

Paul continues to experience opposition from non-believers throughout Acts 13. This is especially evident when he is at the synagogue in the city of Pisidian Antioch. When he is asked to give a word of exhortation,

---

2. His full name would then have been Gaius Titius Justus. Cf. D. J. Moo, *The Epistle to the Romans*, NIGTC (Grand Rapids: Eerdmans, 1996), 935.

Paul gives a lengthy exhortation from Scripture and history. He then recounts the appearance of Jesus before John the Baptist and Pontius Pilate, and states that Jesus has died and been resurrected. His speech concludes by urging the Jewish leaders in Pisidian Antioch to believe the resurrection of Jesus (Acts 13:13–41). While these leaders are at first interested in Paul's message, they become jealous of Paul and contradict and defame him (Acts 13:44–45). Several verses later, Luke records that Paul was persecuted for his efforts (Acts 13:50).[3]

Paul experiences frequent resistance from outside opposition in other places in his missionary activities, leading up to his time at Corinth. In Acts 14, he endures threats of being stoned to death at the city of Iconium (Acts 14:6). In Lystra, Paul is stoned and left for dead (Acts 14:19). At Philippi, Paul is falsely accused by the merchants of the city. Paul is beaten by rods and then ends up in jail (Acts 16:22–23). In Acts 17, a mob forms as a result of his teaching. Paul and his companion Silas had to flee by night to escape the resistance (Acts 17:10). These are all examples of resistance from those who were not in the church. Paul experienced severe resistance even before planting the church at Corinth.[4]

The resistance that Paul faces in his first encounter with the Corinthians within Acts 18 fits in line with the resistance he experienced in other cities. As in previous instances within his missionary work, Paul faced opposition from Jewish leaders. There is a particular overlap with Luke's prior record of Paul's visit to Pisidian Antioch. Paul preaches in the synagogue and the Jewish religious leaders become enraged and revile him. Luke even uses the same word from the Pisidian Antioch incident from Acts 13:45 in Acts 18:6. The ESV translates this as "revile," but other versions, such as the KJV and NASB, use the word "blaspheme," which better draws out the meaning of the word βλασφημέω. Afterwards, Paul turns to the Gentiles at Corinth, just as he declares plainly in Pisidian Antioch (Acts 13:46; 18:6).

From the beginning of Paul's church planting work at Corinth, he faced strong and unfair opposition from other leaders. They reviled and blasphemed him, indicating that they felt that his work was not only wrong but also opposed to the one true God. Despite the opposition, Paul becomes

---

3. Note that the same word διωγμός is used in Acts 13:50 as the persecution that arose following the stoning of Stephen in Acts 8:1.

4. For further discussion of resistance to the gospel message within the book of Acts, see the following article. B. Rapske, "Opposition to the Plan of God and Persecution," in *Witness to the Gospel: the Theology of Acts*, ed. I. H. Marshall and D. Peterson (Grand Rapids: Eerdmans, 1998), 235–56.

divinely reassured that there are many people within the city for the Lord, and thus he continues his work (Acts 18:9f).[5]

This, then, begins the second phase of his church planting ministry in Corinth. Paul remains in the city for about 18 months. His ministry is directed to the Gentiles. As a result of his efforts, he becomes the founder of the church in Corinth (1 Cor 4:14–15). After the church was founded, Paul left for Ephesus in A.D. 51.

Paul's Second Opponent: The Influx of Pagan Social Values

While the church had been established in Corinth in A.D. 51, it was unstable for many years. Paul wrote several letters and had several subsequent visits, both activities of which there is evidence within 1 and 2 Corinthians. The first of these letters was written a few years later. This is the letter prior to 1 Corinthians. While there is no copy of it that remains, evidence of it can be found within 1 Cor 5:9–13. The second letter is 1 Corinthians. The third letter is the "severe" letter, which is considered to be a lost intermediary letter.[6] There are evidences of what was in the "severe letter" within 2 Corinthians. The final correspondence that we have from Paul to the Corinthians is 2 Corinthians.[7] Since 2 Corinthians is dated from A.D. 56, the contents of these four letters reveal the opposition that Paul faced in the early years of the church at Corinth, a time when the church plant was still fragile.

Scholars have considered several sources for the problems within the Corinthian church after Paul left Corinth the first time. Earlier studies placed the blame on Gnosticism that infiltrated the Corinthian church.[8] Gnosticism, however, is a second century phenomenon, and most

---

5. Note how this, too, is a theme within Acts where the Holy Spirit reassures at key moments (cf. Acts 5:18f; 7:55f; 12:5–15; 16:26; 23:11). Rapske, "Opposition to the Plan of God and Persecution," 251–4.

6. While there is controversy regarding which letter is the severe letter, it is best to take the severe letter as an intermediary letter. See M. J. Harris, *The Second Epistle to the Corinthians*, NIGTC (Grand Rapids: Eerdmans, 2005), 3–8.

7. For discussion about the integrity of 2 Corinthians, cf. Harris, *Second Epistle to the Corinthians*, 8–50.

8. W. Schmithals, *Gnosticism in Corinth: an Investigation of the Letters to the Corinthians* (Nashville: Abingdon, 1971), and M. Winter, *Pnuematiker und Psychiker in Korinth: zum religionsgeschichtlichen Hintergrund von 1 Kor. 2,6–3,4* (Marburg: Elwert, 1975).

scholarship has now discarded this opinion.[9] Some have placed blame on false teaching that infiltrated the church. This has ranged from charismatic teaching to a misunderstanding of baptism to an over-realized eschatology or a misunderstanding of the resurrection.[10] Paul, however, never specifically addresses false teaching or teachers. While some of these may be symptoms, it appears that there is a greater problem affecting Corinth. Indeed, the true nature of the problems at the church in Corinth has been a matter of dispute for nearly half a century,[11] but recent scholarship is settling upon Greco-Roman pagan values as the chief cause. For example, B. W. Winter writes

> The problems which arose subsequent to Paul's departure [from Corinth] did so partly because the Christians were "cosmopolitans" i.e., citizens of this world and, in particular, citizens or residents of Roman Corinth, and thus the primary influences on the responses of the Christians were derived principally from *Romanitas*.[12]

In his commentary on 1 Corinthians, Richard Hays states about the Corinthians, "[they] are uncritically perpetuating the norms and values of the pagan culture around them."[13] David Garland concludes similarly when he writes, "The influences upon them [the Corinthian believers] were more amorphous and their behavior was swayed by culturally ingrained habits from their pagan past and by values instilled by a popularized secular ethics."[14] Similar conclusions are found also in the commentaries by Thiselton and Schrage.[15] Greco-Roman secular practices had infiltrated the church.

---

9. Note that Wilckens who once supported this viewpoint changed his view. See U. Wilckens, "Zu 1 Kor. 2,1–16," in *Theologia Crucis – Signum Crucis: Festschrift für E. Dinkler zum 70 Geburtstag*, ed. C. Andersen and G. Klein (Tübingen: Mohr, 1979), 516–37.

10. Cf. R. Baumann, *Mitte und Norm des Christlichen: eine Auslegung von 1 Korinther 1,1–3,4* (Münster: Aschendorff, 1968); J. H. Schütz, *Paul and the Anatomy of Apostolic Authority* (Cambridge: CUP, 1975); A. Thiselton, "Realized Eschatology at Corinth," *NTS* 24 (1978) 510–26; and E. Käsemann, *Jesus means Freedom: a Polemical Survey of the New Testament* (London: SCM, 1969).

11. Cf. D. G. Horrell and E. Adams, eds., *Christianity at Corinth: the Quest for the Pauline Church* (Louisville: John Knox, 2004), 16–23.

12. B. W. Winter, *After Paul Left Corinth: the Influence of Secular Ethics and Social Change* (Grand Rapids: Eerdmans, 2001), 27–28.

13. R. B. Hays, *First Corinthians* (Louisville: Westminster John Knox, 1997), 71.

14. D. B. Garland, *1 Corinthians* (Grand Rapids: Baker, 2003), 13.

15. A. C. Thiselton, *The First Epistle to the Corinthians* (Grand Rapids: Eerdmans,

Many ethical problems could be identified within 1 Corinthians. Despite the disparity, several of these could be grouped under immorality and idolatry. These two vices were common within Greco-Roman secular society. Furthermore, Gentiles were characterized by these two vices. In Jewish literature that was contemporary with Paul's writing, immorality and idolatry were seen as critical problems. In the Sibylline Oracles, for example, there are numerous injunctions against these two vices. These documents, which range from the mid-second century B.C. to the seventh century A.D., present Jewish exhortations directed to the sins of the culture. While there are many ethical problems that are identified, they can be effectively summarized under the sins of immorality and idolatry.[16]

In the Jewish and Christian interpretation of the Ten Commandments from the time of Paul's writing, immorality and idolatry were becoming increasingly distinguished amongst these commandments. William Loader has noticed how the prohibition against idolatry was used by Jewish and Christian interpreters to summarize the first five commandments. The commandment against immorality heads the second half of the Ten Commandments.[17]

In several places in Paul's letters, immorality and idolatry have also been used to represent the Greco-Roman pagan culture that rejects God. According to Romans 1:21–28, these vices were well rooted within pagan culture. As Romans 1:21 indicates, ". . . although they knew God, they did not honor him as God or give thanks to him, but they became futile in their thinking, and their foolish hearts were darkened." As a result, they "exchanged the glory of the immortal God for images resembling mortal man and birds and animals and reptiles (Rom 1:23)." This then degenerates into immorality in which God gives them up to perverse practices. Several other places within the New Testament identify immorality and idolatry as key aspects of Greco-Roman pagan culture (cf. Acts 15:20, 29; 21:25; Eph 5:5; Col 3:5; Rev 22:15).

2000), xviii; W. Schrage, *Der erste Brief an die Korinther*, 4 vols. (Zürich: Benzinger, 1991–2001), 1:42.

16. See also the *Sibylline Oracles* which denounce idolatry and immorality and identifies them as pagan vices. Cf. J. J. Collins, "Sibylline Oracles," in *Old Testament Pseudepigrapha* ed. J. H. Charlesworth (New York: Doubleday, 1983), 1:323. "The sins in which the Sybil expresses most interest are idolatry and sexual offenses."

17. W. Loader, *The Septuagint, Sexuality and the New Testament* (Grand Rapids: Eerdmans, 2004), 7.

Immorality

The first two letters that Paul wrote to Corinth indicate that immorality and idolatry were significant problems within the church. Paul's first letter to the church plant in Corinth indicates that immorality had infiltrated the life of the church. This became a problem nearly a year after his leaving.

The first letter that Paul wrote the Corinthians was written approximately in A.D. 51. This is not 1 Corinthians, but a letter written earlier. Evidence of some of its contents can be seen from 1 Corinthians 5:9–13. That letter chided the Corinthians for their sexually immoral behavior and forbade them from associating with immoral people.

> I wrote to you in my letter not to associate with sexually immoral people—not at all meaning the sexually immoral of this world, or the greedy and swindlers, or idolaters, since then you would need to go out of the world. But now I am writing to you not to associate with anyone who bears the name of brother if he is guilty of sexual immorality or greed, or is an idolater, reviler, drunkard, or swindler—not even to eat with such a one.[18]

Moral standards had slipped within the life of the church following Paul's departure. The sexually immoral were mixing with the brothers in Corinth, and Paul was urging them not to engage in immoral practices.

This problem of sexual immorality continued into 1 Corinthians, which Paul wrote in A.D. 55. In 1 Corinthians 5, Paul rebukes the Corinthians for accepting a man living with his father's new wife. Two men of the same family were having the same woman! Even those outside of the church had trouble dealing with this (1 Cor 5:1). The Corinthian church is to remove the immoral man in 1 Corinthians 5:1–11. This continues further into 1 Corinthians 6. In 1 Corinthians 6:9–10, the Corinthians are to avoid immorality of any kind: "neither the sexually immoral, nor idolaters, nor adulterers, nor men who practice homosexuality, nor thieves, nor the greedy, nor drunkards, nor revilers, nor swindlers will inherit the kingdom of God." The Corinthians are to "flee sexual immorality" (1 Cor 6:18).

In 1 Corinthians 6:12–17, the Corinthians are called to avoid prostitution. There is debate as to what type of prostitution is involved in this chapter. Some have suggested that this is sexual immorality of any kind.[19]

---

18. All Scripture texts in this essay are taken from the English Standard Version (ESV) unless otherwise noted.

19. See G. Fee, *The First Epistle to the Corinthians*, NICNT (Grand Rapids: Eerdmans,

Paul's explicit mention of prostitution in 6:15–16 seems to point to a specific situation, rather than a general one. Some have advocated that Paul was rebuking the participation in sacred prostitution as a part of pagan worship.[20] This is unlikely, due to the lack of sacred prostitution in Paul's day.[21] The temple of Aphrodite that is often appealed to with its many sacred prostitutes was destroyed in 146 B.C., and then rebuilt well after the time that Paul was present.

There are two other possibilities for the prostitution that Paul rebukes. Paul could be addressing temple or secular prostitution. Several of the temples in Corinth hosted dinners after which prostitutes were available. The prostitute would have been a part of the event rather than having any special ritual significance. Feasting and prostitution was connected within Jewish and Christian writing.[22] Oftentimes, the brothel keepers would take their prostitutes to great festive occasions.[23] Various ancient texts reveal that sexual pleasure was expected following a banquet (cf. Cicero, *Phil.* 2.104–5; *De fin.* 2.23; Seneca, *Ep.* 47.7; 95.23).[24]

Secular prostitution may equally have been the problem. Jewish texts link immorality with greed as distinguishing marks of Gentiles. For example, sexual immorality was seen as one of the three nets of Belial in the *Damascus Document* (CD 4:15–17). Other places within the Old Testament treat immorality as sin. Joseph flees Potiphar's wife in Genesis 39:9, since lying with her would constitute wickedness and be a sin against God. Similar ideas are repeated by David in Psalm 51:3, his psalm of penitence. Considering that the Corinthians felt as if they had the right to do anything (1 Cor 6:12), it is just as likely that a general temptation to immorality may be envisioned.[25]

1987), 250; A. Robertson and A. Plummer, *A Critical and Exegetical Commentary on the First Epistle of St. Paul to the Corinthians*, ICC (Edinburgh: T. & T. Clark, 1911), 121.

20. K. van der Toorn, "Cultic Prostitution," *ABD* 5:510.

21. Cf. J. Murphy-O'Connor, *St. Paul's Corinth: Texts and Archaeology* (Collegeville, MN: Liturgical, 1990), 56.

22. B. S. Rosner, "Temple Prostitution in 1 Corinthians 6:12–20," *NovT* 40/4 (1998): 348–50.

23. Cf. B. W. Winter, *Seek the Welfare of the City: Christians as Benefactors and Citizens* (Grand Rapids: Eerdmans, 1994), 174.

24. C. Edwards, *The Politics of Immorality in Ancient Rome* (Cambridge: Cambridge UP, 1993), 188.

25. R. E. Ciampa and B. S. Rosner, *The First Letter to the Corinthians* (Grand Rapids: Apollos, 2010), 248–50.

Obstacles for a Church Planter

Whatever the case, Paul rebukes loose sexual practice that had infiltrated the church. He then issues guidelines for faithful sexual practice in 1 Corinthians 7. Following his rebuke of loose sexuality, Paul advocates for self-control in 1 Corinthians 7, whether single or married. Rather than succumbing to immorality, the Corinthians are to have sexual relations with one's spouse (1 Cor 7:2). Married couples are to maintain sexual relations rather than refuse their spouse (1 Cor 7:1–7). Even if one is married to a non-believer, Paul encourages that they remain married (1 Cor 7:12–16). If one is not married, Paul encourages self-restraint (1 Cor 7:25–38). Rather than succumbing to sexual temptation, the Corinthians are urged to glorify God in their bodies. Thus, 1 Corinthians 7 completes Paul's "holiness code" that he began in 1 Corinthians 5.[26]

Idolatry

The first letter that Paul wrote to the Corinthians (seen in 1 Cor 5:9–13), as well as his second letter (1 Corinthians), reveal a second obstacle from Greco-Roman pagan culture which Paul faced as a church planter. This issue is idolatry which had infiltrated the church.

Greco-Roman Corinth was filled with idols.[27] The second century traveler Pausanias identified a large number of Greek, Roman, and Egyptian deities that were worshipped within ancient Corinth. There was a large temple dedicated to Apollo, the sun god.[28] Corinthians would seek healing from Asclepius, the god of healing and medicine. There were also temples to Roman imperial personalities, such as a temple to Octavia, the sister of Emperor Augustus. Other gods also were worshipped, such as Dionysius, Neptune, Pan, Artemis, Zeus, Athena, Poseidon, Isis, Tyche, Poseidon, Kthonios, Hyposistos, Athena, and Aphrodite. The Corinthians would certainly have identified with the statement that Paul makes in 1 Corinthians 8:5: ". . . there may be so-called gods in heaven or on earth—as indeed there are many 'gods' and many 'lords.'"

---

26. Ciampa and Rosner, *First Letter to the Corinthians*, 266.

27. Cf. Pausinius 2.2–5. R. M. Grant, *Paul in the Roman World: the Conflict at Corinth* (Louisville: Westminster, 2001), 64.

28. Dinsmoor called this temple the largest on the Peloppenesian peninsula. W. D. Dinsmoor, "The largest temple in the Peleponnesos" *Hesperia Supplement* 8 (1949): 104–15.

It is evident that idolatry was a concern within the church at Corinth. The first letter to the Corinthians reveals that Paul was urging them not to associate with someone who calls himself a brother but who is an idolater (1 Cor 5:11). Several chapters within 1 Corinthians address concerns related to idolatry. In 1 Corinthians 8, Paul urges people not to participate in an activity that they consider to be idolatrous. In 8:7, some of the weaker brothers in the Corinthian church struggled with eating food offered to idols. As a result, Paul urges the stronger brothers among them not to eat food sacrificed to idols. By their eating, they were causing those with weaker consciences to be vulnerable to idolatry (1 Cor 8:10–11).

Then, in 1 Corinthians 10, Paul warns against stronger brothers who do not take the concerns of idolatry seriously enough. While they may believe that they are innocent, their actions reveal that they are participating in idolatry. Paul urges them to remember the history of their predecessors in the faith. He exhorts them to remember the failings of those at the time of the Exodus, which specifically concern idolatry. Paul is explicit when he writes in 1 Corinthians 10:6–7, "Now these things took place as examples for us, that we might not desire evil as they did. Do not be idolaters as some of them were." They were unaware of their own vulnerability (1 Cor 10:11–12); thus, Paul issues the plea that they flee idolatry just as he urges the Corinthians to flee immorality (1 Cor 6:18; 10:14).[29]

The dangers of idolatry are explained further within 1 Corinthians 10. Participation in pagan meals compromises the Christian's participation within the Lord's Supper. Paul contrasts the food offered to idols with the Lord's Supper. Participating in the Lord's Supper precludes participating in idolatrous feasts. The sacrifices of demons are offered to demons and not to God. There is no part that one can have in the participation with demons when one celebrates the one true sacrifice that has been offered to God (1 Cor 10:14–22).

Besides these explicit instances that forbid participating in idolatry, there are several times within 1 Corinthians where Paul uses language that asserts the superiority of the Christian God over these idols. In 1 Corinthians 8:6, he writes, "yet for us there is one God, the Father, from whom are all things and for whom we exist, and one Lord, Jesus Christ, through whom are all things and through whom we exist." In 1 Corinthians 15:24–28, he asserts the superiority of the Christian God.

---

29. Note that Paul urges the flight from idolatry with the same verb (φεύγετε) that he urges the flight from immorality in 1 Cor 6:18.

> Then comes the end, when he delivers the kingdom to God the Father after destroying every rule and every authority and power. For he must reign until he has put all his enemies under his feet. The last enemy to be destroyed is death. For "God has put all things in subjection under his feet." But when it says, "all things are put in subjection," it is plain that he is excepted who put all things in subjection under him. When all things are subjected to him, then the Son himself will also be subjected to him who put all things in subjection under him, that God may be all in all.

Passages like these imply that there is a conflict with idolatry that must be resolved.

Other sections within 1 Corinthians present a positive reply to idolatry. Instead of worshipping other idols, 1 Corinthians 11–14 presents the proper way that the sovereign God is to be worshipped. Instead of revering other gods, the Corinthians are to glorify God through their own worship. This entails having order with husbands and wives in the marital relationship, respect for each other in partaking of the Lord's Supper, and order in relation to the use of spiritual gifts.[30]

This volume of texts illustrates that Paul was confronting idolatry within the church. It was a major concern that occupied several chapters within Paul's first letters to the Corinthian congregation.

Conflict with Christian Leaders from Changing Church Dynamics

A final major obstacle that can be seen in Paul's correspondence with the Corinthians through his writing of 1 Corinthians is changing church dynamics. This is something overlooked often, but it is a significant factor in the crisis at Corinth.

Paul Barnett, in *The Corinthian Question: Why did the Church oppose Paul?*, provides a list of these changing relationships from 1 Corinthians. The italicized portions show how many were directly related to Paul's responses to the critical attitude of the Corinthians.

- *Factions* (1:10–12; 3:3–4)
- *Fascination with rhetoric* (1:17–25; 2:1–5)
- Spirit of elitism among the wealthy towards the poor (1:26–31)
- *Elite's judgment and snobbery towards Paul* (4:1–20)

30. Ciampa and Rosner, *First Letter to the Corinthians*, 24.

Not Weary of Well Doing

- Toleration of incest (5:1–2)
- Litigation between members in public (6:1–8)
- Visits to temple brothels (6:9–20)
- Ascetical attitudes to sexuality and marriage (7:1–40)
- Men of knowledge a stumbling block to the weak (8:1–13)
- *Paul's defense for declining payment (9:1–27)*
- Rebuke to those who continue to attend temples (10:1–22)
- Uncaring attitudes to unbelievers and Jews (10:23–11:1)
- Wives praying and prophesying bareheaded (11:2–16)
- Selfishness of "haves" to "have nots" at the Lord's Supper (11:17–34)
- Spiritual elitism by tongues-speakers (12:1–14:25)
- Echo inspired chaos at church meetings (14:26–40)
- "There is no resurrection of the dead" (15:12)
- *Apollos will not be returning (16:12)*
- *Foreshadowing the visit of Timothy (16:10–11; cf. 4:17)*
- *Request for recognition of Stephanas (16:15–18)*[31]

When viewed in this manner, changing church dynamics can account for approximately four chapters within 1 Corinthians. Barnett notes this significant problem when he states, "It was that in the previous three years the character and membership of the church had changed and no longer recognized Paul's leadership, a leadership that had been eclipsed in the meantime by the arrival of Paul and Cephas."[32] The church at Corinth has changed in its leadership and composition from the time when Paul was present in Corinth. This, indeed, is a significant obstacle.

The significance of this is accentuated by the lengthy sections in which Paul addresses the church's social dynamics and leadership. Within 1 Corinthians 1–3, Paul counters the party spirit that was found. It is the first concern that he addresses within 1 Corinthians 1. Interestingly, he chooses not to support any of the different parties found within 1 Corinthians 1:12. Most notably, he does not select his own party or the Christ party. Instead,

---

31. P. Barnett, *The Corinthian Question: Why did the Church oppose Paul?* (Nottingham: Apollos, 2011), 82–83.

32. Barnett, *Corinthian Question*, 101.

he chooses to counter their problem with the cross of Christ. This problem of party factions and divisions then extends into 1 Corinthians 3. Instead of encouraging allegiance to one party leader, he urges the Corinthians to think of themselves as all part of one field, one building, and one temple under the Lord's leadership (1 Cor 3:6–17).

He counters hard-headed leaders in 1 Corinthians 4. He urges them not to live as worldly people, counting their wealth and glorying in their position. This he states in 1 Corinthians 4:7–13:

> For who sees anything different in you? What do you have that you did not receive? If then you received it, why do you boast as if you did not receive it? Already you have all you want! Already you have become rich! Without us you have become kings! And would that you did reign, so that we might share the rule with you! For I think that God has exhibited us apostles as last of all, like men sentenced to death, because we have become a spectacle to the world, to angels, and to men. We are fools for Christ's sake, but you are wise in Christ. We are weak, but you are strong. You are held in honor, but we in disrepute. To the present hour we hunger and thirst, we are poorly dressed and buffeted and homeless, and we labor, working with our own hands. When reviled, we bless; when persecuted, we endure; when slandered, we entreat. We have become, and are still, like the scum of the world, the refuse of all things.

He counters their snobbery with cross-like behavior.[33]

Other sections within 1 Corinthians may also contain overtones of conflict with the Corinthian leaders. In 1 Corinthians 9, for example, Paul provides a lengthy description of his conduct. While he had certain rights to receive money for his labors or to take a believing wife, he chooses to forgo these. He chooses not to make use of these rights so as to keep obstacles from the way of the gospel of Christ (1 Cor 9:12). Such a mention implies that the current leaders at Corinth were putting obstacles in Paul's path.

Throughout 1 Corinthians, Paul will confront divisive behavior.[34] In 1 Corinthians 11:17–22, he will confront those who are coming together in a divided manner for the Lord's Supper. Some come together having already

---

33. See further R. Pickett, *The Cross in Corinth: The Social Significance of the Death of Jesus* (Sheffield: Sheffield Academic Press, 1997).

34. Note how this is a major theme brought out through in M. Mitchell, *Paul and the Rhetoric of Reconciliation: An Exegetical Investigation of the Language and Composition of I Corinthians* (Louisville: Westminster, 1992).

eaten, while others go hungry. He concludes that they are divided, saying in 1 Corinthians 11:19, "there must be factions among you in order that those who are genuine among you may be recognized."

How would these relationships have become so strained between Paul and the Corinthians? It is likely that one cause was the changing relationships that took place at Corinth. Paul had arrived in A.D. 49, and by the time that he is writing 1 Corinthians, there would have been a sizable number of changes in relationships in the seven years.

Paul had stayed with the Corinthians for a year and a half. The size of the Corinthian congregation during Paul's time has been estimated at approximately 80 people. This would have included Paul, Silas, Timothy, and a handful of families. It would have increased when Crispus, the synagogue official, and his household came to faith. Several other household groups would have formed after this. This would have increased the church to around 200 members by the time that Paul wrote 1 Corinthians.[35]

The dynamics had changed substantially by the time that he wrote 1 Corinthians. This can be seen by the difficulties with factions forming. Some wanted to follow Paul, others Cephas, and some Apollos (1 Cor 1:12). This had been encouraged by the visits of these other leaders to the city. Apollos may particularly have drawn the church after himself. In Acts 18:27–28, it appears that he stimulated the growth of the church. His skills in refuting the Jews in public gave confidence to the church and allowed it to increase. Those who arrived later may have inadvertently obscured Paul's leadership.

The church also had grown since Paul had left. In 1 Corinthians 1:1, Paul addresses believers *in every place*. This might even include the port of Cenchrea (Rom 16:1). A growing church can also be seen in 2 Corinthians 1:1, where Paul addresses believers in *the whole of Achaia*, which implies expansion into the whole province.[36] The growing numbers created new relational problems.[37]

The dynamics within the church were also enflamed by Greco-Roman values that can be traced to a traveling group of speakers known as the Sophists. This group of rhetoricians would enter major cities within the Greco-Roman world and speak persuasively with rhetorical wisdom. They

---

35. Barnett, *Corinthian Question*, 225–7.

36. Barnett, *Corinthian Question*, 80–81.

37. Barnett estimates that there may have been as many as 200 when the whole church met at the time Paul wrote 2 Corinthians. Barnett, *Corinthian Question*, 225–7.

encouraged their hearers to give of their money and to form factions. They supported the values of power and wealth, and liked to boast in their own abilities. There is evidence that there were several Sophists who influenced Corinth.[38]

The language of the Sophists is evident within 1 Corinthians. Particularly, there are notable overlaps with the language of 1 Corinthians 1:17–2:5.[39] Words such as σοφία, λόγος, and ἀπόδειξις were known and used by the Sophists. The ideas of boasting were plain within Corinth (1 Cor 1:26–31). The effect of division was evident from Paul's rebuke of party factions (1 Cor 1:12; 3:4, 22). Furthermore, the Corinthians' love for power and wealth could have emerged from the values that these traveling speakers provided from their rhetorical wisdom. Their influence intensified the changing dynamics of the Corinthian church and provided another obstacle for Paul.

Direct Conflict with a Specific Leader

Paul faced further obstacles with the young church in Corinth after writing 1 Corinthians. After he had written this letter, Paul then returned to his work in Ephesus with the expectation that he would travel to Corinth with the collection (1 Cor 16:5–8). Meanwhile, he sent Timothy to visit the Corinthians (1 Cor 16:10–11; cf. Acts 19:22). When he arrived in Corinth, Timothy found that problems were much greater than what he expected. As a result, Paul decided to visit Corinth immediately. He would then go on to Macedonia and return for a second visit on his way to Jerusalem (2 Cor 1:15–16). He was expecting that his arrival at Corinth would provide a "second experience of grace," and his sincere conduct would be proved. Instead of solving problems, however, this visit turned into what scholars call the "painful visit," the next great obstacle for the church planting work (2 Cor 2:1).

During this second visit to Corinth, the relational problems became great. There was at least one person who had caused Paul personal pain and in turn had disturbed the Corinthian congregation (2 Cor 2:5). The

---

38. See B. W. Winter, *Philo and Paul among the Sophists: A Hellenistic-Jewish and a Christian Response* (Cambridge: Cambridge UP, 1996), 109–40.

39. Cf. D. A. Litfin, *St. Paul's Theology of Proclamation: 1 Corinthians 1–4 and Greco-Roman Rhetoric* (Cambridge: Cambridge UP, 1994).

opponent was punished by the rest of the congregation, but still Paul felt hurt personally (2 Cor 7:12).

There are some things that are known about the person who opposed Paul. He was from the Corinthian church. This is evident, since 2 Corinthians 2:6 states that the offender received "punishment by the majority." Paul would not have called for punishment of an outsider but rather for dismissal. Furthermore, Paul would not have asked for forgiveness and comfort for the repentant one since this would have indicated that the man would have been allowed to return to fellowship (2 Cor 2:7).[40]

The person who opposed Paul may have been the man in incest from 1 Corinthians 5:1. Barnett takes this opinion, seeing that the man identified in incest within 1 Corinthians would likely have become bitter and enraged. It appears to be too much of a coincidence that one person is identified in both 1 Corinthians 5 and 2 Corinthians 2. A powerful person within the church would have been able to get away with incest and then unleash his rage at Paul.[41]

Despite this viewpoint, it is more likely that the one who caused Paul so much heartache at the painful visit was someone else. Paul does not recall a rebuking of the entire church within 2 Corinthians 2 as he recounts what took place during the painful visit. In 1 Corinthians 5, he did point to the culpability of the entire church when he addressed the one in incest. Furthermore, Paul's retelling of the confrontation within 2 Corinthians shows no reference to sexual immorality, but rather a direct confrontation with Paul's authority (2 Cor 7:12).[42] Thus, these two conflicts seem unrelated. It is more likely that this is a new confrontation that arose separate from the incestuous affair.

It is likely that the dispute between Paul and the other leader involved a conflict between personal relationships and was not a doctrinal dispute. The confrontation was most likely a verbal attack that took place at some time between Paul's painful visit and the severe letter. He may have been a spokesman for an anti-Pauline group. He may have objected to the process of church discipline.[43] Perhaps the person took advantage of the collection

---

40. Harris, *Second Epistle to the Corinthians*, 224–5.

41. See Barnett, *The Corinthian Question*, 141. This has been a viewpoint supported by others. E.g., P. E. Hughes, *Paul's Second Epistle to the Corinthians* (Grand Rapids: London, 1962), 59–65.

42. Harris, *The Second Epistle to the Corinthians*, 224–7.

43. Harris, *The Second Epistle to the Corinthian*, 227.

funds for Jerusalem.⁴⁴ While these are conjecture, it is apparent that the confrontation was severe and caused Paul grief. Personal emotional pain was thus another obstacle that Paul faced in the establishment of the church at Corinth.

Opponents from Outside the Church

While most of the opposition that Paul faced with the Corinthian church came from within the church, there was one group that he opposed which came from outside the church. These were the "super apostles." This group had entered the church following the painful visit and before the writing of 2 Corinthians. Titus had reported their presence.

Paul labels these new missionaries in various different ways. He calls them "peddlers of God's word," "super-apostles," and "false apostles" (2 Cor 2:17; 11:5, 13; 12:11). These designations all refer to the same opponents. They were a rival apostolate, and Paul worried whether he had preached the gospel in vain to them (2 Cor 6:1).

He condemns them in strong terms. He calls them false apostles, deceitful workmen, and servants of Satan in 2 Corinthians 11:12–15, which states the following:

> And what I do I will continue to do, in order to undermine the claim of those who would like to claim that in their boasted mission they work on the same terms as we do. For such men are false apostles, deceitful workmen, disguising themselves as apostles of Christ. And no wonder, for even Satan disguises himself as an angel of light. So it is no surprise if his servants, also, disguise themselves as servants of righteousness. Their end will correspond to their deeds.

These opponents are introducing a rival apostolate with a different message. Moreover, they are trying to eclipse Paul and supplant him. They call themselves ministers and apostles (2 Cor 6:3; 11:5, 13, 23) but, while they preach Jesus, they preach a different gospel (2 Cor 4:5; 10:14; 11:4).

There have been many options proposed for the identification of these super apostles which can be reduced to four principal categories: Hellenistic Jewish propagandists, pneumatics, Gnostics, and Judaizers.⁴⁵ Of these

44. M. E. Thrall, *2 Corinthians 1–7: A Critical and Exegetical Commentary on the Second Epistle to the Corinthians,* ICC (London: T & T Clark, 2004), 66–69, 171, 495.

45. For a more complete listing of possibilities see Harris, *Second Epistle to the*

options, it appears best to view the opponents as Jews who thought they were Christians but were self-appointed agents of a Judaizing agenda. It is evident that they envision themselves to be Christians from references such as 2 Corinthians 10:7, where Paul says, "If anyone is confident that he is Christ's, let him remind himself that just as he is Christ's, so also are we." Their Jewish and Christian background can also be seen from 2 Corinthians 11:22–23: "Are they Hebrews? So am I. Are they Israelites? So am I. Are they offspring of Abraham? So am I. Are they servants of Christ? I am a better one."[46]

While they carried a Judaizing agenda, these super apostles were not Judaizers. Within 2 Corinthians, there is no mention of circumcision, dietary laws, Sabbath, or Jewish festivals. These are the concern of the Judaizers in Galatia and Philippians, but they are not found within 2 Corinthians. Jewish ideas were a part of their teaching, as is evident by the amount of Jewish concepts that fill 2 Corinthians, such as the discussion of the old and new covenants in 2 Corinthians 3. It is possible that they stressed the Mosaic covenant alone and righteousness that derives from the letter.[47]

It is clear that these super-apostles stressed outward appearance rather than inward reality. This is evident from the way that Paul contrasts himself with these deceitful workers. They promoted outward appearances, rather than simplicity and sincerity of heart (2 Cor 1:12). They carried letters of recommendation, rather than counting on a ministry commended by the people and by the Lord himself (2 Cor 3:1). In 2 Corinthians 5:12, Paul states this contrast plainly when he writes, "We are not commending ourselves to you again but giving you cause to boast about us, so that you may be able to answer those who boast about outward appearance and not about what is in the heart."

They had no place for suffering, but only profit making. For much of 2 Corinthians, Paul speaks of his suffering apostolic ministry (cf. 2 Cor 4; 6; 10, 12). This is encapsulated within 2 Corinthians 2:14–16, where he presents his apostolic motivation. In this section, he presents himself as led in triumphal procession. As a result of being a captive to the Lord and his subsequent suffering, he acts as an aroma of death—to death for some, but life to life for others. His suffering becomes the revelatory vehicle of the

---

Corinthians, 79–80.

46. Cf. 2 Cor 11:13.

47. Barnett, *The Corinthian Question*, 168–9.

glory of God.⁴⁸ In contrast to Paul's manner are the super apostles, who are represented in 2 Corinthians 2:17. They "peddle" the word of God for profit. It is possible that this Greek word (καπηλεύω) could even carry the meaning of "adulterate" or "sell at illegitimate profit." Trickery and greed were associated with the word. Murray Harris accuses the super-apostles of "huckstering the word of God."⁴⁹

These super-apostles were also boastful. They claimed influence in areas that they did not affect. In 2 Corinthians 10:13–15, Paul writes:

> But we will not boast beyond limits, but will boast only with regard to the area of influence God assigned to us, to reach even to you. For we are not overextending ourselves, as though we did not reach you. We were the first to come all the way to you with the gospel of Christ. We do not boast beyond limit in the labors of others.

While Paul is willing to commend himself within his own sphere of influence, he claims that the super-apostles overextended their influence. They took credit for Paul's ministry and his labors. Theirs was a self-deceptive boast in irrelevant human standards and unsuitable for being truly commended (2 Cor. 10:12–13).⁵⁰ Later, he claims that they boasted according to the flesh (2 Cor 11:18).

Conclusion

While there were many obstacles that Paul encountered at Corinth, this essay has identified five significant ones. He first faced opposition from other religious leaders. The problems then became related to the secular culture of Greco-Roman Corinth, specifically that of immorality and idolatry. There were also changing relational issues. As the church grew, there were church dynamic problems. Then there was significant confrontation with a leader from within, which caused Paul great personal pain. Afterwards, there was the great challenge posed by the infiltration of false apostles. Even after facing the previous difficulties, Paul was still concerned in A.D. 56 as

---

48. S. J. Hafemann, *Suffering and the Spirit: An Exegetical Study of 2 Cor. 2:14–3:3 within the context of the Corinthian Correspondence*, WUNT 19 (Tübingen: Mohr, 1986), 163–74.

49. Harris, *The Second Epistle to the Corinthians*, 254.

50. Cf. S. J. Hafemann, "'Self-Commendation' and Apostolic Legitimacy in 2 Corinthians: A Pauline Dialectic?" *NTS* 36 (1990): 77.

to whether he had labored in vain. Great were the difficulties in the church planting work at Corinth.

Despite the great opposition, the church plant at Corinth succeeded. Following Paul's writing of 2 Corinthians, his third visit to Corinth seemed positive (cf. Acts 20:2–4; Rom 15:24, 28; 16:21–23). Particularly, the passages in the book of Romans, a letter written from Corinth, do not reveal any sense of turmoil within the Corinthian church. The sense of stability and calm within the letter likely indicates that the troubles had been overcome.[51]

Forty years later, another letter was written to the church at Corinth, written by Clement, the bishop of the church in Rome to the church in Corinth. The letter is known as *First Clement*. Its opening verses and its formal tone indicate that the work had been established.[52] While Paul underwent much opposition and heartache in his work, he was revered later, as Clement writes in 1 Clement 47:1: "Take up the epistle of the blessed Apostle Paul. What did he write to you at the time when the Gospel first began to be preached? Truly, under the inspiration of the Spirit, he wrote to you." Paul faced great opposition, but through the work of the Spirit the church was founded.

---

51. Barnett, *Corinthian Question*, 195–208.

52. 1 Clement 1:1 reads, "The Church of God which sojourns at Rome, to the Church of God sojourning at Corinth, to those who are called and sanctified by the will of God, through our Lord Jesus Christ: Grace to you, and peace, from Almighty God through Jesus Christ, be multiplied." Unless otherwise indicated, all quotes from 1 Clement are from *The Ante-Nicene Fathers: Translations of the Writings of the Fathers Down to A.D. 35*, vol. 1, ed. Alexander Roberts and James Donaldson (repr., Grand Rapids, Eerdmans, 1981).

God's Word and Life as it was Meant to Be

EDWARD M. CURTIS

A few years ago, my wife and I drove across the country and spent some time in the Canadian provinces of Ontario and Quebec. As we were driving back into Maine from Quebec, we were greeted by a sign that said, "Welcome to Maine: Life as it was meant to be." While it is difficult to evaluate those things, the people of Maine can make a pretty good case for their slogan from what I saw of the state. We were struck by the lack of congestion, the beautiful scenery throughout the state, the abundant wildlife, and the relaxed feel of the parts of the state that we experienced. Perhaps a winter in Maine would disabuse me of the impressions that I got from our week there, but I was fascinated by their take on "life as it was meant to be."

It is commonplace for evangelical students and congregations to enthusiastically affirm that Scripture is the final authority for faith and practice, but it is much less common to find them actually living all of life under its authority. Perhaps this is understandable. After all, most of us would never think of depending on a ten year old computer or driving a twenty year old car across the country. When we are faced with necessary medical procedures, we want those things done at a facility where the latest equipment and technology are available. In some respects, then, it is not surprising that many are somewhat skeptical about depending on three thousand-year old instruction for living our lives. We have been conditioned to prefer the latest advice from the most knowledgeable experts, and the idea does not seem realistic for most people—even those in the Church—that the Bible would be the final source of teaching about marriage, parenting, business ethics, personal relationships, or morality in the twenty-first century, despite our affirmation of its authority.

Not Weary of Well Doing

Three psalms focus on God's *Torah* or instruction and affirm the potential that this teaching has for transforming life. An understanding of the benefits that the Word brings to the disciple, and an awareness of the characteristics of the disciple who receives these blessings, can help us see why holding fast to God's faithful Word is essential for "life as it was meant to be." As we will see, this goes well beyond what the state of Maine has in mind with their slogan, appealing as that sounds. Psalms 1, 19:7–14, and 119 are wisdom psalms that focus on the Word of God, presenting different aspects of how that instruction benefits God's people, and how those benefits can become a reality for the disciple.

The potential is expressed in Psalm 1. The person who meets the criteria presented there is described in terms of a tree planted[1] by canals of water, which produces it fruit in season, and its foliage does not wither. The person prospers or succeeds in everything that he does. The luxuriant, productive tree that is deeply rooted in the soil and is in constant touch with a source of water is a metaphor that we all want to characterize our lives. This is especially the case when we consider the contrast that the psalm makes between the flourishing, stable tree and chaff that is blown away by the wind. In the parallel to this passage found in Jeremiah 17:5–8, the firmly established and thriving tree is contrasted with a bush in the desert that struggles just to survive.

Psalm 1 presents the potential in another interesting way, as well. The first words of the psalm (אַשְׁרֵי־הָאִישׁ, translated "How blessed is the man" (NAS); "Blessed is the man" (NIV, NKJ); or "Happy are those" (NRSV) are set off from the poetic structure of the psalm, presumably to put special emphasis on the important theme that is being introduced.

The word אֶשֶׁר is not the normal Hebrew word for "blessed," though it is used a number of times in the Old Testament wisdom literature. According to Sarna, the word reflects "the discriminating judgment of an observer who expresses wonderment and admiration over another's enviable state of being."[2] The word is always used to describe one person's judgment about another's enviable situation. It is never used by God to describe a person. The psalm's claim is that living according to the principles taught therein

---

1. The word שׁתל sometimes means "to transplant" (e.g., Ezekiel 17:22–23). According to Nahum Sarna, *On the Book of Psalms: Exploring the Prayers of Ancient Israel* (New York: Shocken Books, 1993), 42, the word here means "well-rooted," not just "planted." He notes that the rabbis emphasized that the normal word for planted was not used here and a somewhat rare word was used instead.

2. Sarna, *Psalms*, 29.

will result in such obvious benefits that others will notice and congratulate us on our enviable state. Sarna says, "the psalmist . . . is describing an existing reality, not offering a cheering promise of a romanticized future. His is not 'the religion of the sad soul,' but the happiness of the religious one."[3] He further points out that the word describes happiness rather than pleasure. He says, "Pleasure may be self-centered . . . frivolous and illusory. By contrast, happiness is deep-rooted; it penetrates to the very depths of one's being, and it is serious and enduring. In fact, it is this last quality which most distinguishes it from pleasure."[4] Further, Psalm 1 begins with a noteworthy expression that is the Hebrew counterpart to the term Jesus uses in the Beatitudes—something that should immediately stir our interest. It seems that the psalm is calling believers to a way of living not entirely unlike that to which Jesus called his disciples in the Sermon on the Mount, and with many of the same results.

Wisdom's Perspective on Life

As we noted, the psalms that we are considering are all wisdom psalms, and thus they share the basic perspective of wisdom. Wisdom thinking is anchored in the doctrine of Creation. This approach begins with the awareness that God created all things that exist, and recognizes that there is order in the universe because God created it that way. That order is reflected in the laws that operate in the physical realm. Water boils at 212-degrees Fahrenheit; gravity exerts its force on all things; a body immersed in a fluid is buoyed up by a force equal to the weight of the displaced fluid. The order that exists throughout the physical realm exists, according to the perspective of the wisdom literature, because God created the world to function in this way, and he sustains that order by his sovereign oversight. The wisdom literature does not see the order that God designed into the world as limited to the physical realm. There are cause-and-effect relationships that exist in the moral, ethical, social, and spiritual realms, as well, and they exist because God designed them into the fabric of the universe.

Wisdom is seen from several different perspectives in Scripture, so a precise definition of the term is difficult to formulate. Wisdom is the ability to formulate a plan that will allow a person to accomplish an objective. According to Proverbs 3:19–20, the Lord utilized his wisdom, understanding,

3. Sarna, *Psalms*, 29.
4. Sarna, *Psalms*, 30.

and knowledge to create the world. The order that is a part of God's design also constitutes wisdom; as Crenshaw points out, "God has embedded truth within all of reality. The human responsibility is to search for that insight and thus learn to live in harmony with the cosmos."[5] He further notes, "The fundamental assumption, taken for granted in every representative of biblical wisdom, consisted of a conviction that being wise meant a search for and maintenance of order."[6]

Proverbs 3:13–18, using the same Hebrew word as that found in Psalm 1:1, attributes blessing to the person who gains wisdom and understanding, and this wisdom and understanding seems to be equated with that which God used to create the world. As Ross concludes, "The wisdom that directs life is the same wisdom that created the universe; to surrender to God's wisdom is to put oneself in harmony with creation, the world around one."[7] Proverbs makes it clear that the search for wisdom requires diligence and resolve (e.g., 2:1–4; 4:1–9, 20–27), but it clearly presupposes that people are capable of discovering this wisdom if they diligently seek it. The wisdom literature recognizes that people made in the image of God have the intellectual and perceptual abilities to discover at least a part of the wisdom that God has built into the universe. Passages such as Isaiah 28:23–29 include such matters as the farmer's knowledge of when and how to plant, cultivate, and harvest his crops—the wisdom that people can discover—and many of the principles found in the wisdom literature touch on matters that do not involve the spiritual or theological areas of life. At the same time, passages such as Proverbs 2:5–6, 9:10, and the psalms that we are considering here make it clear that the knowledge of God is included in this wisdom, and that such wisdom comes from the mouth of God (Prov 2:6).[8] Wisdom, then, includes both what we call general revelation and special revelation. Psalms 1, 19, and 119 make it clear that God's revelation in his Word plays a central role in providing his people critical elements of the wisdom that is needed for knowing God intimately and for living life as it was meant to be.

---

5. James Crenshaw, *Old Testament Wisdom* (Atlanta: John Knox Press, 1981), 18.

6. Crenshaw, *Old Testament Wisdom*, 19.

7. Allen P. Ross, "Proverbs," in *The Expositor's Bible Commentary*, vol. 5, ed. Frank E. Gaebelein (Grand Rapids: Zondervan, 1991), 919.

8. As Derek Kidner puts it, the starting point for this knowledge "is revelation—specific (words) and practical (commandments); its method is not one of free speculation, but of treasuring and exploring received teachings so as to penetrate to their principles." Derek Kidner, *Proverbs* (Downers Grove, IL: InterVarsity Press, 1964), 61.

As we noted above, wisdom presents a worldview, an understanding of reality, and wisdom's view of reality differs significantly from that of our culture in several important ways. The claim of Scripture is that the biblical understanding provides an accurate description of "the way things are," even for the modern world. The claim throughout the wisdom literature is that life lived in harmony with the way it was designed by God will result in blessing, happiness, and contentment that will be apparent to others and a basis for envy and congratulation.

Nonetheless, while a cause-and-effect relationship between action and outcome is seen by the wisdom literature as extending beyond the physical realm into every area of life, the relationship is seen in general terms, rather than in invariable and absolute ones. At first glance, the proverbs may appear to leave no room for exceptions but, as Garrett notes, this conclusion results from:

> . . . our failure to grasp the hermeneutics of wisdom literature. By its very nature and purpose, wisdom emphasizes the general truth over some specific cases and, being a work of instruction, frames its teachings in short pithy statements without excessive qualification. It is not that the wisdom writers did not know that life was complex and full of exceptions, but dwelling on those cases would have distracted attention from their didactic purposes. . . . [G]eneral truths are the stock in trade of Proverbs.[9]

In fact, wisdom books such as Job and Ecclesiastes make it clear that the sages recognized that exceptions do occur to the general principles, and these books reflect some of the tensions that result when experience seems to be at variance with traditional understandings of how things work in the world.

The wisdom authors also clearly recognized that wisdom is limited by God's sovereignty, and God's purpose is that which ultimately determines outcomes. Proverbs 16:9 says, "The heart of man plans his way, but the Lord establishes his steps." Proverbs 21:30–31 says, "No wisdom, no understanding, no counsel can avail against the Lord. The horse is made ready for the day of battle, but the victory belongs to the Lord." As von Rad says, the purpose of such statements is not to discourage people from acquiring and using wisdom in every area of life.

---

9. Duane Garrett, *Proverbs, Ecclesiastes, Song of Solomon*, The New American Commentary (Nashville: Broadman Press, 1993), 57.

> Its aim is, rather, to put a stop to the erroneous concept that a guarantee of success was to be found in practicing human wisdom and in making preparations. Man must always keep himself open to the activity of God, an activity which completely escapes all calculation, for between the putting into practice of the most reliable wisdom and that which then takes place, there always lies a great unknown.[10]

With the important qualifications that have been noted, wisdom recognizes that there is order built into the fabric of the universe by God's design and maintained by his sovereign oversight. The person who begins the search for wisdom with the fear of the Lord can find many of those principles of order from a careful study of God's world and from God's revelation in Scripture. According to Estes, "In the thought of Proverbs, wisdom is skill in living according to Yahweh's order. Folly is choosing to live contrary to the order he embedded in the universe."[11] According to this same perspective, the person who lives life according to the principles that God designed and revealed will experience certain benefits as he lives in harmony with Yahweh's created order, and those benefits will be such that others will take notice and declare such people blessed. Psalms 1, 19, and 119 describe some of those blessings or benefits in more detail, and it is to those psalms that we now want to turn.

The Blessings of God's Word

While the blessings noted in these psalms primarily belong in the realm of the spiritual or emotional, the benefits offered also may go beyond these categories. The metaphor of the tree in Psalm 1 suggests a vitality that extends to every area of life, and the statement made by the psalmist in verse 3, "In all that he does, he prospers," suggests that, as well.

Two of the expressions used in Psalm 19 also allude to blessings that encompass all of life. The effect of God's instruction in 19:7 is "reviving the soul." While the expression often is translated "restoring the soul," the use of the idiom elsewhere suggests an effect that goes beyond what most people understand by *soul*. The expression is used in 1 Kings 17:21 of restoring

---

10. Gerhard Von Rad, *Wisdom in Israel*, trans. James Martin (Nashville: Abingdon Press, 1972), 101.

11. Daniel Estes, *Hear, My Son: Teaching and Learning in Proverbs 1–9*, New Studies in Biblical Theology (Grand Rapids: Eerdmans, 1997), 26.

God's Word and Life as it was Meant to Be

the life of a widow's dead child. It is used in Psalm 35:17 of the relief that comes when one is rescued from those who are relentlessly attacking. The expression is used in Ruth 4:15 of the emotionally energizing effect of the birth of a grandson on Naomi, a woman who had been beaten down by the discouraging rigors of life. Similarly, the expression is used in Lamentations 1:16 of the encouraging effect of a comforter on those despairing because of a long siege that had left them with no resources or hope. Finally, in Job 33:30, the term is used of the effect of God's discipline in bringing a wayward person back from the brink of destruction into the fullness of life lived according to wisdom. The expression suggests that God's instruction, welcomed and applied, results in blessings that affect the whole person. Both emotional and physical well being are nourished by his truth.

A second expression in Psalm 19 suggests a similar conclusion. Verse 8 tells us that the commandment of the Lord has the effect of "enlightening the eyes." The use of this expression elsewhere in the Old Testament suggests that the blessing involves something different than illumination. As Psalm 13:3 makes clear, "enlightening the eyes" means "to give life" or "allow to live." It is the opposite of sleeping in death. The expression is used in Ezra 9:8 to describe the revitalization of people set free from bondage and oppression. 1 Samuel 14:27, 29 illustrates what is described by the term. Jonathan, exhausted from an all-night battle against the Philistines, sees some honey in a log. He eats some of it, and "his eyes brightened." The words describe the energizing and invigorating affect of honey on a person weary from lack of sleep and great exertion. As Sarna notes, the expression "does not refer to intellectual enlightenment, but rather to revitalization of physical vigor."[12]

The restoration of life is the theme of several verses in Psalm 119, though the psalmist uses a different expression than those noted above from Psalm 19. This word means "to cause to live," and is used in several different contexts. Often it describes the restoration of life and vitality that accompanies deliverance from a threat, such as persecution or illness (for example, vv. 25, 88, 107, 149, 154, 156, 159). In a few cases (vv. 37, 40, and perhaps 93), it is the "very keeping of God's law that is restorative and life giving,"[13] and this idea also is affirmed elsewhere in the Bible. Proverbs 4:4 says, "Let your heart hold fast my words; keep my commandments, and

---

12. Sarna, *Psalms*, 86.

13. Derek Kidner, *Psalms 73–150*, vol. 14b of Tyndale Old Testament Commentaries (Downers Grove, IL: InterVarsity Press, 1975), 421.

live." Deuteronomy 30:15–20 also relates life to loving God and keeping his commandments.

The Old Testament recognizes that life is more than simply the opposite of physical death. Life in its fullest sense is experienced in a right relationship with God (that is, in loving God and obeying his commandments). Only through faith and obedience can people experience life as it was meant to be. Certainly a part of what Deuteronomy 30 has in view is the enjoyment of the blessings of the Covenant in the promised land. But by identifying Deuteronomy 6:5 as the great commandment, Jesus seems to make it clear that loving God and obeying him results in life—not just under the Mosaic Covenant, but today as well. This is a timeless principle reflecting the order that God has designed into the world. Obeying God's instruction is an essential element in living life as it was meant to be. God's Word, embraced by faith, is restorative and life-giving in every age.

In addition to these broad descriptions of the blessings that God's revelation is designed to produce, these psalms also identify the kinds of blessings in more specific terms. Among the benefits are knowledge, understanding, and insight. Psalm 19:7 states, "the testimony of the Lord is sure, making wise the simple." The simple person is a well-known character; almost all of the occurrences of the word are located in the wisdom literature. This is not a person who is lacking intellectual ability; rather, he is naïve and uninformed. Sarna says that this is a person "who is wholly inexperienced in the ways of the world, whose moral consciousness is underdeveloped, and who, through . . . ignorance, lacks the critical ability to weigh ethical issues and to make prudent decisions."[14] Fortunately, by wisdom this person can be delivered from his naiveté and become wise. Scripture makes it clear that human beings made in God's image are capable of marvelous things and can discover many aspects of the wisdom that God has designed into the world. At the same time, human beings are significantly limited in the truth that they can discover. People, by God's design, are finite creatures who need both God and others to function to the full. In addition to human finiteness, people are fallen creatures, and the effects of the fall further limit our ability to discover truth and understand reality. God's revelation in Scripture has significant potential for instructing those who are naïve, whether because of finitude, fallenness, or simple lack of experience in the world, and it can make them wise. As Psalm 119:130 says, "The unfolding of your words gives light; it imparts understanding to the simple."

14. Sarna, *Psalms*, 85.

As Kidner points out, verses like 119:105 ("Your word is a lamp to my feet and a light to my path") make the practical nature of the knowledge apparent. He says that "this is light to walk by, not to bask in."[15] While knowledge is imparted through the revelation, the real goal of the instruction seems to be skills in living. The idea is similar to that found in Deuteronomy 17, where the king is instructed to make a copy of the Law for himself. He is to read that instruction "that he may learn to fear the Lord his God by keeping all the words of this law" (Deut 17:19). The knowledge gained from God's truth warns the disciple (Ps 19:11). It helps him to avoid sin and keep his life pure (Ps 119:9, 11), and it allows him to identify and reject what is false (Ps 119:29, 104, and 128). The author of Psalm 19 prays that he may be acquitted of hidden faults (v. 12); God's instruction is essential in illuminating such faults. As Kidner notes, "a fault may be hidden not because it is too small to see, but because it is too characteristic to register."[16] The knowledge gained from God's revelation in Scripture enables the disciple to remain on the right path despite pressure from others (119:21–24; 42), and even in the presence of dissenting opinions from "experts" (119:97–100).

Many of the benefits extolled by the psalmist involve the emotional or psychological aspects of life. The psalmist sees God's revelation as a source of strength and comfort in times of affliction and grief (Ps 119:28, 50, 52, 76), and this is the reason for the psalmist's hope (Ps 119:49–50; 166). This hope is based on the faithfulness of God (Ps 119:89–93) and the knowledge that God can be trusted to do what he says. Misplaced trust can leave a person embarrassed or disappointed when the person trusted fails to do what he has promised. The Old Testament commonly describes that situation using a Hebrew word that literally means "to have a red face." The prophets often describe the end result of trusting idols or foreign alliances in these terms. In contrast to those who trust idols or human resources, those who depend on God will not be left with a red face because God did not do what he promised. As Isaiah 45:16–17 puts it, "All of them are put to shame and confounded; the makers of idols go in confusion together. But Israel is saved by the Lord with everlasting salvation; you shall not be put to shame or confounded to all eternity." History attests to God's faithfulness, as is clear in Psalm 25:2–3: "O my God, in you I trust; let me not be put to shame; let not my enemies exult over me. Indeed, none who wait for you shall be put to shame; they shall be ashamed who are wantonly

15. Kidner, *Psalms*, 421.
16. Kidner, *Psalms*, 100.

treacherous." It is this awareness of God's faithfulness in the past, nourished by God's Word, that gives the psalmist hope in the midst of difficulty. It is this promise about which the psalmist reminds God throughout Psalm 119 (vv. 31, 46, 116).

God's instruction brings joy and delight to the disciple, as Psalms 19 and 119 make clear. The psalmist both delights in the instruction and also finds delight in it. He finds God's words sweeter than honey (19:10; 119:103). They are better to him than gold and silver (19:10; 119: 14, 72, 162). No doubt, many reasons exist why the disciple finds delight in God's truth. As noted earlier, God's instruction is life-giving and energizing to the person who embraces it. It gives comfort and guidance that keeps a person from harm. God's Word received by faith nourishes the intimacy with God that is the prerequisite for life as it was meant to be (Ps 25:14 and numerous New Testament passages). The early chapters of Proverbs make it clear that the search for wisdom will produce many benefits, and the fruits produced through this search most likely will encourage further pursuit, since most people will repeat a behavior that brings them pleasure. Thus, the delight produced through embracing wisdom motivates the further pursuit of it. As Kidner notes about verse 103, the taste for God's Word is "an acquired taste."[17]

The psalmist sees God's Law in very different terms than most Christians today. Most people think of words like "restrictive," "oppressive," and "limiting" when they think of Law. The psalmist sees God's instruction, not as confining or narrow, but rather as in verse 45: it brings him out into a broad place. As Davidson says,

> What is remarkable about this section [of the psalm] are the words used to describe the psalmist's attitude to and response to Torah; 'liberty,' 'freedom' (v. 45), 'delight' or joy, and the repeated 'love' (vv. 47–48). These are not words which you find in the context of a harsh legalism. They are words which the New Testament uses again and again to describe the Christian's relationship with and response to Christ.[18]

Kidner says that what we see in Psalm 119 is "true piety: a love for God not desiccated by study, but refreshed, informed and nourished by it."[19] Several verses in these psalms indicate that a significant benefit of God's instruc-

---

17. Kidner, *Psalms*, 427.
18. Robert Davidson, *The Vitality of Worship* (Grand Rapids: Eerdmans, 1998), 394.
19. Kidner, *Psalms*, 419.

tion is that it delivers the disciple from sin (119:11) and unrighteousness (119:3). God's Word helps a young man keep his way pure (119:9), and these verses may provide significant insight into the psalmist's perspective.

Most people today see freedom in terms of being able to do what they please. The biblical authors typically began at a different place, and perhaps a place that reflects the way God created the world to work. The biblical perspective on freedom begins with the recognition that people are in bondage to sin. True freedom means that we are delivered from our bondage to sin and freed up to live the way God intended his people to live. That way is presented to us in God's Word. Thus, the psalmist sees the Law as liberating, not restrictive and confining. God alone has the power to free us from our bondage, and it is his instruction in Scripture that shows us how life was meant to be lived. The psalmist sees obedience to God's Law as an agent of grace, rather than something that stands in opposition to it.

The Blessed Disciple

Even a brief survey of the benefits and blessings that God's faithful Word brings to the disciple makes clear the essential role that God's instruction should play for the believer and in the Church. At the same time, it is important to recognize the characteristics of the blessed disciple mentioned in these psalms. The disciple appears to be determined in his commitment to know and obey God's revelation; yet this very clearly is not a commitment driven by duty and obligation, but rather by love and delight. The psalmist's love for God's Law is mentioned numerous times in Psalm 119 (vv. 47, 48, 97, 113, 119, 127, 132, 140, 159, 163, 165, 167). While it is God's Law that is the focus of the psalmist's love, it is clear that this flows out of his relationship with God himself. He says in verse 2 that those who are blessed are those who observe his testimonies and who seek God with all their heart. In verse 10, the psalmist says, "With my whole heart I seek you." He says in v. 57, "the Lord is my portion." He says in v. 94, "I am yours." His prayers are directed to the Lord. He desires the Lord's lovingkindness so that he may live (v. 77). His praise is directed to the Lord (v. 164). He wants God's face to shine on him (v. 135).

Oesterely says, "As he constantly emphasizes, the Law is the expression of the divine will; it is not the Law, *per se*, that he loves. . . , he loves the Law because it tells of God's will; and he loves it because he loves God first."[20] Kirkpatrick says, "The close personal relationship of the Psalmist to God is one of the most striking features of the Psalms in general, and in few psalms is it more marked than in this."[21]

The psalmist delights in God's instruction and intensely longs for it (119:14, 16, 20, 40, 47, 72, 92, 111, 131, 162). No doubt that delight encourages the meditation and song (vv. 15, 23, 48, 54, 78, 97, 148) that Psalm 1:2–3 says is the secret of the godly person's success and prosperity. He treasures the teaching (119:11) just as the wise person does in Proverbs 2:1. The psalmist trusts in God's instruction (119:42, 66, 74, 81, 114) because he knows that God is characterized by truth, righteousness, and faithfulness (vv. 89–90). The disciple is teachable and welcomes God's instruction. He recognizes his need for guidance and instruction, especially when it comes from God (vv. 24, 26, 33, 73, 125, 128). He recognizes, if only in hindsight, that God's discipline is good (vv. 65–72), and that even in painful correction, "God is good, and he does good" (v. 68). He regularly asks God to teach him.

Perhaps the characteristic of the disciple that stands out above everything else is his commitment to obedience. Over and over in Psalm 119, he expresses his determination to obey (for example, vv. 2–5; 8, 10, 22, 30, 33, 51, 55, 57, 60, 129, 145–45, 168, and many others). The disciple is deliberate in his obedience. He chooses the faithful way (v. 30). He obeys promptly and with enthusiasm. He says, "I will run in the way of your commandments" (v. 32). He says in v. 60, "I hasten and do not delay to keep your commandments." He expresses his determination to obey in v. 106, "I have sworn an oath and confirmed it, to keep your righteous rules." He persists in obeying even when he is in difficulty, or when there are significant pressures not to obey (vv. 69, 87, 110, 141, 157).

Even as the psalmist expresses his love for God's Law and his determination to obey it, he also clearly recognizes that he must have God's help for this to occur. As Kirkpatrick notes, "If sometimes his professions of obedience seem to savor of self-righteousness, his prayers for grace fully recognize that strength to obey must come from God."[22] The psalmist recognizes that his understanding of God's truth must come from God. He asks God to teach him (vv. 12, 19, 27, 29, 33, 38, 66, 68, and others), and to show him wonderful things in the Law (v. 18). He understands that his faithful

---

20. W. O. E. Oesterely, *Psalms* (London: S. P. C. K., 1959), 499.
21. A. F. Kirkpatrick, *The Book of Psalms* (Cambridge: University Press, 1906), 701.
22. Kirkpatrick, *Psalms*, 701.

obedience is possible only if God helps him and empowers him. He says in verse 10, "let me not wander from your commandments!" He says in vv. 35–36, "Lead me in the path of your commandments . . . Incline my heart to your testimonies." He prays in v. 133, "Keep steady my steps according to your promise, and let no iniquity get dominion over me." Clearly, the disciple described in the psalm—the disciple who receives the blessings imparted by God's Word—is one who deeply loves God and appreciates the great treasure that God has given us in Scripture. He deeply desires to know that truth and diligently seeks to put it into practice in his life. At the same time, he clearly is aware of his own inability to understand God's truth, to keep God's Law, and to persist in faithfulness to God. This is a disciple who, to the degree possible for him, understood Paul's exhortation in Philippians 2:12–13 to "work out your own salvation with fear and trembling, for it is God who works in you, both to will and to work for his good pleasure."

Conclusions

The worldview of the wisdom literature flows out of the firm conviction that God created everything that exists; the order that is part of God's design continues because of his sovereign oversight of all that he created. Life lived in harmony with God's order flourishes, while life lived at variance to that order will not prosper. The wisdom perspective sees this order in terms that move beyond the physical and extend into the relational, the moral, and the spiritual realms, as well. People made in God's image are able to discover many elements of wisdom, as they carefully observe life and the world, but the limitations posed by human finitude and human sinfulness often produce mixed results. As the early chapters of Proverbs make clear, the human search for wisdom must begin with a clear acknowledgment of God's authority over his creation. It is this relationship with God that Kidner describes as "worshipping submission to the God of the Covenant."[23] The Old Testament calls this the fear of the Lord. Life lived in this relationship is what the New Testament calls living by faith. The early chapters of Genesis make it clear that people are designed to function in a relationship with God. Apart from that relationship of trusting dependence on God, life as it was meant to be is not possible.

As these psalms make clear, God's revelation in Scripture plays a central role in understanding reality and the order that is a part of God's

23. Kidner, *Proverbs*, 59.

design. The reality envisioned by these wisdom psalms sees God as the central focus. Life as it was meant to be flows out of a relationship with him, and is informed and sustained at every point by his revelation. It is this revelation that gives certainty to moral understanding, and that warns us of hazards in a fallen world that can otherwise cause disaster. It is this revelation that allows us to confidently embrace truth in a world where plausible arguments by various experts can be brought forth to support almost any idea. It is this revelation that enables us to live with hope and confidence when the difficulties of life assail and batter us. It is this revelation that comforts us in grief and gives us stability as we navigate uncertain waters. The promise that is offered in this psalm is summed up in Psalm 119:165, "Great peace have those who love your law; nothing can make them stumble." It is hard to imagine a greater contrast than that between the promise of the psalm and the outcomes generated by embracing the values of our world and culture.

While the psalms do not present it in exactly the same terms, the contrast between the invitation of the psalms and that of the world appears to be essentially the same as that between Jesus and the world, as he concludes the Sermon on the Mount.

> Enter by the narrow gate. For the gate is wide and the way is easy that leads to destruction, and those who enter by it are many. For the gate is narrow and the way is hard that leads to life, and those who find it are few. (Matthew 7:13–14)

> Everyone then who hears these words of mine and does them will be like a wise man who built his house on the rock. And the rain fell, and the floods came, and the winds blew and beat on that house, but it did not fall, because it had been founded on the rock. And everyone who hears these words of mine and does not do them will be like a foolish man who built his house on the sand. And the rain fell, and the floods came, and the winds blew and beat against that house, and it fell, and great was the fall of it. (Matthew 7:24–27)

It is those who hear the message of these psalms and put it into practice about whom others will say, "Blessed are those who keep his testimonies, who seek him with their whole heart (Ps 119:2). These are the people who have discovered life as it was meant to be.

Christian Preaching and the Old Testament

JORDAN M. SCHEETZ

Since the time of Marcion, Christians have been wrestling with the relationship between the texts inherited from the Hebrews and the texts from the early Church.[1] Although mainstream Christianity replied with a resounding affirmation of both the texts inherited from the Hebrews and the early church, there is still a sense that somehow the text of what became known as the Old Testament is somehow only real Scripture, inasmuch as it is read only through the lens of the New Testament. The reverse is usually not true. The problem is oftentimes shrouded in ignorance and massive anachronisms.

From a personal standpoint, I encountered this exact issue after teaching on Isaiah 52:13–53:12, making clear parallels between the Servant of the Lord and Jesus. What I was trying to do was allow the text from Isaiah to inform our understanding of Jesus in the Gospels. One of my colleagues was clearly distressed that I would take such an approach, and I found myself meeting with the head of this particular ministry. At a certain point, this leader, who was very well meaning, made it clear that he was striving to be just like Paul in the way he taught. The implications were clear: I was not teaching like Paul. Somehow this person had missed the fact that Paul's "Bible" was what we would call the Old Testament, and further that Paul was not walking around with copies of Matthew, Mark, Luke, and John, since they had not yet been written.

---

1. Martin Ebner, "Der christliche Kanon," in *Einleitung in das Neue Testament*, ed. Martin Ebner and Stefan Schreiber (Stuttgart: Kohlhammer, 2008), 25–28, demonstrates the very hermeneutical nature of Marcion's canon.

Not Weary of Well Doing

In a recent text on preaching the Old Testament, Sidney Greidanus illustrates the point from more nuanced perspective:

> In 1976, while a pastor in Delta, British Columbia, I preached a series of sermons on Ecclesiastes. After hearing one of these theocentric sermons, a retired pastor approached me and said, "I appreciated your sermon, Sid, but could a rabbi have preached your sermon in a synagogue?" I was dumbfounded by the question, but it set me to thinking about the issue of Christocentric preaching. Of course, a rabbi and I have the Old Testament in common. Moreover, since wisdom is a reflection on "customary 'orders' in the world."..., the message of wisdom literature would be the same for the church as for the synagogue. So yes, a rabbi could have preached that sermon in a synagogue without causing offense. But if that was the case, had I preached an "Old Testament sermon" instead of a "Christian sermon"?[2]

This type of questioning foreshadows Greidanus's conclusion: "I concluded that sermons based on Old Testament passages cannot merely be theocentric sermons but must be Christocentric."[3] The question of the value of an Old Testament text (for preaching) is based on its validation through New Testament (Christocentric) texts.

The difficulty that this creates from a practical standpoint is that the Old Testament is Scripture only as much as it is informed by the New Testament. This creates a directional impact where the authoritative texts, New Testament Christocentric texts, become the appropriate context in which the Old Testament is to be read. This unidirectional reading misses the ambition of the early Christian writers, who were obviously looking to place their own writings in the context of their own authoritative books, the books of the Hebrews. These books were viewed as authoritative in their own right, without any further qualification. The New Testament books were added to this already authoritative collection.

The Books of the Hebrews

Eusebius's *Ecclesiastical History* demonstrates that, from an early time, the church viewed the books of the Hebrews, the Old Testament, as the key

---

2. Sidney Greidanus, *Preaching Christ from Ecclesiastes: Foundations for Expository Sermons* (Grand Rapids: Eerdmans, 2010), x.

3. Greidanus, *Preaching Christ from Ecclesiastes*, x.

Christian Preaching and the Old Testament

group of authoritative texts to which the early authoritative Christian writings, the New Testament, were added. In this sense, Eusebius quotes from two earlier authorities to establish both the names and order of these books.

The first discussion is found in *Ecclesiastical History* IV.26.12-14, where Eusebius quotes from Melito, who was bishop of Sardis and died around A.D. 190,[4] establishing both the grouping and order of the Old Testament (τῆς παλαιᾶς διαθήκης):

> Ἀλλὰ ταῦτα μὲν ἐν τῷ δηλωθέντι τέθειται λόγῳ· ἐν δὲ ταῖς γραφείσαις αὐτῷ Ἐκλογαῖς ὁ αὐτὸς κατὰ τὸ προοίμιον ἀρχόμενος τῶν ὁμολογουμένων τῆς παλαιᾶς διαθήκης γραφῶν ποιεῖται κατάλογον· ὃν καὶ ἀναγκαῖον ἐνταῦθα καταλέξαι, γράφει δὲ οὕτως· "Μελίτων Ὀνησίμῳ τῷ ἀδελφῷ χαίρειν. ἐπειδὴ πολλάκις ἠξίωσας, σπουδῇ τῇ πρὸς τὸν λόγον χρώμενος, γενέσθαι σοι ἐκλογὰς ἔκ τε τοῦ νόμου καὶ τῶν προφητῶν περὶ τοῦ σωτῆρος καὶ πάσης τῆς πίστεως ἡμῶν, ἔτι δὲ καὶ μαθεῖν τὴν τῶν παλαιῶν βιβλίων ἐβουλήθης ἀκρίβειαν πόσα τὸν ἀριθμὸν καὶ ὁποῖα τὴν τάξιν εἶεν, ἐσπούδασα τὸ τοιοῦτο πρᾶξαι, ἐπιστάμενός σου τὸ σπουδαῖον περὶ τὴν πίστιν καὶ φιλομαθὲς περὶ τὸν λόγον ὅτι τε μάλιστα πάντων πόθῳ τῷ πρὸς τὸν θεὸν ταῦτα προκρίνεις, περὶ τῆς αἰωνίου σωτηρίας ἀγωνιζόμενος. ἀνελθὼν οὖν εἰς τὴν ἀνατολὴν καὶ ἕως τοῦ τόπου γενόμενος ἔνθα ἐκηρύχθη καὶ ἐπράχθη, καὶ ἀκριβῶς μαθὼν τὰ τῆς παλαιᾶς διαθήκης βιβλία, ὑποτάξας ἔπεμψά σοι· ὧν ἐστι τὰ ὀνόματα· Μωυσέως πέντε, Γένεσις Ἔξοδος Ἀριθμοὶ Λευιτικὸν Δευτερονόμιον, Ἰησοῦς Ναυῆ, Κριταί, Ῥούθ, Βασιλειῶν τέσσαρα, Παραλειπομένων δύο, Ψαλμῶν Δαυίδ, Σολομῶνος Παροιμίαι ἡ καὶ Σοφία, Ἐκκλησιαστής, Ἆισμα Ἀισμάτων, Ἰώβ, Προφητῶν Ἡσαΐου Ἰερεμίου τῶν δώδεκα ἐν μονοβίβλῳ Δανιήλ, Ἰεζεκιήλ, Ἔσδρας· ἐξ ὧν καὶ τὰς ἐκλογὰς ἐποιησάμην, εἰς ἓξ βιβλία διελών." καὶ τὰ μὲν τοῦ Μελίτωνος τοσαῦτα.[5]

But these things were put in a discussion having been made known. But in the *Extracts* having been written by him, the same man according to the preface, beginning, made a list of the agreed upon writings of the Old Testament, which it is necessary to recount, and so he writes, "Melito to Onesimos, the brother, greeting. Since you many times thought, yearning in zeal for the word, to be produced for you extracts from the Law and the Prophets concerning the

---

4. F. L. Cross, ed., "St. Melito," in *The Oxford Dictionary of the Christian Church* (London: Oxford University Press, 1957), 884.

5. Eusebius, *Ecclesiastical History*, vol. 1, trans. Kirsopp Lake (Cambridge, MA: Harvard University Press, 1926), 390, 392.

Savior and all our faith, and still also you desired to learn well the exactness of the ancient books, how many the number and of what sort the order. I was eager to do so, knowing your earnest way concerning the faith and one fond of learning concerning the word that indeed these things you prefer especially of all things longing for God, fighting concerning the eternal salvation. Therefore, having gone back into the East and until the place, being there where it was preached and it was done, and having accurately learned the books of the Old Testament, having appended I sent to you, of which are the names: Five of Moses, Genesis, Exodus, Numbers, Leviticus, Deuteronomy, Joshua Nun, Judges, Ruth, four of Kings, two of Omissions, Psalms of David, Proverbs, also the Wisdom of Solomon, Ecclesiastes, Song of Songs, Job, of Prophets, Isaiah, Jeremiah, the Twelve in one book, Daniel, Ezekiel, Esdras. From which I also made the *Extracts*, having divided into six books." And so much are these things of Melito.[6]

Clearly, the purpose of Melito's enumerating the Old Testament is Christocentric, but it is also its own standalone witness to the Savior and the whole faith: "γενέσθαι σοι ἐκλογὰς ἔκ τε τοῦ νόμου καὶ τῶν προφητῶν περὶ τοῦ σωτῆρος καὶ πάσης τῆς πίστεως ἡμῶν."[7] Further, his concern was not simply to give a random list of these books, but both their number and actual order: "ἔτι δὲ καὶ μαθεῖν τὴν τῶν παλαιῶν βιβλίων ἐβουλήθης ἀκρίβειαν πόσα τὸν ἀριθμὸν καὶ ὁποῖα τὴν τάξιν εἶεν, ἐσπούδασα τὸ τοιοῦτο πρᾶξαι."[8] He lists the books of Moses as five in the unique order of Genesis, Exodus, Numbers, Leviticus, and Deuteronomy: "Μωυσέως πέντε, Γένεσις Ἔξοδος Ἀριθμοὶ Λευιτικὸν Δευτερονόμιον."[9] The second group of books has no special title, but clearly comes after the five books of Moses, and is distinguished from the Prophets that close the list, which, in order, are Joshua, Judges, Ruth, four books of Kings (1–2 Samuel and 1–2 Kings), two books of Omissions (1–2 Chronicles), Solomon's Proverbs and Wisdom (Proverbs and Wisdom of Solomon), Ecclesiastes, Song of Songs, and Job: "Ἰησοῦς Ναυῆ, Κριταί, Ῥούθ, Βασιλειῶν τέσσαρα, Παραλειπομένων δύο, Ψαλμῶν Δαυίδ, Σολομῶνος Παροιμίαι ἡ καὶ Σοφία, Ἐκκλησιαστής, Ἆισμα Ἀισμάτων, Ἰώβ."[10] The final section is identified as the Prophets and

6. All English translations of the Greek text are the author's.
7. Eusebius, *Ecclesiastical History*, vol. 1, 392.
8. Eusebius, *Ecclesiastical History*, vol. 1, 392.
9. Eusebius, *Ecclesiastical History*, vol. 1, 392.
10. Eusebius, *Ecclesiastical History*, vol. 1, 392.

is ordered as Isaiah, Jeremiah, the Twelve, Daniel, Ezekiel, and Esdras: "Προφητῶν Ἡσαΐου Ἱερεμίου τῶν δώδεκα ἐν μονοβίβλῳ Δανιήλ, Ἰεζεκιήλ, Ἔσδρας."[11] These books in this order are viewed as foundational to understanding the Savior and all the faith, to the point that Melito compiled extracts from the Old Testament that filled six books: "ἐξ ὧν καὶ τὰς ἐκλογὰς ἐποιησάμην, εἰς ἓξ βιβλία διελών."[12]

The second discussion is found in *Ecclesiastical History* VI.25.1-2, where Eusebius quotes from Origen, who was an Alexandrian biblical scholar and lived around A.D. 185-254,[13] cataloguing the Holy Scriptures of the Old Testament (τῶν ἱερῶν γραφῶν τῆς παλαιᾶς διαθήκης):

> Τὸν μέν γε πρῶτον ἐξηγούμενος Ψαλμόν, ἔκθεσιν πεποίηται τοῦ τῶν ἱερῶν γραφῶν τῆς παλαιᾶς διαθήκης καταλόγου, ὡδέ πως γράφων κατὰ λέξιν· "οὐκ ἀγνοητέον δ' εἶναι τὰς ἐνδιαθήκους βίβλους, ὡς Ἑβαῖοι παραδιδόασιν, δύο καὶ εἴκοσι, ὅσος ἀριθμὸς τῶν παρ' αὐτοῖς στοιχείων ἐστίν." Εἶτα μετά τινα ἐπιφέρει λέγων· "εἰσὶν δὲ αἱ εἴκοσι δύο βίβλιοι καθ' Ἑβραίους αἵδε· ἡ παρ' ἡμῖν Γένεσις ἐπιγεγραμμένη, παρὰ δ' Ἑβραίοις ἀπὸ τῆς ἀρχῆς τῆς βίβλου Βρησιθ, ὅπερ ἐστὶν 'ἐν ἀρχῇ'· Ἔξοδος, Ουελλεσμωθ, ὅπερ ἐστὶν 'ταῦτα τὰ ὀνόματα'· Λευιτικόν, Ουϊκρα, 'καὶ ἐκάλεσεν'· Ἀριθμοί, Αμμεσφεκωδειμ· Δευτερονόμιον, Ελλεαδδεβαρειμ, 'οὗτοι οἱ λόγοι'· Ἰησοῦς υἱὸς Ναυῆ, Ιωσουεβεννουν· Κριταί, Ῥούθ, παρ' αὐτοῖς ἐν ἑνί, Σωφτειμ· Βασιλειῶν α' β', παρ' αὐτοῖς ἕν, Σαμουηλ, 'ὁ θεόκλητος'· Βασιλειῶν γ' δ' ἐν ἑνί, Ουαμμελχδαυιδ, ὅπερ ἐστὶν 'βασιλεία Δαυιδ'· Παραλειπομένων α' β' ἐν ἑνί, Δαβρηϊαμειν ὅπερ ἐστὶν 'λόγοι ἡμερῶν'· Ἔζρας α' β' ἐν ἑνί, Εζρα, ὅ ἐστιν 'βοηθός'· βίβλος Ψαλμῶν, Σφαρθελλειμ· Σολομῶνος παροιμίαι, Μελωθ· Ἐκκλησιαστής, Κωελθ· Ἄισμα ἀσμάτων (οὐ γάρ, ὡς ὑπολαμβάνουσίν τινες, Ἄισματα ἀσμάτων), Σιρασσιρειμ· Ἡσαΐας, Ιεσσια· Ἱερεμίας σὺν Θρήνοις καὶ τῇ Ἐπιστολῇ ἐν ἑνί, Ιερεμια· Δανιήλ, Δανιηλ· Ἰεζεκιήλ, Ιεζεκιηλ· Ἰώβ, Ιωβ· Ἐσθήρ, Εσθηρ. ἔξω δὲ τούτων ἐστὶ τὰ Μακκαβαϊκά, ἅπερ ἐπιγέγραπται Σαρβηθσαβαναιελ."[14]

At least expounding the first Psalm, an exposition was made of the list of the Holy Writings of the Old Testament, so in some way

---

11. Eusebius, *Ecclesiastical History*, vol. 1, 392.

12. Eusebius, *Ecclesiastical History*, vol. 1, 392.

13. Cross, "Origen," 991.

14. Eusebius, *Ecclesiastical History*, vol. 2, trans. J. E. L. Oulton (Cambridge, MA: Harvard University Press, 1932), 72-74.

writing as the phrase goes, "But not to be ignorant about the books committed to writing, as the Hebrews passed down, two and twenty, as much is the number of the letters among them." Then after something he adds, saying, "And the twenty-two books according to the Hebrews are these: The one inscribed among us Genesis, but among the Hebrews from the beginning of the book *Bresith*, which is "In the beginning." Exodus, *Ouellesmoth*, which is "These are the names." Leviticus, *Ouikra*, "and he called." Numbers, *Ammesfekodeim*. Deuteronomy, *Ekkeaddebareim*, "These are the words." Joshua son of Nun, *Iosouebennoun*. Judges, Ruth, among them in one, *Softeim*. Of Kings 1, 2, among them one, *Samouel*, "The One Called of God." Of Kings 3, 4, in one, *Ouammelxdauid*, which is "Kingdom of David." Omissions 1, 2, in one, *Dabreiamein*, which is "Words of Days." Esdras 1, 2, in one, *Ezra*, which is "Assisting." Book of Psalms, *Sfarthelleim*. Solomon's Proverbs, *Meloth*. Ecclesiastes, *Koelth*. Song of Songs (for not as some understand, Songs of Songs), *Sirassireim*. Isaiah, *Iessia*. Jeremiah with Lamentations and the Epistle in one, *Ieremia*. Daniel, *Daniel*. Ezekiel, *Iezekiel*. Job, *Iob*. Esther, Esther. And outside of these are the Maccabees, which have been inscribed *Sarbethsabaneiel*."

As with the list from Melito, Origin's list is viewed as an inherited group of authoritative literature. Eusebius's preface calls this body of literature "the Holy Writings of the Old Testament" (τῶν ἱερῶν γραφῶν τῆς παλαιᾶς διαθήκης).[15] Origen makes clear that these texts were handed down as a group from the Hebrews (ὡς Ἑβραῖοι παραδιδόασιν) and that they were twenty-two in number, corresponding to the letters of the Hebrew alphabet (δύο καὶ εἴκοσι, ὅσος ἀριθμὸς τῶν παρ' αὐτοῖς στοιχείων ἐστίν).[16] Origen's list gives various bits of information, including the Greek name of the book, sometimes what books are considered one book, sometimes a transliteration of the Hebrew name of the book, and sometimes including a translation of the Hebrew title: e.g, "Παραλειπομένων α' β' ἐν ἑνί, Δαβρηϊαμειν ὅπερ ἐστὶν 'λόγοι ἡμερῶν.'"[17] What is extremely interesting is that, although Origen's list is given in Greek, he claims that he is representing the books as they are actually found in Hebrew. Because of the complicated nature of the description of these books, the following lists give the English equivalents in the main text with further clarification in the parenthesis: 1) Genesis, 2) Exodus, 3) Leviticus, 4) Numbers, 5) Deuteronomy, 6) Joshua, 7) Judges

15. Eusebius, *Ecclesiastical History*, vol. 2, 72.
16. Eusebius, *Ecclesiastical History*, vol. 2, 72.
17. Eusebius, *Ecclesiastical History*, vol. 2, 72.

Christian Preaching and the Old Testament

(Judges and Ruth in one book), 8) Samuel (1 and 2 Samuel in one book), 9) Kings (1 and 2 Kings in one book), 10) Chronicles (1 and 2 Chronicles in one book), 11) Ezra (1 Esdras, Ezra, and Nehemiah in one book), 12) Psalms, 13) Proverbs, 14) Ecclesiastes, 15) Song of Songs, 16) Isaiah, 17) Jeremiah (Jeremiah, Lamentations, and the Letter of Jeremiah in one book), 18) Daniel, 19) Ezekiel, 20) Job, 21) Esther, and 22) the Maccabees. It could be questioned whether the Maccabees should be included in the list, since Origen notes that they are outside of these (ἔξω δὲ τούτων ἐστὶ τὰ Μακκαβαϊκά),[18] but without the Maccabees, there are clearly only twenty-one books instead of twenty-two.[19]

Beyond these two texts found in Eusebius, another key list from early Christianity in relation to the Old Testament is found in Athanasius's "Thirty-Ninth Festal Letter" (Ἕκτη τῆς λθ ἑορταστικῆς ἐπιστολῆς), written in A.D. 367 for Easter:[20]

> ἔτι τοίνυν τῆς μὲν παλαιᾶς διαθήκης βιβλία τῷ ἀριθμῷ τὰ πάντα εἰκοσιδύο· τοσαῦτα γάρ, ὡς ἤκουσα, καὶ τὰ στοιχεῖα τὰ παρ' Ἑβραίοις εἶναι παραδέδονται. τῇ δὲ τάξει καὶ τῷ ὀνόματί ἐστιν ἕκαστον, οὕτως· πρῶτον Γένεσις, εἶτα Ἔξοδος, εἶτα Λευτικὸν, καὶ μετὰ τοῦτο ἀριθμοί, καὶ λοιπὸν τὸ Δευτερονόμιον. ἑξῆς δὲ τούτοις ἐστὶν Ἰησοῦ ὁ τοῦ Ναυῆ, καὶ Κριταί. καὶ μετὰ τοῦτο ἡ Ῥοῦθ. καὶ πάλιν ἑξῆς Βασιλειῶν τέσσαρα βιβλία· καὶ τούτων τὸ μὲν πρῶτον καὶ δεύτερον εἰς ἓν βιβλίον ἀριθμεῖται· τὸ δὲ τρίτον καὶ τέταρτον ὁμοίως εἰς ἕν· μετὰ δὲ ταῦτα παραλειπόμενα α καὶ β, ὁμοίως εἰς ἓν βιβλίον ἀριθμούμενα, εἶτα Ἔσδρας α καὶ β ὁμοίως εἰς ἕν, μετὰ δὲ ταῦτα βίβλος ψαλμῶν, καὶ ἑξῆς παροιμίαι. εἶτα ἐκκλησιαστής, καὶ

---

18. Eusebius, *Ecclesiastical History*, vol. 2, 74.

19. In comparing the two lists, a clear case of the missing book could be made for the Twelve. Roger Beckwith, *The Canon of the New Testament Church* (Grand Rapids: Eerdmans, 1985), 186, notes in this regard, "The omission of the Minor Prophets, whether due to Origen himself or to Eusebius through whom we receive the list, must be accidental, since their canonicity was never disputed, and Origen both appeals to their authority in his extant writings and wrote a commentary on them, now lost."

20. David Brakke, "Canon Formation and Social Conflict in Fourth-Century Egypt: Athanasius of Alexandria's Thirty-Ninth *Festal Letter*," *Harvard Theological Review* 87/4 (1994), 395-6, notes in relation to the importance of this particular document, "In histories of the formation of the Christian biblical canon, the thirty-ninth *Festal Letter* of Athanasius of Alexandria, written for Easter 367, holds a justifiably prominent place. Not only is this letter the earliest extant Christian document to list precisely the twenty-seven books that eventually formed the generally accepted canon of the New Testament, but Athanasius is also the first Christian author known to have applied the term 'canonized' (κανονιζόμενα) specifically to the books that made up his Old and New Testaments."

ἆσμα ἀσμάτων. πρὸς τούτοις ἔστι καὶ Ἰὼβ, καὶ λοιπὸν προφῆται· οἱ μὲν δώδεκα εἰς ἓν βιβλίον ἀριθμούμενοι. εἶτα Ἡσαΐας, Ἱερεμίας, καὶ σύν αυτῷ Βαροὺχ, θρῆνοι καὶ ἐπιστολὴ, καὶ μετ' αὐτὸν Ἐζεκιὴλ καὶ Δανιήλ. ἄρχι τούτων τὰ τῆς παλαιᾶς διαθήκης ἵσταται.[21]

Yet therefore all the books of the Old Testament are twenty-two in number. For so, as I have heard, are also the number of letters among the Hebrews, they have been passed down. But the order and each name are so: First Genesis, then Exodus, then Leviticus, and with this Numbers, and the rest, Deuteronomy. And next are Joshua the one of Nun and Judges and after this Ruth. And again next are four books of Kings. And of these, first and second are counted in one book. And third and fourth likewise are in one book. And after these are Omissions 1 and 2, likewise being counted in one book, then 1 Esdras and 2 Esdras likewise in one, and after these are Book of Psalms and next Proverbs. Then are Ecclesiastes and Song of Songs. To these are also Job, and the rest of the Prophets. The Twelve are counted in one book. Then are Isaiah, Jeremiah, and with it Baruch, Lamentations, and the Epistle, and with it Ezekiel and Daniel. Until these ones are set the ones of the Old Testament.

Athanasius's statement contains many of the elements that have already been noted in the lists from Melito and Origen. Just like Melito and Origen, he calls these texts "the Old Testament" (τῆς μὲν παλαιᾶς διαθήκης).[22] Just like Origen, he notes that they are twenty-two in number (τῷ ἀριθμῷ τὰ πάντα εἰκοσιδύο) which corresponds to the number of letters in the Hebrew alphabet (τὰ στοιχεῖα τὰ παρ' Ἑβραίοις).[23] In agreement with both Melito and Origen, these books have been passed down in a lump sum from the Hebrews (τὰ παρ' Ἑβραίοις εἶναι παραδέδονται).[24] Further, as with Melito's list, Athanasius is not just giving a group of books, but also their order (τῇ δὲ τάξει καὶ τῷ ὀνόματί ἐστιν ἕκαστον).[25] Athanasius lists the books in order as: 1) Genesis, 2) Exodus, 3) Leviticus, 4) Numbers, 5) Deuteronomy, 6) Joshua, 7) Judges (Judges and Ruth in one book), 8) 1 and 2 Kings (1 and 2 Samuel in one book), 9) 3 and 4 Kings (1 and 2 Kings in

---

21. Athanasius, "Ἕκτη τῆς λθ ἑορταστικῆς ἐπιστολῆς," in *Quellensammlung zur Geschichte des Neutestamentlichen Canons bis auf Hieronymus*, ed. Johannes Kirchhofer (Zürich: Meyer and Zeller, 1844), 8.

22. Athanasius, "Ἕκτη τῆς λθ ἑορταστικῆς ἐπιστολῆς," 8.

23. Athanasius, "Ἕκτη τῆς λθ ἑορταστικῆς ἐπιστολῆς," 8.

24. Athanasius, "Ἕκτη τῆς λθ ἑορταστικῆς ἐπιστολῆς," 8.

25. Athanasius, "Ἕκτη τῆς λθ ἑορταστικῆς ἐπιστολῆς," 8.

one book), 10) 1 and 2 Omissions (1 and 2 Chronicles in one book), 11) 1 and 2 Esdras (1 Esdras, Ezra, and Nehemiah in one book), 12) Psalms, 13) Proverbs, 14) Ecclesiastes, 15) Song of Songs, 16) Job, 17) the Twelve (the Minor Prophets in one book), 18) Isaiah, 19) Jeremiah (Jeremiah, Baruch, Lamentations, and the Letter of Jeremiah in one book), 20) Ezekiel, and 21) Daniel. Just as with Origen's list, Athanasius is actually one book short. Although it may be tempting to add the mystery book as Esther, Athanasius lists this book and several others as outside those canonized in the Old and New Testament, including: 1) the Wisdom of Solomon, 2) Ecclesiasticus, 3) Esther, 4) Judith, 5) Tobit, 6) the Didache, and 7) the Shepherd of Hermas:

> ὡς ὅτι ἐστὶν καὶ ἕτερα βιβλία τούτων ἔξωθεν· οὐ κανονιζόμενα μὲν τετυπωμένα δὲ παρὰ τῶν πατέρων ἀναγινώσκεθαι τοῖς ἄρτι προσερχομένοις καὶ βουλομένοις κατηχεῖσθαι τὸν τῆς εὐσεβείας λόγον· σοφία Σολομῶντος, καὶ σοφία Σιρὰχ, καὶ Ἐσθὴρ, καὶ Ἰουδίθ, καὶ Τοβίας, καὶ διδαχὴ καλουμένη τῶν ἀποστόλων, καὶ ὁ ποιμήν.[26]

> As that there are also other books outside of these, ones not being canonized but having been modeled by the fathers to be read to the ones just coming to and desiring to be instructed the word of piety: the Wisdom of Solomon and the Wisdom of Sirach and Esther and Judith and Tobias and the Teaching (being called of the Apostles) and the Shepherd.

This may very well indicate that the missing book was Maccabees. However, it is noteworthy that both Origen and Athanasius had their main list and a supplementary list. Of course, this is only a group of books in Origen's case in relation to the Old Testament, namely, the Maccabees (τὰ Μακκαβαϊκά)[27] and the seven books just mentioned in relation to both Testaments from Athanasius.

Although other lists could be included, the main point has already been illustrated. These books as a whole were viewed as being passed down directly from the Jewish people. As such, they are understood as the foundational Jewish texts to which other (Jewish) texts, the New Testament, were added. In a very real way, Melito's statement points to a key earlier context in which the Savior and the whole faith were to be understood. In this sense, the Old Testament becomes the right context. The distinction of the term "Old Testament" that was used in each of these lists seems

---

26. Athanasius, "Ἕκτη τῆς λθ ἑορταστικῆς ἐπιστολῆς," 9.

27. Eusebius, *Ecclesiastical History*, vol. 2, 74.

to designate, not "out of date," but the reality that these texts significantly predate those texts from the apostolic era. They were not produced by early Christianity; instead, they were inherited.[28] A further curious point, especially with regard to recent canonical approaches to the Old Testament, is that both the collection and the order of the books were emphasized in these lists.

The New Testament

In this same line of investigation, the New Testament writers also assume the foundational authority of the Old Testament, even if there may be lingering questions about the *exact* shape and size of this corpus in the first century A.D.[29] In brief, the obvious focus of the New Testament is the anointed Jesus. The Gospels of Matthew and Mark make this focus explicit with their superscriptions:

> Mt 1:1 Βίβλος γενέσεως Ἰησοῦ Χριστοῦ υἱοῦ Δαυὶδ υἱοῦ Ἀβραάμ.
>
> Mt 1:1 The book of the descent of the anointed Jesus, son of David, son of Abraham.
>
> Mk 1:1 Ἀρχὴ τοῦ εὐαγγελίου Ἰησοῦ Χριστοῦ υἱοῦ θεοῦ.
>
> Mk 1:1 The beginning of the good news of the anointed Jesus, son of God.

However, what is equally clear is that all of the details of the anointed Jesus are to be read and understood in a much larger context. Matthew opens by connecting the genealogy of Jesus with two key people, David and Abraham, who are of course two key people in the Old Testament. Further, as

---

28. Erich Zenger, "Heilige Schrift der Juden und der Christen," in *Einleitung in das Alte Testament*, 8th ed., ed. Erich Zenger and Christian Frevel (Stuttgart: Kohlhamer, 2012), 28, notes in relation to early Christianity's authoritative books, "Das *Urchristentum* hat für sein 'Altes Testament' keinen eigenen Kanon geschaffen, sondern hielt die Bücher für kanonisch, die auch das Judentum, aus dem es hervorging, für kanonisch hielt."

29. Differing recent views on this issue can be found in Stephen B. Chapman, *The Law and the Prophets* (Tübingen: Mohr Siebeck, 2000); Johann Maier, *Studien zur jüdischen Bibel und ihrer Geschichte* (Berlin: Walter de Gruyter, 2004), 3–136; Karel van der Toorn, *Scribal Culture and the Making of the Hebrew Bible* (Cambridge, MA: Harvard University Press, 2007), 205–64; and Georg Steins, "Zwei Konzepte – ein Kanon," in *Kanonisierung – die Hebräische Bibel im Werden* (Neukirchen-Vluyn: Neukirchner, 2010), 8–45.

Christian Preaching and the Old Testament

the events of Jesus' life unfold, they are read in the context of passages from the Old Testament. Matthew 1:22–23 states:

> τοῦτο δὲ ὅλον γέγονεν ἵνα πληρωθῇ τὸ ῥηθὲν ὑπὸ κυρίου διὰ τοῦ προφήτου λέγοντος· ἰδοὺ ἡ παρθένος ἐν γαστρὶ ἕξει καὶ τέξεται υἱόν, καὶ καλέσουσιν τὸ ὄνομα αὐτοῦ Ἐμμανουήλ, ὅ ἐστιν μεθερμηνευόμενον μεθ' ἡμῶν ὁ θεός.

> And all this happened in order that the word of the Lord through the prophet might be fulfilled saying, "Behold the virgin will be pregnant and she will give birth to a son and they will call his name Emmanuel, which translated is 'God with us.'"

Jesus' direct speech demonstrates his own consciousness of this connection to the Old Testament in Matthew 5:17–18:

> Μὴ νομίσητε ὅτι ἦλθον καταλῦσαι τὸν νόμον ἢ τοὺς προφήτας· οὐκ ἦλθον καταλῦσαι ἀλλὰ πληρῶσαι. ἀμὴν γὰρ λέγω ὑμῖν· ἕως ἂν παρέλθῃ ὁ οὐρανὸς καὶ ἡ γῆ, ἰῶτα ἓν ἢ μία κεραία οὐ μὴ παρέλθῃ ἀπὸ τοῦ νόμου, ἕως ἂν πάντα γένηται.

> "Do not think that I came to abolish the Law and the Prophets. I came not to abolish but to fulfill. For truly I say to you, until heaven and earth might pass away, one iota or hook might not pass away from the Law, until all things come to pass."

Paul's epistles carry the same focus on the anointed Jesus with the Old Testament as the broader context in which his life and ministry are to be viewed. The theme verse of Romans is not a new theological statement, but is a quotation about righteousness from Habakkuk 2:4. Romans 1:17 states:

> δικαιοσύνη γὰρ θεοῦ ἐν αὐτῷ ἀποκαλύπτεται ἐκ πίστεως εἰς πίστιν, καθὼς γέγραπται· ὁ δὲ δίκαιος ἐκ πίστεως ζήσεται.

> For the righteousness of God has been revealed in this, from faith to faith, just as has been written, "And the righteous will live by faith."

Further, when Paul begins his detailed explanation of justification by faith, he begins with this statement in 3:21–22:

> Νυνὶ δὲ χωρὶς νόμου δικαιοσύνη θεοῦ πεφανέρωται μαρτυρουμένη ὑπὸ τοῦ νόμου καὶ τῶν προφητῶν, δικαιοσύνη δὲ θεοῦ διὰ πίστεως Ἰησοῦ Χριστοῦ εἰς πάντας τοὺς πιστεύοντας.

> But now a righteousness of God apart from law has been revealed, being testified by the Law and the Prophets, but a righteousness of God through faith of the anointed Jesus for all the ones believing.

The New Testament views all of Jesus' life in relation to the broader context of the Old Testament.

With this said, Jesus is both the fulfillment and the pinnacle of God's revelation. John 1:18 describes Jesus in this unique way:

> Θεὸν οὐδεὶς ἑώρακεν πώποτε· μονογενὴς θεὸς ὁ ὢν εἰς τὸν κόλπον τοῦ πατρὸς ἐκεῖνος ἐξηγήσατο.

> No one has ever seen God. Only the unique God, the one being in the bosom of the father, this one, explained [him].

In this regard, Paul also states in Colossians 1:15:

> ὅς ἐστιν εἰκὼν τοῦ θεοῦ τοῦ ἀοράτου, πρωτότοκος πάσης κτίσεως.

> Who is the image of the invisible God, first born of all creation.

This appears to be the reason that no further definitive (canonical) books were added to those after the time of the Apostles. Jesus is the fulfillment and pinnacle of revelation. Although other books have been viewed as helpful or useful, the highpoint has already been reached in the eyewitness accounts of the Apostles, or at the very least those who were privy to their direct insight.

This brief survey of the New Testament brings a few issues to the forefront. First, although the anointed Jesus is the focus of the New Testament, his life and ministry at every turn are to be read in light of the Old Testament. The Old Testament is the specific context in which the New Testament is to be read. Second, Jesus is viewed as the fulfillment and pinnacle of God's revelation. What appears to have been an open process of gathering, collecting, and ordering of God's revelation, comes to a conclusion with the witness to Jesus' life and ministry found in the eyewitness accounts of the Apostles. Third, there is a layering of reading, where the Old Testament is the foundation. Fourth, quotations from the Old Testament function, on the one hand, to give the context from which Jesus' life and ministry are to be understood, but they also create a new context for these quotes. These texts are taken from the Old Testament and their particular contexts and are now used in relation to Jesus' life and ministry, or even in relation to the emerging "assemblies" forming wherever the good news of the anointed Jesus was preached.

Christian Preaching and the Old Testament

Although the previous two sections clearly demonstrate a strong bond between the Old Testament and a Christological perspective, they also argue for the continued foundational role of the Old Testament in early Christianity. These texts were certainly authoritative before there were any written New Testament documents, and they continued to be so even after the New Testament was completed, collated, ordered, and added to the Old Testament. Another way of saying this is that the Old Testament continued to be authoritative for the church even after the New Testament was added to it.

From a hermeneutical standpoint, the early church did clearly have a Christological perspective. One could view this as a foreign way of reading the Old Testament, somehow mishandling the Jewish text. But it could be equally argued, since the Jewish reception history represented in the New Testament does this, that the actual text itself contains these Christological/Messianic themes, of which the New Testament does not represent an exhaustive exposition.

However, it should be noted that Old Testament texts were not only used for Christological purposes in preaching in early Christianity. As an example, Ephesians 6:1–2 combines an exhortation to children supported from Exodus 20 and Deuteronomy 5:

> Τὰ τέκνα, ὑπακούετε τοῖς γονεῦσιν ὑμῶν ἐν κυρίῳ· τοῦτο γάρ ἐστιν δίκαιον. τίμα τὸν πατέρα σου καὶ τὴν μητέρα, ἥτις ἐστίν ἐντολὴ πρώτη ἐν ἐπαγγελίᾳ, ἵνα εὖ σοι γένηται καὶ ἔσῃ μακροχρόνιος ἐπὶ τῆς γῆς.
>
> Children, obey your parents in the Lord. For this is right. Honor your father and mother, which is the first command in a promise, in order that it may be well to you and you might be a long time upon the earth.

Although this passage is broadly constructed under Ephesians 5:21, "Submitting to one another in the fear of Christ (Ὑποτασσόμενοι ἀλλήλοις ἐν φόβῳ Χριστοῦ)," the exhortation in 6:1–2 uses the quotations from Exodus 20 and Deuteronomy 5 as its immediate basis. Examples of this kind could be multiplied, not only with texts found in the New Testament, but by other writers in early Christianity.[30] Presumably, this type of case is also not exhaustive in its representation in early Christianity.

When these various strands are brought together, a few key statements seem to be appropriate in considering Christian preaching and the Old Testament. First, Christians should allow Old Testament texts to inform their reading of New Testament texts, since this is what the New Testament writers were doing. Second, Christians should be preaching Old Testament texts, at times with a Christocentric perspective, and at other times for ethical reasons, or maybe even combining the two. Third, New Testament texts should inform the reading of Old Testament texts, in the sense that what was once interpretively open may now be particularized (fulfilled) in the New Testament. In many instances, the rabbi and the preacher should be saying the same thing. It is just that the preacher may at times be able to be even more particular.

As a way of illustrating these points, I will quote from sermons that were freely delivered at Crossroads International Church in Amsterdam. The first is a straightforward exposition of Jonah 3 with no reference to the New Testament. The second follows the highlights from Abraham's life and ends with Jesus. In both cases, I have striven to be faithful to the biblical texts at hand, believing them to have value as authoritative Scripture, yet at times making reference to other texts both in the Old and New Testaments. All of the Bible quotations in block quotes are from the New Revised Standard Version (NRSV); the others are mine.

Jonah 3: Sweet Sorrow

Adversity can be explained from two different perspectives. One kind of adversity is found in an incredible tragedy, where bad things simply happen. There is really nothing that can be done to avoid this form of adversity, but there is something that we can do about how we respond to it. The stories that come from this form of adversity speak with power to those who witness the tragedy and its response. However, there is another type of adversity that we can bring on ourselves. This type of difficulty follows the law of the sower; we reap what we sow. Difficulty that comes to those

---

30. 1 Corinthians 9:9–10 represents an interesting example in this regard, in that Paul first quotes from a text from Deuteronomy 25:4, and then seems to support his case with a text from Sirach 6:19. This seems to support Athanasius's categories of canonized texts, Deuteronomy 25:4, and texts that are beneficial reading, Sirach 6:19.

who have sown in a destructive direction is usually no surprise, and even at times there is a sense of thankfulness from those who have been affected.

However, to those who have been sowing in a destructive direction, there can be a sense of hopelessness. They believe that they are beyond any form of forgiveness, and so they continue in the same destructive lifestyle until they fulfill their own prophecy of destruction. For some, this is reinforced as their own concept of God is somehow one dimensional, and so God is unable to forgive them.

As we work our way through Jonah, we can see that God is proving himself to be multidimensional in relation to his character. In chapter 1, God calls Jonah to cry out against Nineveh because of their evil (1:2). God brings a storm, so serious that even sailors think that the ship is going to be destroyed, just to get Jonah's attention during his rebellion against God's word to him. But this is matched by God's deliverance of Jonah from the sea and miraculous transport back to dry land. The emerging picture from the book of Jonah is that God is multidimensional in his character; he relents from bringing disaster on those who believe in him and as a result turn from their evil ways.

Body

After being in the belly of a big fish three days and nights, Jonah was vomited onto dry ground (2:1, 11). While in the belly of the fish, he confessed the reality of what he believed to be true, namely that God's presence was the real desire of his life (2:5, 8), and that salvation only comes from YHWH (2:10). Jonah's poetic prayer ends with the two key themes that will dominate the whole of chapter three when Jonah concludes in the last part of 2:10, "What I have vowed, I will repay. Salvation is of YHWH."

Jonah is given a chance to repay his vow, as 3:1–4 makes clear:

> The word of the Lord came to Jonah a second time, saying, "Get up, go to Nineveh, that great city, and proclaim to it the message that I tell you." So Jonah set out and went to Nineveh, according to the word of the Lord. Now Nineveh was an exceedingly large city, a three days' walk across. Jonah began to go into the city, going a day's walk. And he cried out, "Forty days more, and Nineveh shall be overthrown!"

Jonah is given a chance to repay his vow to YHWH when the word of YHWH comes to him a second time. After three days and nights in the belly of the fish, the radical call of YHWH to go and give a message of pending destruction to a people known by their evil and violence was received with simple obedience. Jonah gets up and goes to Nineveh, undoubtedly driven by a deep confidence in YHWH due to his own miraculous deliverance. Jonah calls out his very difficult message, "Yet forty days and Nineveh will be overturned," one day into his projected three-day journey. Through this second word of YHWH, Jonah was allowed to repay his vow by boldly proclaiming a difficult message, to an evil and violent people: *God is a God of second chances.*

It appears that Jonah's journey was cut short through the surprising response of the people of Nineveh after only one day, as 3:5–9 makes clear:

> And the people of Nineveh believed God; they proclaimed a fast, and everyone, great and small, put on sackcloth. When the news reached the king of Nineveh, he rose from his throne, removed his robe, covered himself with sackcloth, and sat in ashes. Then he had a proclamation made in Nineveh: "By the decree of the king and his nobles: No human being or animal, no herd or flock, shall taste anything. They shall not feed, nor shall they drink water. Human beings and animals shall be covered with sackcloth, and they shall cry mightily to God. All shall turn from their evil ways and from the violence that is in their hands. Who knows? God may relent and change his mind; he may turn from his fierce anger, so that we do not perish."

Everything that the Ninevites do flows out of the one simple statement in verse 5, "they believed in God." The fasting, the wearing of sackcloth, and the proclamation of the king all flow from the fact that they believed in God. They believed that God had a right to judge them, which led to acts of humility and mourning. However, the proclamation of the king also demonstrates that they believed that God may also be something different. God may actually be forgiving and even change his plan of destroying them. In their belief in God and hope that God may relent from bringing disaster on them, the king calls for the people to turn from their evil and violence. *Belief gives way to life change.*

The concluding verse of the chapter in 3:10 demonstrates the reality of God's character. "When God saw what they did, how they turned from their evil ways, God changed his mind about the calamity that he had said he would bring upon them; and he did not do it." God sees the response of the Ninevites and relents in his plan to bring disaster on them. This is not to be understood as some sort of radical shift in relation to God, but instead

God is being completely consistent to his character. In YHWH's self-revelation to Moses in Exodus 34:6–7, he makes his character abundantly clear:

> The Lord passed before him, and proclaimed, "The Lord, the Lord, a God merciful and gracious, slow to anger, and abounding in steadfast love and faithfulness, keeping steadfast love for the thousandth generation, forgiving iniquity and transgression and sin, yet by no means clearing the guilty, but visiting the iniquity of the parents upon the children and the children's children, to the third and the fourth generation."

God is both able to judge and forgive.

Conclusion

In this short chapter, God's multifaceted character is revealed. He is a God of second chances to his people who choose to run in the opposite direction from his clear word. He is a God who can rightly speak a message of judgment. He is a God who will relent of bringing disaster on those who believe and, as a result, turn away from their evil ways.

As we are gathered here today, the question is, "Who are we in relation to this God?" If you are God's child and have been running from his clear word, he calls you to a second chance. If you are living a life of evil and violence, he calls you to believe in him, to believe that he has a right to judge you—but further to believe that you will find his kindness as you turn to him.

Abraham

The real world in which we live is a messy place. On the one hand, we experience things that are right: the warmth of a hug from those we love, the celebration of life when our children are born, and a peaceful meal with family and friends. On the other hand, we experience things that are wrong: being hurt by those who are closest to us, hurting those who are closest to us, destroyed relationships due to the sin of others or even our own sin. Life as we all experience it in this world is filled with this messy reality, where right and wrong and good and evil exist side by side in our life. This extends not only to the relationships we have with one another, but also to our relationship with God, who is not some abstract concept, but the creator of all things, including us.

The very real question then is how can we, as people who live in this messy world, be in a right relationship with God? The conscious answer to this question will change the whole direction of our life. If a right relationship with God starts with keeping rules, then we either orient the whole of lives around following the rules, or try to make up somehow for the rules that we broke. This, of course, begs two questions: Which rules need to be followed? How do we know they are the right rules? Religious people all around the world have been attempting this kind of pursuit of God since the beginning of time.

From the earliest chapters of the Bible, we see that there are commands, both positive and negative. Humanity is given these commands in Genesis 1:28–30:

> God blessed them, and God said to them, "Be fruitful and multiply, and fill the earth and subdue it; and have dominion over the fish of the sea and over the birds of the air and over every living thing that moves upon the earth." God said, "See, I have given you every plant yielding seed that is upon the face of all the earth, and every tree with seed in its fruit; you shall have them for food. And to every beast of the earth, and to every bird of the air, and to everything that creeps on the earth, everything that has the breath of life, I have given every green plant for food." And it was so.

The man is given this command in Genesis 2:16–17. "And the Lord God commanded the man, 'You may freely eat of every tree of the garden; but of the tree of the knowledge of good and evil you shall not eat, for in the day that you eat of it you shall die.'" Certainly these commands are important, and breaking them brings radical consequences to the whole of what God has created. However, it seems that the greatest value in these rules is pointing out the problem, namely that we are prone to break them. This is not to say that commands and rules are bad or even should not be kept, but rather that the key to being in a right relationship with God will not be found primarily in focusing on them.

In considering this question of how we can have a right relationship with God, one person in particular from the Bible is highlighted in both the Old and the New Testament: Abraham. By following his life, we see the messy reality of this world, but we also see a key example of how we can be right with God even with this mixed reality.

Body

Abraham, who was first known as Abram, is introduced in grand fashion when he receives this command and these promises from YHWH in Genesis 12:1–3:

> Now the LORD said to Abram, "Go from your country and your kindred and your father's house to the land that I will show you. I will make of you a great nation, and I will bless you, and make your name great, so that you will be a blessing. I will bless those who bless you, and the one who curses you I will curse; and in you all the families of the earth shall be blessed."

Out of all of the people YHWH could have chosen, Abram is singled out and commanded to leave everything familiar to him, including his country and his broader family. He is called to go to a place that he had not seen, but somewhere that YHWH would show to him. Related to this command are the promises that YHWH would make him into a great nation, and YHWH would bless him. Beyond this, Abram's blessing was meant to be extended to others, a blessing that would spread to all people. This blessing extends to those who will bless Abram, while cursing extends to those who curse Abram.

Abram responds to YHWH's command with simple obedience in Genesis 12:4. "So Abram went, as the Lord had told him; and Lot went with him. Abram was seventy-five years old when he departed from Haran." However we may understand Lot's presence with Abraham, we find that Abram goes just as YHWH told him; far from this being some kind of radical youthful behavior, Abram was 75 years old when he responded to YHWH's call.

Sometime after this, Abram finds himself in the land that YHWH had shown him, and YHWH speaks to him again in Genesis 15:1–5:

> After these things the word of the Lord came to Abram in a vision, "Do not be afraid, Abram, I am your shield; your reward shall be very great." But Abram said, "O Lord God, what will you give me, for I continue childless, and the heir of my house is Eliezer of Damascus?" And Abram said, "You have given me no offspring, and so a slave born in my house is to be my heir." But the word of the Lord came to him, "This man shall not be your heir; no one but your very own issue shall be your heir." He brought him outside and said, "Look toward heaven and count the stars, if you are able to count them." Then he said to him, "So shall your descendants be."

Not Weary of Well Doing

This time, the word of the Lord comes not to call Abram to leave everything, but to comfort him, to let him know that he is not alone. YHWH is his shield, and Abram will have a great reward. Through Abram's answer, it appears that Abram's fear revolved around the hard reality that he, an old man, who had obeyed YHWH's command and left everything, had no child of his own to inherit everything that YHWH had blessed him with. Now he will leave everything to a slave born in his house. This is to say that Abram had left everything because of the promise that YHWH would make him into a great nation, and now Abram is left with the prospect of not being a great nation, and even being on the furthest extreme: childless. YHWH reassures Abram, letting him know that his descendants will be like the innumerable stars in the sky.

To this reaffirmation of YHWH's promise, this profound response is recorded in Genesis 15:6, "And he believed the Lord; and the Lord reckoned it to him as righteousness." After hearing YHWH's response and reassurance that his obedience was not in vain, Abram not only believes in this promise, but maybe even more foundationally, he believes in the one who is making the promise. To this response of belief, it says that YHWH reckoned it to him—not "as" or "like" righteousness—but that "he reckoned it to him, righteousness (ויחשבה לו צדקה)." This is to say that Abram was right with God because of his belief, his trust in God. Directly after this statement of belief and resulting righteousness, the Lord makes yet another promise to Abram in 15:7. "Then he said to him, 'I am the Lord who brought you from Ur of the Chaldeans, to give you this land to possess.'"

These promises, including the land, are taken up again in Genesis 17, but with important changes. Genesis 17:4–10 explains the nature of this covenant:

> "As for me, this is my covenant with you: You shall be the ancestor of a multitude of nations. No longer shall your name be Abram, but your name shall be Abraham; for I have made you the ancestor of a multitude of nations. I will make you exceedingly fruitful; and I will make nations of you, and kings shall come from you. I will establish my covenant between me and you, and your offspring after you throughout their generations, for an everlasting covenant, to be God to you and to your offspring after you. And I will give to you, and to your offspring after you, the land where you are now an alien, all the land of Canaan, for a perpetual holding; and I will be their God." God said to Abraham, "As for you, you shall keep my covenant, you and your offspring after you throughout their

> generations. This is my covenant, which you shall keep, between me and you and your offspring after you: Every male among you shall be circumcised."

In this key passage, all of the previous promises are connected together and demonstrated to be a formally binding relational agreement among God, Abraham, and Abraham's descendants, complete with the physical sign of circumcision of Abraham and all his male descendants. As is often the case in the Hebrew Bible, names carry a particular meaning. Abram, (אברם) which means "exalted father,"[31] would now be changed to Abraham (אברהם), which is explained "because I have made you a father of a multitude of nations (כי אב המון גוים נתתיך)" (17:5). From God's side of this relational agreement, he promises nations, kings, and the land of Canaan, all descendants from Abraham and to be given to Abraham's descendants. The expectation from Abraham and his descendants in the relational agreement is that YHWH would be their God. As a physical sign of this covenant, all the males were to be circumcised: "And you will circumcise the flesh of your foreskin and it will be for a sign of a covenant between me and between you (ונמלתם את בשר ערלתכם והיה לאות ברית ביני וביניכם)" (17:11).

The enduring nature of this covenant is made clear after Abraham's death, when YHWH appears to Isaac, Abraham's promised son, in Genesis 26:1–5:

> Now there was a famine in the land, besides the former famine that had occurred in the days of Abraham. And Isaac went to Gerar, to King Abimelech of the Philistines. The Lord appeared to Isaac and said, "Do not go down to Egypt; settle in the land that I shall show you. Reside in this land as an alien, and I will be with you, and will bless you; for to you and to your descendants I will give all these lands, and I will fulfill the oath that I swore to your father Abraham. I will make your offspring as numerous as the stars of heaven, and will give to your offspring all these lands; and all the nations of the earth shall gain blessing for themselves through your offspring, because Abraham obeyed my voice and kept my charge, my commandments, my statutes, and my laws."

Similar to Genesis 12 where YHWH first commanded Abraham, so now Isaac is to go to the land which YHWH will "say" to him (cf. 12:1

---

31. Francis Brown, S. R. Driver, and Charles A. Briggs, *A Hebrew and English Lexicon of the Old Testament with an Appendix Containing Biblical Aramaic*, 2nd ed. (Oxford: Oxford UP, 1952), 4.

Not Weary of Well Doing

"אשר אראך" and 26:2 "אשר אמר אליך"). The emphasis is not on the physical sign of the covenant (circumcision), but on YHWH's promises to Abraham about descendants. The emphasis is also upon the land, along with YHWH's blessing and real presence with Isaac. Furthermore, all nations would be blessed through Abraham's descendants.

What is striking about this promise from YHWH is the final verse: "... as a consequence that Abraham listened to my voice and he kept my charge, my commandments, my statutes, and my instructions (עקב אשר שמע אברהם בקלי וישמר משמרתי מצותי חקותי ותורתי)" (26:5). This statement goes much further than what has actually been given in the book of Genesis, and includes a collection of words that only begin to occur together after YHWH gives Moses his instruction on Sinai, hundreds of years after the time of Abraham. It appears that this statement is given to demonstrate that Abraham kept YHWH's charge, commandments, statutes, and instructions, without even knowing them. The key to understanding this statement appears to be that Abraham lived in a right relationship with God, not through "keeping all the rules" in a strict sense, but instead through faith. In the words of Genesis 15:6, "And he believed in YHWH and he reckoned it to him, righteousness (והאמן ביהוה ויחשבה לו צדקה)."[32]

Conclusion

When we look at Abraham, we see a very key ancestor of the Jewish people. He was given the promise of descendants, the promise of land, and the promise of YHWH's blessing. All of this is an enduring covenant with the descendants of Abraham, the Jewish people. However, there is also the reality that all nations are blessed through him, through his descendants, and through his descendant, Jesus, whose first ancestor listed in Matthew 2 is Abraham. Ultimately, YHWH's covenant with Abraham leads to blessing being brought on all nations through the forgiveness and eternal life that are found in Jesus, the promised descendant of Abraham.

Further, Abraham is the key example, whether Jew or Gentile, of how we can be in a right relationship with God. It starts just as each of these passages makes clear, with God's living word speaking to our lives. This happens where he, as the creator of all things, puts a call on our lives to come and follow him with all of his promises. We could say that this

---

32. John H. Sailhamer, *The Pentateuch as Narrative: A Biblical-Theological Commentary* (Grand Rapids: Zondervan, 1992), 77–78.

involves doing what he commands, but there is a more basic starting point, a foundational belief in God, a foundational trust in him that spills over into a trust of his promises.

If we try to start with rules and regulations as the foundation to a relationship with God, they are bound to show us sooner or later that we are prone to break them. However, if the foundation is trust in God, we shift away from reliance on our own performance and onto the one who has called, commanded, and even made promises to us. God calls us today to come and go to the place he will show us, that we might receive all the blessings he has promised. The call is to believe in him, to trust him. Jesus, *the* descendant of Abraham, through whom all nations are blessed, called out almost two thousand years ago, "Repent! For the kingdom of heaven has come near (μετανοεῖτε· ἤγγικεν γὰρ ἡ βασιλεία τῶν οὐρανῶν)" (Matthew 4:17). The call still remains open for all who will believe, following the example of Abraham almost four thousand years ago, in the messy world in which we all live.

Recognizing and Affirming the Personhood of the Senior Adult in the Church

GERALD C. ERICSON

"They still bear fruit in old age; they are ever full of sap and green, to declare that the Lord is upright;" (Psalm 92:14–15a, ESV)[1]

There are notable declines in the death rates of famous people preceding their birthdays, followed by higher than normal death rates in the months subsequent to their birthdays.[2] This is suggestive of the inner human need for recognition and companionship. It may also be indicative of the effect of the senior adult's will power in shaping his attitudes, some of which may eventually alter the state of his physical health. Each person's life narrative is unique, but the events of everyone's life apparently are interpreted through the grid of their general outlook.

The foci of this study, viewed through a biblical perspective on life, are centered on the senior adult, who for purposes of this investigation is any person sixty-five years of age and older. They lead us more specifically through an overview of older personhood in the Bible and in the contemporary church.[3] Our purpose is to consider what can be done to a greater

---

1. This and all subsequent Scripture quotations are from *The Holy Bible: English Standard Version* (Wheaton: Crossway Bibles, 2001).

2. D. P. Phillips, "Deathday and Birthday: An Unexpected Connection," in *Statistics: A Guide to the Biological and Health Sciences*, ed. J. M. Turner, et al. (San Francisco: Holden-Day Company, 1977), 111–125, cited by Joseph Hartog, ed. et al. in *The Anatomy of Loneliness* (New York: International Universities Press, 1980), 5.

3. The term "older adult" is employed synonymously in this manuscript with "senior adult."

extent to recognize and affirm the senior adult in and through the church. A perspective on the senior adult's outlook on life will aid in setting the tone for relating to him.

Older Personhood in the Bible

The Nature of Older Persons

Happy is the senior adult who is being affirmed and motivated toward biblically based spiritual growth, for he is one who is understood and accepted both by God and at least a few family members, friends, and acquaintances. In more concrete, biblical terms, the senior adult who is justified by the grace of God through the redemption that is in Christ Jesus needs to be actively pursuing life in Christ in community with others. He is blessed in Christ Jesus by the God and Father of our Lord Jesus Christ, and subsequently his hope in Christ translates into a desire to live his life to the praise of God's glory (Rom 3:24; Eph 1:3–5, 12–13).

A starting point for encountering the biblical foundation for human worth is the profound statement in Genesis 1:26: "Then God said, 'Let us make man in our image, after our likeness. And let them have dominion over the fish of the sea and over the birds of the heavens and over the livestock and over all the earth and over every creeping thing that creeps on the earth.'" Moreover, the *imago dei* concept, temporarily tarnished by sin, must be traced throughout the Bible. This must be done in order to comprehend why it is difficult for many senior adults to understand themselves and their relationship to God, even those who are attempting to pursue life in Christ.

When our original parents sinned, they had chosen to partake of the forbidden fruit of the tree of good and evil in direct disobedience to God's command (Gen 2:16; 3:1–7). Immediate and permanent consequences ensued for them and the entire human race. Adam was overcome with uncertainty, and he started blaming Eve and God (Gen 3:10–13). Evil permeated the environment. The entire creation experienced the same curse of conflict, pain, misery, toil, and death. All people, including senior adults, are affected adversely today.[4] However, the senior adult who is pursuing life in Christ can gratefully accept the liberating paradox of his existence

---

4. Woodrow Kroll and Don Hawkins, *Prime of Your Life* (Grand Rapids: Revell, 1999), 19–20.

by recognizing that the "inner nature is being renewed day by day" while the outer nature gradually wastes away (2 Cor. 4:16).[5] To be able more fully to appreciate this inner renewal process, the utter pathos of man's total depravity must not be underestimated. Because sin came into the world (Rom 5:12), the *imago dei* no longer adequately reflected the divine glory. The profound problem of man's lostness and incapacity to please God was resolved definitively by the potential reconciliation of the believer through the death of Jesus Christ (2 Cor 5:11–21).[6]

The sacrificial death of Jesus Christ for the penalty of one's sin is accepted by faith through the grace of God. A quantum leap then is taken in resolving the sin problem and enabling man to rejoice in his own justification before God. The senior adult, who is in this sense leaping for joy, walks on a firm foundation upon which he can humbly hold his head high, but not because he has done anything at all to merit his positive standing before his Creator. God has allowed him to pursue new life in Christ with a renewed mind and heart and a new capacity to please Him by discerning what is the "good and acceptable and perfect" will of God (Rom 12:1–2). This is the nature of the older person who is redeemed by Christ.

The Place of Older Persons in OT and NT Societies

Essential spiritual characteristics of older persons in history who have been redeemed by faith in the saving promises of God contribute to a greater understanding of their value to society. The designated elders in Old Testament society were viewed as qualified to govern a particular village or tribe by virtue of their age. Justice was normally meted out by them in accordance with traditional practices. Priests were called upon to dispense justice in complicated situations that required a superior knowledge of the Pentateuchal law.[7]

---

5. J. Oswald Sanders, *Enjoying Your Best Years* (Grand Rapids: Discovery House Publishers, 1993), 83ff.

6. This writer remembers Francis Schaeffer's chapel lectures at Wheaton College in 1966, when he affirmed and explained without reservation, "Man is not junk!" Cf. Francis A. Schaeffer, *Escape From Reason* (Downers Grove: Inter-Varsity Press, 1968), 21, 26, 53–56, 83, 87; and Francis A. Schaeffer, *The God Who Is There* (Downers Grove: Inter-Varsity Press, 1968), 105–106, 131–132.

7. John Bright, *A History of Israel* (Philadelphia: The Westminster Press, 1959), 151.

The word "elder" in the Septuagint is most often derived from πρεσβύτερος.[8] It is also translated "old" and "presbyter" throughout the Old and New Testaments.[9] In applicable contexts, a person with advanced age and seniority acted upon the accumulated experience of many years. His acquired skills were applied to many areas of life: religious, social, economic, and legal.[10]

Beginning with the patriarchs in Genesis, and including many subsequent leaders and prophets, the aged among them were perceived as spokesmen who exercised strategic roles in national development. Moses, Joshua, Caleb, Gideon, and Eli represent individuals used by God to fulfill significant leadership roles in their later years.

An evaluation of a person's usefulness to society and church is not necessarily dependent totally on quantifiable measures of work productivity. Bearing spiritual fruit in all stages of life, including the later years, is a reflection of Christian character, the fruit of the Holy Spirit (Gal 5:22–23), as well as any other gift received from God that "leads to sanctification and its end, eternal life" (Rom 6:21–22). The parables of Jesus related to work, worth, and rewards do not emphasize the interplay between productivity and compensation so much as they elevate the importance of values such as accountability and faithfulness to one's calling.[11] The word "require" is not used lightly in either the Old or the New Testaments, and the accompanying emphasis on accountability is consistent throughout. "What does the Lord your God require of you?" The answers in Scripture are compatible with the words: ". . . to serve the Lord your God with all your heart and with all your soul, and to keep the commandments and statutes of the Lord" (Deut 10:12–13). Micah (6:8) provides a similar answer to the question, "What does the Lord require of you?" It is necessary "to do justice, and to

---

8. There are 230 passages in the OT and apocryphal books where the word πρεσβύτερος appears. Cf. Edwin Hatch and Henry A. Redpath, *A Concordance to The Septuagint and the Other Greek Versions of the Old Testament, Including the Apocryphal Books* (Graz, Austria: Akademische Druck—U. Verlagsanstalt, 1954), II–1201. A partial list follows of passages that deal with the events and actions surrounding the elders of Israel: Exod 3:16–20; 4:29–31; 12:21–28; Num 11:16–29; Deut 19:12; 21:1–4; Josh 7:6; 8:33; Ruth 4:2; 1 Sam 30:26; 2 Sam 17:1–16; Ezra 5:1–12; Ezek 8:1–13.

9. *The New International Dictionary of New Testament Theology*, s.v. "πρεσβύτερος."

10. In communities that were entirely Jewish, the same men would act both as elders of the synagogue (in assumedly the post-exilic context) and as officers or heads of the communities. See W. N. Stearns, "Elder in the OT," *The International Standard Bible Encyclopedia* (Grand Rapids: Eerdmans, 1939), 2:923.

11. Cf., for example, Matthew 25:14–30 and Luke 12:35–48.

love kindness, and to walk humbly with your God."[12] This is the calling that the spiritually mature, adult obeys, and it can be followed just as satisfactorily in any stage of life.

Very instructive for modeling balanced living in the later years of life is the example left by the Lord Jesus Christ in the Gospels. He certainly realized that his life on earth was short, but he never appeared to be in a rush. He seemed to have extensive time for dialogue and encounters with individuals, even though his mission concerned the welfare of all creation.[13]

In New Testament society, the Jewish elders are visible and identifiable for their rejection of the apostles' message (Acts 4:1–8; 5:17–27; 24:1). Apparently, the churches' elders arose naturally from the Jewish tradition (Acts 11:30), and Paul's appointment of elders in the established churches confirms their strategic leadership role (Acts 14:23). An inference is that they were mature men, seasoned with years of experience.

Worthy of note is the group of women over sixty years of age mentioned in 1 Timothy 5:9–10. The older widows are to be enrolled for service in the church, representing it in special ways, such as in social outreach to those in need. They are placed in a special class apart from younger widows (1 Tim 5:11–15) in part by virtue of their moderation in the area of sexuality.

Older women are also invested with the responsibility of training younger women "to love their husbands and children, to be self-controlled, pure, working at home, kind and submissive to their husbands, that the word of God may not be reviled" (Titus 2:3–5). Older men are reminded that they fulfill an important role in being "sober-minded, dignified, self-controlled, sound in faith, in love, and in steadfastness" (Titus 2:2).

Wisdom and discernment in the life of the older adult are exemplified in the lives of the apostles and other writers of the books of the New Testament. Luke, John, Peter, James, and Jude are some of those who, inspired by the Holy Spirit, composed and recorded without error God's revelation to man in their gospels or letters found within the New Testament.[14] These manuscripts were immediately and increasingly recognized for their divine origin and authority. They were profound in their language usage, purpose,

---

12. Earl G. Dahlstrom, "Toward a Theology of Aging," *The Covenant Quarterly* (February 1979), 10–11.

13. Johnnie C. Godwin, *Life's Best Chapter: Retirement* (Birmingham: New Hope Publishers, 2000), 233.

14. These are inerrant within the original autographs which are represented within our canonical New Testament.

meaning, and application to the lives of countless people through the ages. These writers arose out of humble origins and presumably improved over time in their assimilation and use of vocabulary and verbal expression. In most cases, it was only in the later years that their unique personalities and developing writing styles were employed by the Holy Spirit to give to the church an inspired and authoritative guide for faith and practice.[15] They exemplify the importance of life-long learning, and the retention and communication of one's life experiences for the benefit of succeeding generations. Collective wisdom is passed on from one generation to the next, and the older adult in this case is the key link in the connective process.

Wisdom is a spiritual gift and service empowered by the Holy Spirit (1 Cor 12:4, 8, 11), and it is enhanced through many years of practical experience in applying knowledge of the Word of God to facilitate the daily decisions of life. There is no better time to begin this journey than at a very young age. The words of the writer of Proverbs 3:1–8 open the door to "favor and good success in the sight of God and man" (verse 4) that accrue from obedience, love, and faithfulness (verses 1 and 3).

In sum, the older adult in the Old and New Testaments assumed leadership roles in society and in the church by virtue of his age, experience, and spiritual qualities. Not only was he a source of practical wisdom in resolving societal, religious, legal, and economic matters, but he was also called upon to act as a role model and practitioner of servanthood and integrity for the benefit of people of all ages.

The Relationship Between Older and Younger Persons

Models for bridging the generation gap in the spheres that encompass human life in general (family, church, and society) are encountered in the Old and New Testaments. Relationships between older and younger persons are accentuated and strengthened by adhering to biblical admonitions and

---

15. Although the important phrase "rule for faith and practice" was discussed and defended many centuries before A. A. Hodge (1823–1886), he defines it succinctly in chapter 5 in *Outlines of Theology*, 1860 (public domain), accessed on "The Highway: A Repository of Historic Christianity and the Reformed Faith" under http://www.the-highway.com/Scripture—Hodge.html: "Whatever God teaches or commands is of sovereign authority. Whatever conveys to us an infallible knowledge of his teachings and commands is an infallible rule. The Scriptures of the Old and New Testaments are the only organs which, during the present dispensation, God conveys to us a knowledge of his will about what we are to believe concerning himself, and what duties he requires of us."

following biblical examples, all of which are divinely inspired and serve as the only infallible rule of faith and practice.

Familial relations in the book of Genesis provide a basis from which to derive sound applications for intergenerational life today. Examples meriting further explanation are the relationship between Noah and his children, when he became drunk (Gen 9:18–27), Abraham's intended sacrifice of Isaac (Gen 22:1–19), Jacob's trickery in gaining the blessing from Isaac (Gen 27:1–46), and Jacob's blessing of Joseph's sons (Gen 48:1–22). All these and other narratives serve as positive and negative examples of both moral and immoral thinking and behavior.

On several occasions in the Pentateuch, the elders resolve problems that arise out of familial relationships. One example is the disposition of the rebellious son who cannot be controlled by his parents (Deut 21:18–21). Parental authority should not be disparaged, but when ongoing overt acts of rebellious children are a detriment to the welfare and foundational structure of the community, due to the breakdown of familial cohesion, the elders may enter to give their judgment on the case. The authority of the parents may appear at first glance to be challenged by the intervention of the elders, but if the parents adhere to the prescribed societal laws for controlling rebellion, it can strengthen their authority.

The book of Ruth portrays in a beautiful manner the ties that bind the older and younger generations together. Naomi's kin (her grandson Obed) was to be a restorer of her life and her sustainer in old age.[16] The promise was secure since Ruth, her daughter-in-law, loved her and was "more to [her] than seven sons" (Ruth 4:13–17). The implication was that she would prepare him to render this service, since she loved Naomi deeply. There is no generation gap in this true story. On the contrary, a high degree of interdependence and mutual commitment is evident, and the way is well prepared for the coming of future generations that ultimately led to the blessed Savior Jesus.

In each town in Israel, there were elders who were appointed to administer the religious and civil affairs under their jurisdiction (Ruth 4:1–12). It has been noted previously that the term "elder" reflects a respect for age as a reliable source of wisdom, although it should be remembered that advanced age is not the only source of wisdom, nor does it guarantee the presence of wisdom. It does appear that the advice of the elders was normally listened to and respected. Rehoboam's rejection of the counsel of

---

16. Frank Stagg, *The Bible Speaks on Aging* (Nashville: Broadman Press, 1981), 53.

the elders regarding his intended manner of ruling over the people is one exception (1 Kings 12:1–15). The recommendation of the elders was later vindicated, however, when events turned against Rehoboam.

Several aspects of familial relationships are mentioned in the book of Proverbs. Typical of these is an admonition to the younger generation: "Listen to your father who gave you life, and do not despise your mother when she is old" (23:22). Listening and affirming demonstrate an attitude of respect for the personhood of the older adult.

Of all the writings in the New Testament, the Pauline epistles address most directly the relationships between younger and older people in the church. Implicit in almost all of the passages is the attitude of mutual respect. The older man, according to 1 Timothy 5:1, is not to be rebuked, but to be encouraged as if he were a father. Old age does not preclude the possibility of error or erratic behavior, and the older adult must indeed be warned when it is necessary and humanly possible. Older women are to be treated as mothers (1 Tim 5:2), meaning that they should be honored (Eph 6:2).

Older men are enjoined to be "sober-minded, dignified, self-controlled, sound in faith, in love, and in steadfastness" (Titus 2:2). It is evident from the need to mention these positive traits that some people are at times vulnerable to intemperance, a behavior that does not merit respect. Some are vulnerable to a lack of self-control, weakness in faith, and inconsistency in love. Some are also susceptible to wavering in self-doubt and questioning the meaning and purpose of their lives. Likewise, some older women may be vulnerable to negative behavior such as irreverence, slandering, addiction to wine, or teaching what is unsound or less than edifying. Older women instead are encouraged to "train the young women to love their husbands and children, to be self-controlled, pure, working at home, kind and submissive to their own husbands, that the word of God may not be reviled" (Titus 2:3–5).

In conclusion, the older adult should be respected and cared for by others in the church. The primary role of older men and women is to serve intentionally as examples of sound Christian living. In general, the older adult is to be viewed in the wider context of societal relationships as a valuable resource for wise counsel.

Not Weary of Well Doing

Further Biblical Observations Related to Older Persons

The following biblical passages and observations complement the previous perspectives. Each passage will be recorded with a short observation following it. These affirm in practical ways the personhood of the older adult in the church.

Leviticus 19:32 reads, "You shall stand up before the gray head and honor the face of an old man, and you shall fear your God: I am the Lord." In this passage, one can observe that respect for the aged and reverence for God are compatible attitudes.

Ruth 4:14–15 states, "Blessed be the Lord, who has not left you this day without a redeemer, and may his name be renowned in Israel! He shall be to you a restorer of life and a nourisher of your old age, for your daughter-in-law who loves you, who is more to you than seven sons, has given birth to him." One notices in these verses that the older adult is renewed and sustained by children and grandchildren who love him.

In Job 12:12–13, one can see that years of life experience provide wisdom and understanding. "Wisdom is with the aged, and understanding in length of days. With God are wisdom and might; he has counsel and understanding." Ultimately, though, God is the reliable source of these traits wisdom and understanding.

Psalm 71:17–18 contains a further statement about the benefits of faithful learning throughout the years. "O God, from my youth you have taught me, and I still proclaim your wondrous deeds. So even to old age and gray hairs, O God, do not forsake me, until I proclaim your might to another generation, your power to all those to come." Here one sees that lifelong learning from God is translated in later years into testimony to the younger generation of God's mighty and righteous deeds.

The toil and trouble of life are witnessed in Psalm 90:10. "The years of our life are seventy, or even by reason of strength eighty; yet their span is but toil and trouble; they are soon gone, and we fly away." The average life span brings toil and trouble, and it appears to be a very short time.

In Psalm 91:14–16, there are promises for the one who follows God over a lifetime. "Because he holds fast to me in love, I will deliver him; I will protect him, because he knows my name. When he calls to me, I will answer him; I will be with him in trouble; I will rescue him and honor him. With long life I will satisfy him and show him my salvation." In this text, we understand that the obedient older follower of God is promised divine deliverance, protection, honor, satisfaction, and salvation.

Recognizing and Affirming the Personhood of the Senior Adult in the Church

In Psalm 92:12–15, there are also promises for the righteous older adult. "The righteous flourish like the palm tree and grow like a cedar in Lebanon. They are planted in the house of the Lord; they flourish in the courts of our God. They still bear fruit in old age; they are ever full of sap and green, to declare that the Lord is upright; he is my rock, and there is no unrighteousness in him." The righteous older adult who began his faith journey in the presence of God continues to bear fruit through his testimony of the uprightness and righteousness of God.

In Ecclesiastes 12:1–5, the writer encourages each one to turn to the Lord early in life. "Remember also your Creator in the days of your youth, before the evil days come and the years draw near of which you will say, 'I have no pleasure in them'; before the sun and the light and the moon and the stars are darkened and the clouds return after the rain, in the day when the keepers of the house tremble, and the strong men are bent, and the grinders cease because they are few, and those who look through the windows are dimmed, and the doors on the street are shut—when the sound of the grinding is low . . . they are afraid also of what is high, and terrors are in the way; the almond tree blossoms, the grasshopper drags itself along, and desire fails, because man is going to his eternal home, and the mourners go about the streets . . . ."

Physical ailments and challenges will come to the older adult who has diminishing physical strength. According to Ryken, this passage compares the troubles of the older adult to a gathering storm. The best time in life to begin living a God-centered life is in the early years, when one is still young enough to give a whole lifetime in service to God. "The call of the Preacher is to remember our creator now, before all these things (the 'gathering storms' of old age) happen to us."[17]

In summation, the biblical references chosen above speak directly to the experiences of the older adult. From the passages cited in this section, the following guiding principles can be derived to bear on a correct methodology for ministering to the older adult in the church. The older adult:

- is wise and understanding
- retains a valuable reservoir of life experience
- suffers diminishing strength
- realizes that life is short

17. Philip Graham Ryken, *Ecclesiastes: Why Everything Matters* (Wheaton: Crossway, 2010), 271.

- needs emotional renewal and spiritual nourishment
- merits respect
- can be an effective and fruitful witness to others of God's person and power

The Bible is truthful and transparent in its treatment of the challenges, opportunities, problems, and suffering of the older adult. A striking contrast is presented between the blessing inherent in spending the later years with God and the horrid dismay of a life journey ending without God. The older adult who trusts in God has a greater capacity to enjoy the simple, everyday things of life.[18] He recognizes that he is a unique being in God's handiwork, created in the image of God and reconciled to Him through the sacrificial death of His Son Jesus Christ.

As he models balanced and God-honoring living, the older adult merits the respect of his peers and of the younger generation. He serves the church in helping confront difficult issues and resolving challenging problems, on the basis of the breadth and depth of his experience. His potential for giving informal counsel and advice should not be overlooked. Also, the older adult has deep, heartfelt, and at times inexpressible needs that require attention and care by family and church. These are primary conclusions derived from previous observations related to the nature, social standing, and relationships of the older adult, as portrayed in the Old and New Testaments. The biblical teaching presented above forms the basis for contemporary practice that bears on the needs, ongoing education, and affirmation of the older adult in the church.

Older Personhood in the Church

Recognizing the Needs of the Older Person

The biblically based starting point for identifying the needs of the older person and educating him successfully to face the challenges of the final phase of life is the recognition of his ongoing identity. Perspectives on life may change with the passing of years, but the core identity based on innate human worth will never change. "The starting point," according to Dick-Muehlke, "is a theology of aging and impairment which rejects societal

---

18. Cf. Ecclesiastes 3:9–13; 8:15; 9:7–10; 11:8.

stereotypes of the elderly and recognizes the continued personhood."[19] Dick-Muelhke's thinking regarding the constancy of the personhood of all older adults, even those who are unfortunately hampered by gradual cognitive decline, is informed by her belief that all people bear the *Imago Dei*, the image of God which, from her perspective, is primarily relational in nature.[20] Since everyone bears the image of God, "no one is insignificant; no one is worthless," avers Elmer, who adds an instructive testimony: "Today, every contact I have with another person becomes either a sacred or profane moment depending on how I see it and handle it. To accept and affirm the dignity of the other will nurture the image of God in them. To devalue that person or fail to show respect will contribute to a further distortion of the image of God in them."[21]

Two basic needs arising from the personhood of all human beings are survival and self-esteem.[22] Most elderly people want to stay alive as long as life holds a promise of hope to them. These needs are a reflection of the inalienable personhood of the older adult, which should never be violated. Zohar, a researcher and teacher in the area of human nature and consciousness, argues for an inversion of Maslow's pyramid of needs (physiological needs for safety, belongingness and love, esteem, and, at the top of the pyramid, self-actualization, meaning a sense of accomplishment and creativity).[23] She attempts to prove that "the need for meaning is primary," and that meaning should not be disassociated from the so-called foundational or lesser needs for material well-being and companionship.[24] The concept of meaning, or self-actualization, as opposed to other basic needs, such as companionship and material well-being, is interpreted in a variety of ways, depending on a person's background, interests, life habits,

---

19. Cordula Dick-Muehlke, "'And Abraham Laughed': A Theology of Aging and Impairment," *Fuller Theological Seminary: Theology, News and Notes* (December 1995), 15.

20. Some theologians are in agreement, but others believe the *imago dei* is primarily rational in nature.

21. Duane Elmer, *Cross-Cultural Servanthood: Serving the World in Christlike Humility* (Downers Grove: IVP Books, 2006), 63, 66.

22. The author has elsewhere attempted to provide a more extensive overview of perspectives on human nature as they relate to motivation and personality. See Gerald C. Ericson, "Encouraging, Affirming and Motivating a Staff," in *My Brother's Keeper*, ed. Thomas J. Marinello and H.H. Drake Williams III (Eugene, OR: Wipf & Stock), 208–213.

23. Abraham H. Maslow, *Motivation and Personality* (New York: Harper & Row, 1978), 20–21, 35, 47, 51–56. Cf. also the 1970 edition, 38.

24. Danah Zohar, *Rewiring the Corporate Brain: Using the New Science to Rethink How we Structure and Lead Organizations* (San Francisco: Berrett-Koehler, 1997), 15–20.

and other perspectives.[25] For some older adults, it may necessitate a daily walk to the park to talk with other people and share a cup of espresso. For others, it may be expressed in highly creative and artistic ways, which for Maslow are at the top of the pyramid. Moberg agrees that meaning should not be separated from the material, emotional, intellectual, and other aspects of human life and behavior, but he goes one step further by saying, "There is a longing for enduring meaning and purpose for life, a search for something that transcends time."[26]

In the discussion of what constitutes meaning for the older Christian adult, it should be remembered that Christians are unique products of God's creation, redeemed by faith through the grace of God, continually maturing and being conformed to the image of Jesus Christ (Rom 8:29; Phil 1:6). A truly holistic spiritual growth process connected to a human being's total needs does not depend primarily on humanly devised methods and processes that supposedly lead to "self-actualization." In the Christian's life, there is constant development, because God is transforming him into the image of "the glory of the Lord" (2 Cor 3:18) and is working in him "both to will and to work for his good pleasure" (Phil 2:13). The fulfillment of God's will in the life of the older adult does not come automatically. Rather, it involves ongoing openness to the guidance of the Holy Spirit in obeying His directives expressed in the Word.

A needs-based perspective on human actualization of the older adult can be partially derived from several sources. For example, according to Erikson's life-cycle model of development in eight life stages, there are two opposite inclinations in each of the stages, which should be balanced to some extent in a state of dynamic tension. The adult in the last stage of life, that of maturity, must in some way encounter equilibrium between ego integrity and despair, while reaching maturity through accumulated wisdom, the desired virtue. Maier, in his understanding of Erikson's eighth life stage, states, "If it is acquired, a sense of integrity provides a successful solution to an opposing sense of despair and disgust of the many life styles, and a fear of death as the end to an unfulfilled life."[27] For the Christian, true

25. Thomas Bradley Robbs, *The Bonus Years* (Valley Forge: Judson Press, 1968), 73.

26. David O. Moberg, "Spiritual Maturity and Aging," *Fuller Theological Seminary: Theology, News and Notes* (December 1995), 3–5, 21.

27. Henry W. Maier, *Three Theories of Child Development* (New York: Harper & Row, Publishers, 1969), 72. Cf. also a commentary on Erikson's study of the life conflicts of Martin Luther in Robert Coles, *Erik H. Erikson: The Growth of His Work* (Boston: Little, Brown & Co., 1970), 253. Source: Erik H. Erikson, *Young Man Luther, A Study in*

wisdom comes from God (Jas 1:5). It is translated by the Holy Spirit into power, yielding hope and peace based on confidence in the promise of God that the decline of bodily and mental functions will eventually be offset by a total transformation in the resurrection (1 Cor 15:20–22).

It is generally assumed that most people desire as they grow older to live as long and as comfortably as they can without being a burden on the family unit. The traditional Latin makeup of the Portuguese family unit, which the author observed during his missionary service in Portugal, tends to be aware of this need, since most children recognize and accept their familial duty to care for elderly parents, even if it means taking them into their home. Mead described this dynamic in cautionary terms: "If there is separation of old people from family life, there is tragedy for both young and old."[28] The generations learn from and enjoy companionship with each other. If there is intentional separation between the generations, misunderstanding, grief, and human tragedy may ensue.

The older person's need for physical well-being and affirmation that emanate from people of all ages is substantiated by this writer's interviews and conversations with many older adults in Portugal and the United States. The older adult needs to be respected by those in his immediate social unit, to enjoy friendships, to live in a suitable and satisfactory relationship with other family members, and to be spiritually content.

Buhler identifies two groups of people unhappy in their old age. Some of them are dissatisfied with the past and apparently have no opportunities to make up the deficiencies. Others feel even worse in the degree of their remorse. They are of the opinion that they have led meaningless lives, and feel guilty because of it. However, Buhler finds that present attitudes are more important than previous actions in dictating happiness. Some older adults go through life with high standards of excellence and are frustrated at the end of life's journey that they did not do better.[29]

Psychoanalysis and History, Austen Riggs Center, Monograph N. 4 (New York: Norton, 1958). For a summary explanation of Erikson's life-cycle model of development, which can be applied to the development of faith in the older adult, see Colleen Benson, "Faith Development in the Elderly," *Fuller Theological Seminary: Theology, News and Notes* (December 1995), 17–21.

28. Margaret Mead, cited in Earl A. Grollman and Sharon Hya Grollman, *Caring for Your Aged Parents* (Boston: Beacon Press, 1978), 104.

29. C. Buhler, "Old Age and Fulfillment of life with Considerations of the Use of Time in Old Age," *Acta Psychologica*, 1961, 19, 126–148, cited by Sheila M. Chown, "Personality and Aging," in *Theory and Methods of Research on Aging* (Morgantown: West Virginia University, 1968), 135–157.

Not Weary of Well Doing

For those who are frustrated because of an unproductive or meaningless past, and for others who can look back on previous achievements with a sense of accomplishment, a positive worldview in the present can be constructed from a combination of independence and interdependence. The older adult thrives on independence that frees him from being an unnecessary burden on anyone else. However, he longs for contact with others with whom he can relate in a transparent manner, because he is experiencing continual loss in his life. The problem is not necessarily that his feelings are changing, but that he copes with formidable challenges, such as a decline in health, different daily responsibilities, and the ongoing loss of friends who are preceding him in death. He adjusts to these changes, but he must do so intentionally and continuously. A wise and understanding friend who recognizes these challenges and talks to him about them can be a genuine source of encouragement.

One older adult delineates with acquired insight the following basic needs of the aging:

- Good health, to the extent possible
- Financial security
- Comfort
- Appropriate and satisfactory living arrangements
- Companionship and affection
- Interpersonal relationships, if possible, across age groups
- Varied occupations, creative activities
- Continued usefulness; being needed in some way
- A settled life philosophy
- A sound faith and close relationship with its organized form (as a church or synagogue)[30]

The church should strive to help the older adult satisfy his basic physiological needs, especially when these needs are not being met by the immediate family or social community. Most of these necessities are driven by finances related to adequate housing, food, clothing, and medical care. The number of older adults who face these pressing needs is increasing around the world.

30. Dorothy Bertolet Fritz, *Growing Old Is a Family Affair* (Richmond: John Knox Press, 1972), 70.

In sum, aging alone does not guarantee spiritual maturity, but the older adult who is growing in spiritual health is becoming spiritually mature. He revels in being loved and affirmed by God and also by others who know him. He retains a purpose for life, recognizing that God has "set eternity into man's heart" (Eccl 3:11) and cares for him (1 Pet 5:7), even though his diminishing health and quality of life may not be what he desires. The spiritually mature older adult rests in the hope that there is a bright future in heaven beyond the grave.

Educating the Older Person

Education of the older person proceeds ideally from the identification of real and felt needs. The older adult is instructed by example and by means of formal or non-formal teaching. Modular training organized in teaching segments that are conducive to interaction and a high degree of dialogue can well include the following components:

- Encountering and developing suitable work and ministry alternatives to former responsibilities
- Finances and budgeting
- Health and nutritional needs
- Personal and social relationships
- Handling the loss of family members and friends and personal preparation for death

All of these topics can be treated biblically and related to the experience of each individual. Moreover, according to Howe, the older adult is helped through preaching and counseling to find a center outside of self, if he doesn't have it already.[31] When he is fulfilling the biblical admonitions to love and serve others, his consciousness of ultimate worth before God is heightened.[32] Love dispels doubt and fear, satisfies real and felt human needs, and benefits others. The spirit of serving others is foundational for encouraging the older adult to thrive in his spiritual life.

---

31. Reuel L. Howe, *How to Stay Younger While Growing Older: Aging for All Ages* (Waco, TX: Word Books, 1974), 129–130.

32. "You shall love your neighbor as yourself" (Matt 19:19).

Not Weary of Well Doing

Contributing to the Ministry of the Church

Older persons can be involved in three forms of active and vital ministry in and through the church. These actions and behaviors are summed up by the words καταγγέλλω, κοινωνία, and διακονία. The older follower of Jesus Christ who is actively participating in these three expressions of service tends to lead a balanced Christian life. Every disciple of Jesus Christ affirms and validates his faith by proclaiming (καταγγέλλω) the message of the gospel to others (1 Cor 11:26). The follower of Jesus Christ thrives on fellowship (κοινωνία) with others of kindred spirit (1 John 1:7). He reaches out in serving (διακονία) others (Eph 4:12), even when personal physical disabilities and limitations are a concern. Ministering to the older adult is enhanced beyond measure when he is shown how he can serve others, taking into account any physical, intellectual, and emotional limitations in his life.

The driving force for ministering to others is not simply the desire to keep active, make new friends, or stimulate the exercise of brain cells in order to prolong physical health and mental acuity. The older person has time to evaluate his life for the purpose of retooling and refocusing on attitudes and behaviors that are conducive to health and balance. However, more profound and biblically based motives for service to others, such as demonstrating love by encouraging and affirming one's neighbor and companion, are just as valid for the older adult as they are for people of any other age. A person who loves others rises above the elemental cravings of hunger and thirst and "self-actualization." Instead, he aspires to goodness, holiness, and righteousness for the glory of God. Enduring peace comes to that person who is assured that he is helping fulfill the purposes of God for people's lives.[33]

The older adult's deep desire to minister to others reflects the blessing of God through the ministry of the Holy Spirit in his life. This attitude is based on eternal values that guide daily behavior. Five core values that lead to fulfillment (love, joy, peace), reality (that which never fades away), and wisdom (applied skill in living), according to Boa are: knowing God, seeking the approval of God, servanthood, integrity/character, and humility. Unfortunately, the older adult, just as anyone else, is tempted to live on the basis of a temporal value system that requires no dependence on God. This

---

33. "Blessed are those who hunger and thirst for righteousness, for they shall be satisfied" (Matt 5:6).

earthly and demonic system leads to the pursuit of temporary pleasure, recognition by others, popularity, wealth, status, and power. It is therefore understandable why many older adults use the words emptiness, delusion, and foolishness to describe their attitude toward life. Their behavior is not based on an eternal value system.[34]

Gray and Moberg aver that some older adults feel neglected by the church, are dependent on younger members for transportation, disapprove of changes made in worship services, and are unable to contribute financially as they used to do formerly.[35] Others appear ill at ease alongside young people. These reactions and perspectives in certain social contexts are not uncommon, especially when the generation gap is not being bridged successfully by spending time together. Any person may occasionally react less than favorably to his immediate environment; yet there are fundamental biblical premises and guidelines for behavior that can dictate and nourish underlying positive attitudes.

An essential question to be asked regarding the older adult and his relation to his church milieu is the following. Does the church intend for him to be only a spectator who watches what is going on around him, or can he be nurtured more effectively by his being a contributor to the ministry of the church? Assuming that the premise of contributing to the ministry of one's church enhances the spiritual quality of one's life, a discerning church asks itself what can be done to integrate the older adult in the life and outreach of its ministry. Integration affords beneficial results: individual spiritual growth in the context of the community of believers and a contribution to the ministry of the church with which the older adult is affiliated.

Key areas of involvement in church ministries serve to integrate the ministries of older adults, such as proclaiming the Gospel to others, enjoying fellowship with others of kindred spirit, and serving others. These are people whose personalities and abilities have been shaped by a minimum of sixty-five years of valuable life experience. The potential for the service and growth to maturity of others is noteworthy. Accordingly, informed leadership in the church scrutinizes and carefully evaluates how the spiritual gifts and abilities of the older adults are employed. A fundamental underlying value in these decisions is the collaboration between older adults and

---

34. Kenneth Boa, *Conformed to His Image* (Grand Rapids: Zondervan, 2001), 65–71, presents most of the ideas in this paragraph in a cogent and compelling manner.

35. Robert M. Gray and David O. Moberg, *The Church and the Older Person* (Grand Rapids: Wm. B. Eerdmans Publishing Company, 1962), 96–115.

people of all ages in the congregation. A myriad of services are possible. Many of these ministries are encapsulated in the following principal areas:

- Participation in worship and devotional activities
- Life teaching and modeling
- Maintaining and improving the church property
- Business and clerical matters
- Participation in and leading special programs and activities for older adults
- Social and relief work

All the above actions reflect involvement in other people's lives. Spiritual growth and well-being, however, are not measured exclusively by the degree of visible, collaborative behavior of the older adult on a daily basis. One of the most important activities, if not the most important activity, is that of prayer. Many older people, including those with delimiting physical challenges, have more discretionary time and volitional resolve than ever before to pray, giving themselves to God and others through praise, confession, thanksgiving, and supplication for a host of people in need, themselves included. For the older adult to contribute in this significant way to the ministry of the church, he should be cognizant of what prayer really means and entails. Hundreds of authoritative biblical and extra-biblical sources touch on the marvelous mystery of prayer.

One perspective that has greatly influenced the practice of prayer by many people was expressed by a pastor whose martyrdom at the hands of the Gestapo in 1945 cut short his earthly life at the age of thirty-nine:

> Here we learn, first, what prayer means. It means praying according to the Word of God, on the basis of the promises. Christian prayer takes its stand on the solid ground of the revealed Word and has nothing to do with vague, self-seeking vagaries. We pray on the basis of the prayer of the true Man, Jesus Christ. This is what the Scripture means when it says that the Holy Spirit prays in us and for us, that Christ prays for us, that we can pray aright to God only in the name of Jesus Christ.[36]

Bonhoeffer states elsewhere that it is a normal behavior in the Christian life to pray together after each one individually has learned the richness of being alone with God with the Word opened in silence and resting

---

36. Dietrich Bonhoeffer, *Life Together* (New York: Harper & Row, 1954), 47.

Recognizing and Affirming the Personhood of the Senior Adult in the Church

within.[37] This behavior is also desirable in the life of the older adult whose prayers are validated by God to exercise His will both in heaven and on earth. This same sphere of influence rightly includes the church. The older adult's participation in prayer-related ministries and meetings is therefore one of the most, if not the most, secure investments of time and energy that glorify and honor God throughout eternity.

Facing Sickness and Death

Some people are reluctant to openly express anger at the seeming injustices of life. Part of the bewildered feeling that an older adult can experience is due to the lack of opportunities to release pent-up feelings regarding apparent inequities. Many of these arise from questions related to sickness and health and life and death.

It is possible in adolescence and early adulthood to suppress thoughts regarding death, intentionally and habitually. This is natural. For the older adult to consciously deny the reality of death is not a healthy thing. In fact, the suppression of the idea of eventual death during any stage of life deprives a person of a realistic and balanced perspective on life and death. If the older Christian adult accepts the fact that he has doubts or even occasional dread in his inner being due to unanswered questions related to death, he takes an important step forward in facing up to the reality of his own demise. Wondering what death will be like, what surprises it will bring, and whether it will be painful or peaceful are all part of a normal curiosity regarding the future. Faith and hope face death with relative serenity in spite of these and other unanswered questions. Tournier has emphasized the correspondence between Christian faith and one's acceptance of the inward truth about himself. Feelings of anxiety are recognized as reflecting one's weakness, and they should be confessed as a person puts his trust in the grace of God.[38] In the context of the appearance of the "chief Shepherd" who will give the "unfading crown of glory," Peter counsels his readers: "Humble yourselves, therefore, under the mighty hand of God so that at the proper time he way exalt you, casting all your anxieties on him, because he cares for you" (1 Pet 5:4, 6–7).

As the older Christian adult is encouraged to openly face sickness and death, the sharing of a biblical perspective on life and death is apropos. The

---

37. Bonhoeffer, *Life Together*, 76–79.
38. Paul Tournier, *Learn to Grow Old* (New York: Harper & Row, 1979), 222.

best (heaven) is yet to be, and one's entire life on earth is simply a short preparation for death and heaven.[39] Preparations for death and heaven are far-ranging, but they obviously don't approach in importance the decision made regarding one's eternal destiny.[40] Other resolutions related to legal and financial matters affect people who are left behind.[41] Also, the mourning and leave-taking of the one dying who is losing loved ones should not be forgotten.[42] Remembering that the person facing death is also going through a grief process is especially important.[43]

It is crucial for one to pray for divine wisdom in the attempt to break into the lonely world of the person who is close to death. Withdrawal from the real world cheats a person out of the last few days, months, or years of his life. It robs him of fellowship and human understanding which he so desperately needs. When the older adult broaches the topic of death, one must not brush it off with a light comment or attempt to change the topic. The person listening at this time is afforded a good opportunity to pursue the matter wherever it may lead. According to Cohen and Gans, many people feel that it is the height of insensitivity to discuss someone's death face to face with him in the same tone he would use to discuss the latest news event.[44] It could be that a person's reluctance to discuss such matters is

---

39. Oswald J. Sanders, *Enjoying Your Best Years* (Grand Rapids: Discovery House Publishers, 1993), 139ff, 147ff.

40. Jeffrey A. Watson provides helpful guidelines for sharing the hope-giving gospel with older adults in "When the Going Gets Tough," *Eldercare for the Christian Family*, ed. Timothy S. Smick, et al. (Dallas: Word Publishing, 1990), 146–149.

41. James W. Duncan, Jr., gives suggestions regarding inciting and maintaining dialogue with the older adult on these and other important issues in "Talking with Your Elderly Parents," *Eldercare for the Christian Family*, ed. Timothy S. Smick, et al. (Dallas: Word Publishing, 1990), 199–213.

42. Jean Beaven Abernathy, *Old Is Not a Four-Letter Word! New Moods and Meanings in Aging* (New York: Abingdon Press, 1975), 137.

43. Psychiatrist Elizabeth Kübler-Ross, basing her data on interviews with terminally ill patients, describes this process in the following stages: denial, anger, bargaining, depression, and acceptance. Hope continues throughout most of the stages, and stages are neither linear nor the same for everyone. Cf. *On Death and Dying* (New York: The MacMillan Co., 1969), 260ff. In *Death: The Final Stage of Growth* (Englewood Cliffs, New Jersey: Prentice-Hall, Inc., 1975), 181ff, Kübler-Ross analyzes her previously-described stages of dying in terms of the height and depth of emotions experienced by a terminally ill patient. In *Working It Through* (New York: MacMillan Publishing Co., Inc., 1982), 144ff, she suggests how to help people cope with pain and terminal illness.

44. Stephen Z. Cohen and Bruce Michael Gans, *The Other Generation Gap: The Middle-Aged and Their Aging Parents* (Chicago: Follett Publishing Co., 1978), 227.

partially due to his own introspection, selfishness, or unbalanced perspective on life. A reluctance to talk openly about the subject of death prevents one from affirming and revealing the integrity of his own personhood.

The matters of sickness and death are raised truthfully with grace, when an older person has the correct perspective and embraces with joy the reality of eternal life. He tends to feel younger than his years on the inside, even though the body is deteriorating. He cultivates a deepening relationship with Jesus Christ with a growing desire to see Him in heaven. He wants to serve God on earth according to the divine time plan. With heaven as his final reference point, his entire life on earth is radically rearranged.

Stowell insightfully emphasizes related critical points on anticipating heaven. Seven aspects of a person's life are affected by having an eternity in heaven as a reference point for life: posture toward God, perspective on possessions, perception of people, perspective on pain, pleasures on earth, purity, and a sense of identity. Since the best is yet to come, all of a person's earthly possessions are both expendable and free to be used for the glory of God.[45]

What motivates the one who cares for the older Christian adult is the deep human need for being miraculously transformed as a result of the Holy Spirit's working in one's life through the power of Christ's efficacious sacrifice for sin on the cross. These servants of God have set their "minds on things that are above, not on things that are on earth" (Col 3:2).

Esteeming the Older Person

The older adult's personhood as a consequence of his being created in the image of God (Gen 1:27) provides the fundamental reason for meriting respect from others. Consequently, his worth is not based primarily on special abilities or gifting, although certain positive qualities that are easily recognizable in an older adult may influence others to respect him. In the case of the older adult who is a Christian, the transforming work of the Holy Spirit in his life produces qualities such as the fruit of the Spirit (Gal 5:22–23) that also encourage others to esteem him even more.

An incontrovertible reason for esteeming the older adult arises directly in response to the commands in the Old and New Testaments that

---

45. Joseph M. Stowell, *Eternity: Reclaiming a Passion for What Endures* (Grand Rapids: Discover House Publishers, 2006), 24, 27, 41, 49, 73, 77, 84–97.

dictate how other people should be treated.⁴⁶ For example, in the context of presenting Christ's magnificent example of humility in Philippians 2:1–11, Paul orders the Philippian church in 2:3: "Do nothing from rivalry or conceit, but in humility count others more significant than yourselves" (ἀλλήλους ἡγούμενοι ὑπερέχοντας ἑαυτῶν). This command assuredly includes people of all age groups, the older adult included.⁴⁷ In the same context, Philippians 2:1 contains four true first-class conditions introduced by the particle εἰ. These conditional clauses assume that there is "encouragement in Christ," "comfort from love," "participation in the Spirit," and "affection and sympathy," and validate the expressed command in Philippians 2:3 to esteem others, looking not only to one's "own interests, but also to the interests of others" (Phil 2:4). The affirming attributes described in Philippians 2:1–4 are not derived from or in response to a person's special abilities or gifting, but from love in Christ (Phil 2:1, 5) which is reflective of Christ's example of humility (Phil 2:5–8).

Consequently, the older Christian adult is respected and esteemed out of the same love (Phil 2:2) by virtue of his being God's "workmanship, created in Christ Jesus for good works" (Eph 2:10). Christ's example of humility in "taking the form of a servant, being born in the likeness of men," and in "becoming obedient to the point of death, even death on a cross" (Phil 2:7–8), is a model for the thoughts and actions of a person who intentionally and lovingly respects and esteems the older Christian adult in the church.

Conclusion

Demonstrating esteem for an older person requires human contact through dialogue in different venues. An older adult who feels loved, trusted, and encouraged will normally reveal any information about his past that is relevant to understanding how he is reacting to a present challenge. The church does well to encourage sharing and self-disclosure on the part of the older adult. This can be affected through small Bible study and fellowship groups,

---

46. Cf. the beginning subsections in this manuscript under the title *Older Personhood in the Bible*, where the mandates related to honoring the elderly are emphasized. Esteeming and honoring are both actions emanating from love.

47. The participle *count* with a double accusative in this instance can be translated *look upon* or *consider*, according to William F. Arndt and F. Wilbur Gingrich, *A Greek-English Lexicon of the New Testament and Other Early Christian Literature* (Chicago: The University of Chicago Press, 1957), 344.

smaller groups in prayer meetings, and pastoral visits. The foundational communication for dialogue and resultant self-disclosure arises from biblical preaching and teaching, Christian education, and a balanced family life. When the older Christian understands and appreciates his position as a child of God, he grows in the recognition of his value as an individual. The affirmation of his worth by those next to him also significantly enhances the manner in which he views himself.

The older adult must not be disparaged just because he may look old and wrinkled. Only the outer shell shows decay. The inner person of the Christian is renewed continuously. Most older people like to be treated as if they are in the prime of life, because that is how they truly feel (with the exception of those with debilitating physical or emotional illness). Activities shared with people of all ages are conducive to the well-being of the older adult. Those who are younger also greatly benefit from enjoying social contact with those who are older.

No person is immune to praise. The older adult thrives on it from people of all ages, especially those with whom there is mutual trust. Friends and family members who minister to and affirm the older adult learn a good lesson: the acquisition of experience, learning, balance, and esteem is distilled into wisdom over a period of time. This is a life-long process that begins in the early years through the input of many people. A person who continues to grow in the later years satisfactorily faces the crises, losses, and frustrations commonly associated with those years, and by God's grace does so with growing faith and fortitude.

Wisdom gained through the years enables the older adult to face death with courage and hope. His needs as a person are recognized and satisfied through the help of others near to him as the Holy Spirit leads them. Saving trust in his God and Savior Jesus Christ is reaffirmed continuously. He is instructed and encouraged to contribute in significant ways to the ministry of the church. He faces sickness through the lens of his broader perspective on life. Death is recognized as part of the life process and also as a continuation of the full experience of living on into eternity for the glory of the Triune God.

Development of the *Evangelische Christengemeenten Vlaanderen*:

Its Characterization, Rapid Growth, and Relationship with the Flemish Roman Catholic Church

THOMAS J. MARINELLO

The *Evangelische Christengemeenten Vlaanderen* (ECV) began as a result of evangelistic church-planting efforts in the Dutch-speaking portion of Belgium (Flanders) as led by a group of Canadian missionaries in the early 1970s. These missionaries were from one of the many distinct, historically Protestant, evangelical movements known as Brethren.[1] More specifically, these missionaries were from the Open Brethren.[2] What began as a series of home-based, evangelistic Bible studies grew into a fully recognized denomination within a few decades of the first study.

The speed was remarkable at which the churches (or "assemblies") were planted. After many decades of little or no growth among the Brethren in Flanders, twenty-six churches were planted in a nineteen year period. In

---

1. For a listing and summary of the various groups that have been called Brethren except for the *Unitas Fratrum*, cf. "Brethren," in *Religions of the World: A Comprehensive Encyclopedia of Beliefs and Practices*, ed. J. Gordon Melton and Martin Bauman (Oxford: ABC-CLIO, 2002), 1:168–9. For information on the *Unitas Fratrum*, cf. J. G. G. Norman, "Moravian Brethren," in *The New International Dictionary of the Christian Church*, 2nd ed., ed. J. D. Douglas (Grand Rapids: Zondervan, 1978), 676.

2. For a further summary history and definition of this particular group of Brethren, cf. Donald Tinder, "Christian Brethren," in *Religions of the World: A Comprehensive Encyclopedia of Beliefs and Practices*, ed. J. Gordon Melton and Martin Bauman (Oxford: ABC-CLIO, 2002), 1:268–269.

Development of the Evangelische Christengemeenten Vlaanderen

addition to these twenty-six, one was planted in the Netherlands, "three" for a time among Belgian solders in Germany, and one pre-existing Open Brethren assembly in Flanders joined the ECV. Further, these Flemish and Dutch assemblies were composed almost exclusively of converts from Roman Catholicism as opposed to transfer growth from other Protestant churches. The purpose of the founders of what would become the ECV was to organize home Bible studies "all over Belgium or in southern Holland" with the goal of planting churches, yet none envisioned the change from an informal movement to a denominational organization recognized by the Belgian government.

The founders and shapers of the ECV did their work at a unique time in the modern religious and social history of Flanders, a time when the cultural paradigm shifted from the centuries-old culture of Roman Catholicism to a much more secular, postmodern construct.[3] The timing of the founding and shaping of the ECV was such that the explosive growth is not unexpected, however, when viewed through the lens of history, especially that of the history of evangelical awakenings.

So how might one characterize the churches of the ECV? What might have been some significant contributing factors to their remarkable growth, outside of the obvious pneumatological factors associated with a God-sent revival? And what was the ECV's relationship with the Roman Catholic Church, the Christian religion which dominated the socio-religious landscape at the founding and shaping of the ECV?

Characteristic Emphases of the ECV

At least four emphases characterized the functional ecclesiology of the ECV. While these four characteristics are consistent with what was taught and practiced in the ECV, they are not necessarily unique to the churches of the ECV, as distinct from the evangelical churches in Flanders, or indeed the body of Christ since its inception at Pentecost. The prominence given some of them, however, is what set apart the ECV from similar evangelical groups in Flanders. Even though organizational changes and

---

3. For a more complete discussion of this change, cf. Karel Dobbelaere and Liliane Voyé, "From Pillar to Postmodernity: The Changing Situation of Religion in Belgium," in *SA.Sociological Analysis: A Journal in the Sociology of Religion*, 51:S (1990): S1–S13; Karel Dobbelaere, "Trends in de Katholieke godsdienstigheid eind 20ste eeuw," in *Tijdschrift voor Sociologie* 24, no. 1 (2003): 9–36.

methodological variances can be traced in these assemblies since their inception in 1972, the ECV continued to keep as primary at least four emphases in its thought and actions. These four emphases were the purposeful, unwavering commitment to the proclamation of the Gospel for the purpose of Church planting; the centrality of the Lord's Supper consistent with Open Brethren thinking; the emphasis on pragmatic, sound teaching; and the types and selection of leadership.

The Unwavering Commitment of the Proclamation of the Gospel for the Purpose of Church Planting

Since the beginning of the Bible studies which would become the ECV, right up through the formation and governmental recognition of the ECV and beyond, the proclamation of an evangelical Gospel had a central role. This proclamation was not for gaining converts alone, but for the purpose of assembling these converts into new churches. Additionally, the ECV missionaries were not satisfied merely with professions of faith as they reported numbers of new converts. Wisely, they frequently mentioned numbers baptized as they counted converts, because "it is quite a step for a Roman Catholic Belgian to get baptized in front of a group of people."[4]

Both Richard Haverkamp and Henk Gelling, the primary founders of the ECV, were committed to evangelism—openly and unwaveringly.[5] One family member noted, "[Gelling] is an evangelist. That's what he lives for; he thrives on it. I am amazed that any conversation he gets into, he can turn it to Christ."[6] Yet, his passion was not merely for evangelism, but that the new converts could be gathered together to form new local churches, new Brethren assemblies. In a letter to supporters, Gelling wrote, "I long to start new assemblies, that is more my gift, but we need to see the existing ones come to maturity."[7]

Haverkamp was equally gifted and passionate about evangelism, especially for the purpose of planting churches. Additionally, one very experienced and respected church planter noted of Haverkamp and his work

---

4. Richard and Marina Haverkamp, letter to supporters, February 1982.

5. Richard Haverkamp, interview by author, St. Martens Latem, Belgium, 25 April 2003.

6. Julie Gelling, interview by author, Houthalen, Belgium, 12 August 2007.

7. Hank and Beryl Gelling, letter to supporters, January 1989.

Development of the Evangelische Christengemeenten Vlaanderen

in Belgium, "I felt that there was nobody at that time that could preach the Gospel as well as he did."[8]

Over the years, the ECV founders and shapers were involved in a variety of evangelistic outreaches. The various methods included (but were not limited to) door-to-door work, evangelistic outreaches using barges on the Flemish canals, evangelistic teams brought in for campaigns, tent evangelism, drama and music, open air campaigns, films such as *Jesus*, and all manner of literature, both in short tracts and longer booklets.

After the founding of the first few assemblies, evangelistic efforts almost always were connected with and under the direction of one of the ECV assemblies. An evangelism committee was formed within every assembly planted by the founders of the ECV and the assemblies that hived-off in the ensuing years. Every ECV newsletter and every church meeting devoted a section to noting the plans and results of these efforts. The creativity and flexibility of the founders and the assemblies they planted was seen in a number of areas, but especially in those efforts designed to find contacts to invite to evangelistic Bible studies. The primary evangelistic tool in the first decades of the founding of the ECV and the most often used evangelistic Bible study was the *Startstudies*.[9] This ten-lesson study was a methodical, apologetic, biblical presentation of the claims of the evangelical faith from the first three chapters of the Gospel of John. After finding a contact, the Bible study leader would tell the person hosting the study to invite family and friends. Haverkamp noted that he would make outrageous statements in order to draw an audience.[10] "One of the methods Richard used was to say, 'I am a guru.' And people were shocked, thinking, 'How can that be?' 'I come to you tonight explaining what that means,' and he did."[11]

ECV evangelistic efforts were not done in isolation from other evangelistic activities in Flanders, however. Over the years, the ECV churches cooperated with crusades by Billy Graham and Luis Palau, as well as the

---

8. Anonymous, interview by author.

9. Richard Haverkamp, "*Startstudies*: 10 Evangelische Bibjbelstudies vanuit Johannes 1–3," (1979?). This series of Bible studies later was published as: Yvan Thomas and Richard Haverkamp, 10 *startstudies, handleiding voor het doorgeven van geloofsprincipes* (Ieper, Belgium: Jered Publishing, 1995).

10. Richard Haverkamp, "Wie der Herr Jesus Christus Gemeinden baut," 8 lectures & 1 question and answer period (Deutsche Gemeinde-Mission, KfG Ostdeutschland, 2002), session 6.

11. Patrick Nullens, interview by author, Heverlee, Belgium, 10 September 2003. Cf. Haverkamp, "Wie der Herr Jesus Christus Gemeinden baut," session 6.

work of Operation Mobilization (OM)—especially when OM sent teams of young people on barges throughout Flanders or conducted door-to-door evangelistic campaigns. These efforts most often were used to find contacts from which *Startstudies* or another type of evangelistic home Bible study could be formed.

Unlike a number of evangelists, the founders of the ECV saw evangelism as the means to an end, not an end in itself. The founders of the ECV did their work in an era when the stadium evangelistic crusades still were very popular for the purpose of "winning converts," as was the annual "week of revival" in many conservative North American churches, but the goal of the ECV's founders was to create "a living, active, independent, multiplying [local] church" as the result of successful evangelism.[12] The ECV founders considered the work of the evangelist incomplete until this goal was attained.

Further, Haverkamp anchored the founding of the Church in creation principles when he passionately emphasized:

> Evangelicals may say Jesus came to die for our sins. They are right, but this is not the first reason. Jesus came to build His Church, and He went to the cross to die to make it possible. The first thing God built was a woman. The thing that Jesus came to build was a Bride for Himself.[13]

Evangelism was not limited to "native" Belgians as efforts were made to reach out to immigrant communities. Specifically, efforts were made to evangelize Muslims. The Haverkamps asked for special prayer for "the thousands of Muslims in Ghent, mainly from Turkey and Morocco."[14] Additionally, *Belgische Evangelische Zending* (BEZ) courses on how to reach Muslims were made known in the main ECV publication, *Nieuwsbrief*.[15] Nonetheless, the reach of the ECV was limited by design to Dutch speakers or those who potentially would integrate into Flemish society.

---

12. Haverkamp, "Wie der Herr Jesus Christus Gemeinden baut," session 3.
13. Haverkamp, "Wie der Herr Jesus Christus Gemeinden baut," session 1.
14. Richard Haverkamp, New Year's letter to supporters, [21] January 1992.
15. "Waar naar toe?" *Evangelische Christengemeenten Vlaanderen Nieuwsbrief*, ed. Koen Schelstraete, vol. 22, no. 2, 2.

The Centrality of the Lord's Supper Consistent with Open Brethren Thinking in the Assemblies of the ECV

As with any local church within the mainstream of the Brethren, the ECV emphasized the importance and centrality of the Lord's Supper in the meetings of the assembly. In keeping with the outlook of the Open Brethren, the ECV founders and shapers held to a nonsacerdotal, nonsacramental, memorial view of the Lord's Supper which served as both a mark of identity and of unity within the body of Christ.[16] The ECV held that all believers were welcome at the Lord's Supper. As Haverkamp said, "We did not receive people into fellowship, because the moment a person was converted, he was baptized. He was part of the universal Church, and he also was *automatically* part of the *local* church."[17] So central to their identity was this "breaking of bread" meeting that the founders of the ECV and the assemblies that they planted used the first Sunday celebration of the Lord's Supper as the date on which each of their home Bible studies was considered as a local church.[18]

The format of the ECV Lord's Supper was an open meeting during which any believer could ask for a song to be sung, give a prayer, or read a passage from Scripture with or without commentary in line with the traditional Brethren customs for conduct during a Lord's Supper service.[19] The meeting would not be led by a clergyman, an elder, or one of the ECV workers because of the commitment in the Brethren to the priesthood of all believers, especially as practiced with a historical aversion and at times hostility to any sort of clergy/laity division.[20] Additionally, the tradition

---

16. Nonsacramental specifically means that the taking of the elements does not provide the recipient with grace, salvific or otherwise. That said, some see a near sacramental presence, though not in the bread and wine, because of an overemphasis on Christ's presence at the celebration of the Lord's Supper based upon Matthew 18:20. Cf. Neil T. R. Dickson, review of "The Lord's Supper in Brethren Ecclesiology: the Mark of Identity, Unity, and for some, Purity," by Thomas J. Marinello in *My Brother's Keeper*, ed. Thomas J. Marinello and H. H. Drake Williams III, *Brethren Historical Review*, vol. 7 [2011]: 98–100.

17. Haverkamp, "Wie der Herr Jesus Christus Gemeinden baut," session 2.

18. Haverkamp, "Wie der Herr Jesus Christus Gemeinden baut," session 8.

19. "Samenkomst van de gemeente," in minutes of the "Werkersvergadering," Berchem, 28 June 1991. In contradistinction with the common practice at the assemblies from which the founders came, women believers also were allowed to participate in much the same manner as the men.

20. Neil Fraser, *The Lord's Supper* (Chicago: Emmaus Correspondence School, 1965),

among the Brethren normally was to have no sort of preplanned course of the service other than a set start time and a general ending time. Visitors who came to the Lord's Supper celebration at one ECV assembly were told, "You will see several people read something from the Bible and give a short thought, ask for a song to be sung, or pray. All of these will be to praise and worship the Lord Jesus Christ."[21] These "remembrance meetings" culminated with the passing of the bread and cup.

Rosario Anastasi, one of the Flemish men who worked fulltime for the ECV, noted that the former Roman Catholics like himself really liked the participatory nature of the ECV services, and particularly its manner of celebrating the Lord's Supper. This was in sharp contrast with the services at the Roman Catholic churches during which the parishioners mostly were spectators. Still he also observed that his own children, as well as many of the children of the original members of the ECV, did not continue with this same appreciation since they grew up in the ECV assemblies.[22] Nevertheless, one of these children remembered that he was encouraged at a young age to take part in the public expressions of worship associated with the Lord's Supper. As young as sixteen, he remembered participating. He did so due to the "openness for the young people [to participate]."[23]

Thus, the characteristic meeting which was central to the ECV churches was a stark contrast to both the beliefs and practices of the Roman Catholicism in which the new converts had been raised.

The Emphasis on Pragmatic, Sound Teaching throughout the ECV

Since nearly all of those who would associate themselves with the churches planted by Haverkamp and Gelling were new converts, the ECV assemblies had a significant need for Bible teaching in order that these new believers could learn more about the faith to which they had converted. While the new converts had some familiarity with Christian ideas, the knowledge they had primarily was that which might have been learned when catechized as members of the Roman Catholic Church. Accordingly, a fundamental

---

5/2–5/3.

21. "Evangelische Christengemeente Houthalen," a pamphlet given to visitors to this Limburg assembly. n.d.

22. Rosario Anastasi, interview by author, Bergneustadt-Wiedenest, Germany, 30 June 2005.

23. Jelle Creemers, interview by author, Heverlee, Belgium, 06 September 2007.

knowledge of the content of the Bible and most of the tenets of an evangelical faith were absent from the minds of the new believers. In the ensuing years, the founders and shapers of the ECV taught the new converts the fundamentals of evangelical Christianity as well as the basic content of Scripture. In addition to the transmission of basic biblical knowledge was a continual emphasis on practical ways to put this knowledge to use in areas such as working with drug-addicted youth, dealing with the occult, and counseling.

These emphases on providing biblical knowledge and encouraging its practical outworking were not a unique approach for a conservative, evangelical group such as the ECV, yet they continued well past the early years and up through the date of this writing, many decades after the founding. Methodologically, the ECV saw the importance of putting to work the ideas of 2 Timothy 2:2 as a way of multiplying the needed teaching and teachers.[24]

The manner in which this two-fold emphasis was delivered was often a bit surprising, given the lack of formal theological education for Gelling, and the friendly teasing that Haverkamp consistently delivered to those with formal theological training.[25] Early on in the work, the missionaries began a time of organized Bible teaching and study for all the new believers associated with the ECV throughout Flanders, the "one day a month" Bible school.[26] In addition to these large gatherings, the newsletters of the ECV in the early 1980s listed a plethora of Bible studies based in an assembly or perhaps among two or three assemblies which were located within a few kilometers of each other. Most often, these studies worked through a New Testament book or a section of Scripture such as the parts of Genesis which contained the life of Joseph. Commonly, these studies were taught by the founders of the ECV or some of the shapers who became full time workers with the ECV. That said, teachers from the Dutch assemblies, as well as other evangelical groups from Flanders, taught these studies as well.

The more formal days for Bible study began with a plan for Saturday classes in Limburg known as the *Limburgse Studiedag Toerusting* (LST).[27]

---

24. Richard and Marina Haverkamp, "The Haverkamp News," letter to supporters, Spring 1986.

25. A good example of this teasing was evident in several of Haverkamp's lectures, "Wie der Herr Jesus Christus Gemeinden baut," during which he mentioned his lack of education versus those with doctorates or those who held teaching positions on theological faculties.

26. Richard and Marina Haverkamp, letter to supporters, November 1977.

27. Henk Gelling, telephone interview by author, 08 December 2008. Interestingly,

Not Weary of Well Doing

This provided a practical solution to the need for a more in-depth understanding of the Bible, but the reach was limited geographically. A national program eventually was proposed by Patrick Nullens, and he and two others brought this proposal to fruition as the *Toerustingscentrum Christengemeenten Vlaanderen* (TCV).[28]

Preaching and courses taught throughout the ECV were not, however, the only means of pragmatic, sound teaching. In 1994 and 1995, one of the ECV's chief shapers, Guido De Kegel, would have his only two books published. In contrast to his normal preaching content, both books contained teaching of a pastoral, practical nature.[29] *Zalf voor je ziel* (*Salve for your Soul*) contained pastoral principles taken the Psalms and then observed in the life of David in 1 and 2 Samuel. De Kegel's second book, *Splinters in je hart* (*Splinters in Your Heart*), was a twelve-chapter presentation dealing with failures and problems seen in the lives of various biblical characters such as Abraham, Moses, Joshua, Elijah, Peter, and others.[30] These books certainly were in line with the changes evident within the ECV assemblies as they altered in membership from primarily new coverts to those who had been believers for a decade or more. This pastoral emphasis also coincided with the focus on marriage and family teaching brought to the fore with the arrival of Canadian Brethren missionary Peter Gifford, as he and his wife observed the marriage and family needs of the new converts.

Gifford also saw a great need for solid teaching aimed at the youth. Accordingly, he designed material specifically aimed at training young men and women who led camps which he oversaw. Foundational to the teaching that he gave these young leaders was the need to help the campers become believers and mature in the faith (Colossians 1:28–29), as well

---

the initial name of this program was to be *Limburgse Studie Dag*, but the resultant initials, LSD, were deemed inappropriate.

28. "Eindelijk wat ik zocht!," *Nieuwsbrief van de christengemeentes*, ed. Eric Rutten, 1989, nr 2, 7. Patrick Nullens would go on to become a systematics professor and later head of the *Evangelische Theologische Faculteit*, an evangelical school which eventually became an accredited university in Heverlee-Leuven, Belgium.

29. The pastorally themed books were the only ones authored by De Kegel. The more complete record of his characteristic teaching emphasis is garnered by perusing the list of his preaching and teaching topics as well as his personal notes which were made for these lectures.

30. Guido De Kegel, *Splinters in je hart* (Ieper, BE: Jered, 1995), 5–6.

Development of the Evangelische Christengemeenten Vlaanderen

as an emphasis on teamwork predicated upon the individual gifting provided each believer by the Holy Spirit (1 Corinthians 12:4–6; Ephesians 4:11–16).[31]

At the end of the 1990s, the *Nieuwsbrief* also began to take on a role as an instrument through which teaching was delivered. Prior to this time, this publication primarily was for information of interest for the believers of the ECV. This information might have included personal testimonies of conversion, requests for prayer, announcements of new *Startstudies*, announcements of the beginning of a new assembly or the anniversary of one already in existence, notices of upcoming conferences, or the appointment of a new full-time Flemish worker or a foreign missionary to work with the ECV. The *Nieuwsbrief* eventually added sections on marriage and family teaching. In the early parts of the twenty-first century, an extended series was given in the *Nieuwsbrief* which covered the tenets of the Roman Catholic faith, comparing and contrasting these teachings with evangelical Christianity. The topics covered included infant baptism, burial of a loved one, the Eucharist, images, and two on Mary, the mother of Jesus.[32]

The emphasis on sound, practical teaching within the ECV led to their cooperation with the BEZ and the *Vrije Evangelische Gemeenten* (VEG) to form the *Evangelische Toerustingschool Vlaanderen* (ETV) in 2005. The ETV was an outgrowth of the *Evangelische Bijbel Scholen*, a practical Bible training effort in the Netherlands which began in 1972.[33] This four-year course of studies would take the student through the entire Bible "to increase the knowledge and experience of the Christian faith." The collaborative nature of the ETV meant that it had a wider aim than just those associated with the ECV. Nonetheless, three of the five teachers were full-timers from the ECV.[34] Courses emphasized biblical studies, systematic theology, and practical theology.

A good summary of the strong emphasis on pragmatic, sound teaching as a fundamental part of the identity of the ECV comes from the observation of one of its workers. He noted that, while many solid, evangelical

31. Peter Gifford, interview by author, St. Die, France, 25 August 2003.

32. Wout Van Wijngaarden, "Rooms Katholieke Gebruiken Onze Houding?" *Evangelische Christengemeenten Vlaanderen Nieuwsbrief*, ed. Koen Schelstraete, vol. 21, no 2, 3, 4; vol. 22, no 1, 2, 3.

33. "Welkom," Evangelische Toerustingschool Vlaanderen, http://www.ets-vlaanderen.be/index.php?id=21 (accessed 09 December 2008).

34. "Programma," Evangelische Toerustingschool Vlaanderen, http://www.ets-vlaanderen.be/index.php?id=27 (accessed 04 August 2008).

works had come to his part of Flanders, the ECV remained the only group which continued to hold and promote a corporate, weekly Bible study such as was held in his assembly.[35] Indeed, this aspect of the ECV was not a passing fad or a church planting technique, but was part of its "DNA" from its founding.

The Types and Selection of Leadership Within Individual Assemblies and Throughout the ECV

One of the earliest challenges in the planting of assemblies by the founders of the ECV was to provide leadership for the local churches after they had been planted. As could have been expected, the leaders of the evangelistic Bible studies were the initial leaders of any subsequent churches. Thus, the founders were the initial leaders of the individual churches; the ones who came later and shaped the movement or became full-time workers from among the Flemish also became leaders. Clearly, the ECV held that good, biblical leadership was essential for each assembly, and that the proper leadership structure was described in the New Testament in 1 Timothy 3 and Acts 20, among other places.[36] Accordingly, the founders and shapers of the ECV were committed to the recognition of at least elders in each local church; ideally, elders and deacons both would be recognized. The requirements for those who held the position of elder were understood to be located in 1 Timothy 3 and Titus 1. As Guido De Kegel would note, "The qualities of leaders are not so much what they can do, but who they are. It is a matter of character."[37] Thus, an ECV worker or workers initially would act as the pastoral leaders and primary teachers of the new assembly. Over time, an assembly would recognize church leadership of some sort, usually *verantwoordelijken* (responsible ones) or elders.[38] The ultimate leadership goal was the recognition of elders.

Elders of local churches, however, were not the only type of leadership. As the ECV matured as an organization, it understood three divisions among the nationwide leadership: evangelists, teachers, and pastoral

---

35. Peter Gifford, interview by author, Saint-Jorioz, France, 19 August 2008.

36. Guido De Kegel, "Leiding in de gemeente," *Nieuwsbrief van de christengemeenten*, ed. Marc Van Den Bogaerde, vol. 10, nr. 4, 5–6.

37. Guido De Kegel, interview by author, Lovendegem, Belgium, 13 August 2007.

38. *Verantwoordelijken* were leaders who acted much like elders, but were not yet formally recognized as elders for various reasons.

Development of the Evangelische Christengemeenten Vlaanderen

workers. In one meeting of the full-time workers in 1986, the evangelists' work was described primarily toward those outside of the local assembly. They would make contacts and lead *Startstudies*. The teachers would preach on Sundays and lead Bible studies during the week. Among the pastoral worker responsibilities was the youth work, but this 1986 meeting also noted that the workers had care for the nine hundred people associated with the ECV.[39]

Perhaps one of the most interesting aspects of the study of the ECV is to witness the change of church government from the planting of the initial churches until the beginning of the 1990s. In some ways, these forms of government parallel the experiences found in the first centuries of the Early Church.[40] The ECV churches transitioned from purely organism to visible organization within a span of fifteen years. This was seen in activities such as council meetings, the formal name change of their group, and the eventual securing of official government recognition and funding.

Rapid Growth of the ECV

While the founders of the ECV envisioned the planting of Brethren assemblies (what they viewed as "New Testament churches") all over Flanders, none of the founders had any vision to create a new denomination, and none foresaw the explosive growth. A number of factors can be identified which suggest that the growth of assemblies from 1972 through 1991 should not be viewed as so surprising, even though it was remarkable in nature. Although a number of reasons can be posited for the way in which the ECV came to be and subsequently developed, two significant reasons are considered below.

Timing of the Founding and Shaping of the ECV

The founders and shapers of the ECV did their work at a unique time in the modern religious and social history of Flanders. The timing of the founding and shaping of the ECV was such that the explosive growth and equally

39. Henk Gelling, "Werkers vergadering—Berchem," from personal diary: blue-denim colored Clairefontaine notebook entitled "Werkers Fall 85," 04 September 1986.

40. For a summary of this process, cf. John Hannah, *Our Legacy: The History of Christian Doctrine* (Colorado Springs: NavPress, 2001), 258ff. Cf. especially the chart on p. 258.

sudden cessation of growth is not unexpected when viewed through the lens of history. Additionally, comparable rapid growth and cessation of growth were also evident among similar evangelical groups in Flanders during the same era; all had a "season of revival."

The evangelical, free churches in Flanders experienced an explosive growth in the numbers of new converts, as well as the local churches which ensued during the same timeframe at the end of the twentieth century. For example, records from the BEZ/VEG archives show that, prior to 1972, the last church it planted in Flanders was in 1944. From the first church in 1919 through 1944, the method of church planting was through the work of colporteurs, tent meetings, and open-air evangelism.[41] The total number of churches planted during those twenty-five years was fifteen or sixteen, nine of which were planted during the 1920s.[42] From 1972 to 1988, however, thirty new churches were planted.

In the same years, the Pentecostal churches also saw explosive growth in Flanders. Up through 1970, one academic study noted that Flanders had twenty-one churches associated with some kind of Pentecostal gathering as categorized in ten identifiable groupings.[43] Using the same identified groupings, the Pentecostal gatherings numbered fifty-six by 1990.[44] Additionally, the number of Pentecostal adherents had grown by three hundred percent in the same twenty-year span.[45]

During the same years, no similar growth was witnessed among those churches associated with the *Verenigde Protestantse Kerken van België* (VPKB), either in Flanders or Wallonia, because they had "no vision for church planting [and] their problem [was] one of decline of membership."[46] Additionally, a serious and accelerating decline was quite evident in the

---

41. Johan Lukasse, "Een lijst van posten en gemeenten gesticht door de B.E.Z." Brussels, Belgium, a summary report by the VEG dated 29 June 1988.

42. Cf. Lukasse's list of the fifteen to the sixteen in "File: POST GEMLYST 2; Report: BEZ-overzicht," a summary report by the BEZ dated 30 December 1988. While the records found in the BEZ versus the VEG differ by one church, both accountings maintain the gap between 1944 until 1972.

43. Ignace Demaerel, "Tachtig jaar pinksterbeweging in Vlaanderen (1909–1989): Een historisch onderzoek met korte theologische en sociologische analyse" (MA thesis, Universitaire Faculteit voor Protestant Godgeleerdheid te Brussel, 1990), 3–8.

44. Demaerel, "Tachtig jaar," 374.

45. Demaerel, "Tachtig jaar," 376.

46. Egbert A. Bos, "Church Planting in Flanders," (MA thesis, Evangelische Theologische Faculteit, 1988), 12.

Development of the Evangelische Christengemeenten Vlaanderen

numbers of practitioners of Roman Catholicism. As an American priest visiting Antwerpen observed in the early nineties, "Antwerp is a city of half a million in a country estimated to be 90 percent Catholic. It bills itself as the 'city of monumental churches.' Its tourist literature, however, does not add that most of them are empty."[47] Similarly, even official Roman Catholic publications noted the paucity of Roman Catholic communicants and priests, as well as the hostility toward the Pope himself among Belgians during the pope's 1995 visit to Belgium. As a speaker quoted in a Roman Catholic periodical said:

> The fact that the pope will spend less than 48 hours in one of the church's traditionally most loyal and most Catholic nations appears hard to understand, given the warm welcome he received in 1985. At best he's expected to draw 10,000 faithful—out of a population of 9 million Catholics.... [T]he clerical model of church in Belgium is fading fast. The average priest is 63, and hundreds of parishes are without a priest.[48]

The only other religious group in Flanders which showed a noteworthy increase in practitioners at the end of the twentieth century was Islam. The reason for its increase, however, was due to increased immigration from countries in which Islam was the predominant religion.[49]

Sociological studies from a number of sources note that the time period from the early 1970s until the turn of the twenty-first century mark a paradigm change from what often is called modernism to postmodernism. A major part of this sociological change was the rapidly diminishing influence of the Roman Catholic Church in Flanders as well as a concurrent rise in secularization.[50] Additionally, "the conjunction of two phenomena—secularization and individualization—probably were amplified by the bursting of the traditional social categories."[51] In fact, Luc de Fleurquin, a Roman

---

47. James Gilhooley, "The Church in the Low Countries," *America* 167, no. 17 (28 November 1992): 430.

48. Patricia Lefevere, "Pope to face disgruntled laity in Belgium," *National Catholic Reporter* 31 (02 June 1995): 13.

49. Meryem Kanmaz, "The Recognition and Institutionalization of Islam in Belgium," in *The Muslim World* 92, no. 1/2 (Spring 2002): 100.

50. This is not an isolated phenomenon, but readily seen in studies of other Roman Catholic countries such as Brazil, Chile, and Guatemala. Cf. Robert Ruby, ed., *Spirit and Power: A 10-Country Survey of Pentecostals* (Washington, DC: The Pew Forum on Religion & Public Life, 2006), 72–77.

51. Liliane Voyé, et al., *Belges Hereux et Satisfaits: Les Valeurs des Belges dan les annees*

Catholic professor of canon law in Belgium, said that "he feared much more the 'indifference and secularization without limit' that is buffeting Belgian society" than he did the changes within the Roman Catholic Church as it attempted to stay relevant.[52]

Studies sponsored by the European Values Study Foundation (EVSF) confirmed what people sensed: secularism was on the rise, and Roman Catholicism was on the decline. Roman Catholicism was in decline according to a measurement of Roman Catholic practices. The EVSF also noted the same decline using self-identification. In 1981, 71.7 percent of respondents stated Roman Catholicism as their religion, but by 1999 this had dropped to 56.9 percent. Interestingly, people identifying themselves as free church/ nondenominational actually increased from .3 percent in 1981 to 1.1 percent by 1999. Belief in no God rose from 11.7 percent in 1981 to 27 percent by 1999.[53] In another study comparing confidence in "the church" for the years 1981 and 1990, affirmative responses dropped from 60 percent to 49 percent.[54] These surveys were in line with the larger picture noted by sociological studies cited earlier, the change sensed by Roman Catholics and the evangelicals alike, and contemporary stories in the popular media.[55]

In a similar vein, Haverkamp noted that people were interested in religion when the founders of the ECV arrived in the early 1970s. Why might have the Flemish listeners been so receptive? One cannot consider the answer without attention to the effects of the Second Vatican Council. So far-reaching were the effects of the Second Vatican Council that one participant wrote:

> It fell upon us like a thunderbolt, called by a charismatic Pope, John XXIII, in a moment of extraordinary insight. As the sessions unfolded from 1962–65, it gathered energy of its own.... Vatican II left all concerned from Paul VI and the Fathers of the Council

---

90 (Brussels: De Boeck-Wesmael, 1992), 228.

52. Lefevere, "Pope to face disgruntled laity," 13.

53. "European and World Values Surveys Four Wave Integrated Data File, 1981–2004, v.20060423," The European Values Study Foundation and World Values Survey Association, http://margaux.grandvinum.se/SebTest/wvs/index_data_analysis (accessed 07 January 2009).

54. Voyé, et al., Belges Hereux et Satisfaits, 202.

55. Cf. Noelle Knox, "Religion Takes a back seat in Western Europe," USA Today, 11 August 2005. While written at the popular level, this article uses statistics from both the Center for the Study of Global Christianity and the World Values Survey Association.

Development of the Evangelische Christengemeenten Vlaanderen

itself, down to the simplest practicing Catholic, somewhat breathless in its aftermath.[56]

A veteran BEZ missionary made four observations about the times in view of this, observations oft repeated by others.[57] All of these were as the result of the pronouncements of the Second Vatican Council or the popes associated with this council.[58] First, "[Protestant Christians] were no longer heretics anymore, but separated brethren."[59] This created an opening for evangelical Christians such as the ECV to meet with Roman Catholics. Second, Pope John XXIII, the convening pope, said that Catholics should read their Bibles.[60] Third, the Mass was now read in the vernacular after centuries of teaching that it could be said only in Latin.[61] This removed some of the sense of mystery associated with the Mass.[62] Finally, Pope Paul VI, the pope at the end of the council, released his encyclical *Humanae Vitae*. This clearly stated the Roman Catholic Church's position with respect to human reproduction and life. The positions concerning contraception and abortion, for example, were directly opposed to the cultural climate in Belgium at the time of the arrival of the ECV founders. As a result, these four points created a climate where "everybody was confused" by the sudden change to centuries of teaching, and "everybody was disappointed" because the teachings on human life did not change.[63] Into this setting came the founders and shapers of the ECV who presented the evangelical Gospel with a slightly apologetic edge, and the results were remarkable.

---

56. Francis J. Moloney, "Vatican II: The Word in the Catholic Tradition," Catalyst for Renewal, http://www.catalyst-for-renewal.com.au/moloney.htm (accessed 28 June 2009).

57. Johan Lukasse, interview by author, Badhoevedorp, Netherlands, 05 December 2003.

58. Cf. Walter M. Abbott, ed., *The Documents of Vatican II*, trans. Joseph Gallagher (Piscataway, NJ: New Century Publishers, 1966).

59. Abbott, *Documents of Vatican II*, 33–34.

60. Pope John XXIII, "The Roman Synod And The Priest" (lecture, Rome, 24 November 1960). Cf. John F. Cronin, *The Encyclicals and Other Messages of John XXIII* (Washington, D.C.: TPS, 1964), 112–128. http://www.catholicculture.org/culture/library/view.cfm?RecNum=3227 (accessed 28 June 2009).

61. Abbott, *Documents of Vatican II*, 159.

62. The author found this change to the use of the vernacular to be a shattering experience for a number of Roman Catholics present in a religion class he taught in the US. The Catholics and former Catholics in the class reasoned that, if such an important practice could be changed after so many centuries, what else could and would be changed?

63. Lukasse, interview, 05 December 2003.

Additionally, Haverkamp and the other ECV founders told people that they had not come to Belgium to start a new organization, but that they just wanted to return to the Bible.[64]

As he looked back at the beginning of the twenty-first century, however, Haverkamp noted,

> Twenty years ago when I would start a home Bible study with ten people, the next week would be twelve, and the next fifteen, and then twenty and twenty-five, and it would keep growing. People would bring relatives and friends. Six months ago I began a Bible study. With about fourteen, the next week was twelve and then ten and now only six. I am doing exactly the same thing, but something strange is going on.[65]

Looking back after two decades in Belgium, Gifford also noted a lack of interest and a change in attitudes. He observed:

> Where there was an openness for the Gospel twenty years ago, there is an overwhelming apathy today. Belgium, a formerly Catholic country has thrown religion overboard and lives in the illusion of self-sufficiency—"I have everything I need. I don't need God."[66]

For Gifford, one of the most obvious examples of this change was in the increase in the number of television stations. He realized that this increase may have been minor in the larger scheme, but all kinds of entertainment took up the potential converts' time. "When we came to Belgium there were three stations, and now there are thirty-three. I remember talking to one man who said, 'Who needs God? We have VTM?'"[67]

The lack of interest among the listeners was not limited to the unconverted, however. Haverkamp again noted that in the early years of the founding of the ECV assemblies, believers would come to two or three Bible studies a week; this was not true by the end of the 1990s and beyond. As Haverkamp noted, "It's like Christians are coming to a smorgasbord and pick here and there. And what suits them, they believe."[68] Sociologists

---

64. Haverkamp, 25 April 2003. This statement is ironic given the change in the relationship among the ECV churches that the founders planted.

65. Haverkamp, "Wie der Herr Jesus Christus Gemeinden baut," session 1.

66. Peter and Joanna Gifford, letter to supporters, May 2005.

67. Peter Gifford, interview by author, St. Die, France, 25 August 2003. VTM is the commercial television station, *Vlaamse Televisie Maatschappij*.

68. Haverkamp, "Wie der Herr Jesus Christus Gemeinden baut," session 1.

noted the same phenomenon, labeling it *religion á la carte* or *bricolage*, and they associated this with what many called the change to a postmodern paradigm.[69] Additionally, as the newly converted believers matured, their faith became merely one part of their life rather than the all-encompassing center around which all other aspects of life orbited. The believers moved toward the typically Western view of faith as a slice of the pie of life, rather than the hub to which all the spokes were held together.

Thus, the founding and growth of the ECV happened in a time during which all the main evangelical, free church groups in Flanders grew, and grew at a rapid pace. These same groups all ceased to grow significantly in numbers of new converts and new local churches by the first few years of the 1990s. Changes of technique or the number of personnel working at the task seemingly made no difference. Hence, a case can be made that the growth of the ECV was part of a revival—a pneumatological reason for both the beginning and the end of the amazing years of church planting and numbers of evangelical conversions as marked by baptisms throughout Flanders. Certainly this was the perspective of the founders and shapers of the ECV; they looked to God as the cause of any success they had seen. As Haverkamp said, "God has to be in it, and God's timing is important."[70]

Overall Vision of the Founders of the ECV

Clearly, the goal of the founders of the ECV was church planting, not merely evangelism, and certainly their goal was not the planting of Brethren assemblies such as had been present in Flanders previously.[71] In a spirit more akin to the founders of the Brethren in the early nineteenth century, the founders of the ECV sought to plant churches based simply on New Testament principles as opposed to Brethren traditions. Where these two worlds overlapped, the traditions were kept. Where they differed, the ECV felt free to follow another course of action.

---

69. Karel Dobbelaere and Liliane Voyé, "From Pillar to Postmodernity: The Changing Situation of Religion in Belgium," in *SA.Sociological Analysis: A Journal in the Sociology of Religion*, 51:S (1990): S4.

70. Haverkamp, "Wie der Herr Jesus Christus Gemeinden baut," session 3.

71. Cf. chapter 2, sections 2.2 and 2.3 of Thomas J. Marinello, "A History of the Evangelische Christengemeenten Vlaanderen: Its Origins and Development, 1971–2008" (Doctoral dissertation, Evangelische Theologische Faculteit, 2009) for a rehearsal of the nature of the Brethren in Flanders before the coming of the ECV.

The founders of the ECV believed that church planting was a supremely important task and that this is what God wanted of them.[72] "The Church is like the Jews in the Old Testament; it is like Jerusalem; it is the city of God. Nehemiah left his position to rebuild the city of God. Building the Church is the most important job on earth."[73] While they may not have expected to help found so many new assemblies in Flanders, they did believe that God would use them to plant churches throughout Flanders. The surprise to their vision would have come with the explosive growth and the subsequent organization which formed over the decades. Nevertheless, after more than thirty years of work in Flanders, both Haverkamp and Gelling maintained their singular focus on evangelism for the purpose of church planting as the primary reason for which they believed "God called" them to Flanders. Their work was the result of a deep-seated evangelical faith, as well as their understanding of the biblical purpose of the evangelical Christian to build the Church of Jesus Christ. Hence, organization was done for pragmatic reasons of furthering this singular purpose, and other reasons for organization were greeted with less enthusiasm by the founders and, at times, even opposed.

Haverkamp looked back on the rapid growth of the ECV and credited the success to God. "God is sovereign. He is the One who does the work."[74] In a series of lectures on Church-planting in 2002, Haverkamp noted this as he looked to God ultimately for any who might undergo evangelical conversion, even in the midst of so few responding. "I believe that God still has His elect here and there."[75] Gelling also was conscious of "God's work" as wrote to supporters, "On the 8th of March we want to begin a [*Startstudies*] in Wellen. Along with that we have meetings (too many it seems sometimes), Bible studies, speaking on Sundays, visitation, evangelism, etc., etc. We are thrilled the Lord allows us to do this."[76] Similarly, Gifford wrote supporters concerning an extended stay in Canada, "It will be good to share with you the way the Lord is working in Belgium both in and through us. .

---

72. This conviction that one is doing what God wants him to do has been noted as the "common dynamic" in contemporary articles examining other successful works. Cf. Thomas Minnery, "Success in Three Churches: Diversity and Originality," in *Leadership* 2, no. 1 (Winter 1981): 65.

73. Haverkamp, "Wie der Herr Jesus Christus Gemeinden baut," session 1.

74. Richard Haverkamp, telephone interview, 06 December 2008.

75. Richard Haverkamp, "Wie der Herr Jesus Christus Gemeinden baut," session 1.

76. Hank and Beryl Gelling, letter to supporters, 19 February 2002.

Development of the Evangelische Christengemeenten Vlaanderen

. we continue to preach Christ and trust Him to awaken a need in people's lives."[77]

One of the surprises for the founders which was not part of their overall vision was the creation of the government-recognized organization, the ECV. As Haverkamp often noted, they had not come to start an organization but to return to the Bible.[78] Nonetheless, a very well-defined organization did result, complete with a carefully enunciated structure, written long range plans, evaluations of the plans in retrospect, and a statement of faith. All this happened primarily through the vision and efforts of De Kegel as well as some others. Still, even De Kegel and others did not help to create a new denomination for its own sake, but as a tool to further the growth and strength of the churches which had been planted.

While this organizational aspect did not turn out as the founders might have expected, the founders' overall vision was achieved by the planting of Flemish churches, churches whose leaders had not come from outside of Flanders and the overall control of which was not outside the country. As Gelling noted in the often repeated statement by Haverkamp, "We came and we knew that God had sent us, and our desire was to see local churches started that were run by local people."[79] Success in this area of local people running the churches is especially evident when a list of ECV workers is compared with that of similar Flemish free church groups such as the BEZ or the VEG.[80] Further, this Flemish character was noted by those who had grown up in the ECV. During his studies at ETF, one young man looked back at his time in the ECV and noted, "I [realize] that the ECV, unlike BEZ and VEG, is probably the only thoroughly evangelical church growth movement in Flanders where the majority of churches are not directly guided by non-Flemish leaders such as Dutchmen or Dutch Canadians."[81]

Thus, the timing of the planting of the ECV, as well as the singular focus of its founders, were significant reasons for the rapid growth. The rapid growth was the result of a God-given revival as led by singularly

---

77. Peter and Joanna Gifford, letter, May 2005.

78. Richard Haverkamp, interview by author, St. Latem Martens, Belgium, 25 April 2003.

79. Henk Gelling, interview by author, 11 September 2003.

80. E.g., "Belgische Vereniging van Vrij Evangelische Gemeenten," March 1987, 14–16.

81. Hans van Nes, "ECV," email to author, 20 September 2004.

focused men who worked at an auspicious historical moment. What about the Christian church which predominated the socio-religious scene during the time prior to the founding and shaping of the ECV? What was the relationship of the ECV with the Flemish Roman Catholic Church?

Relationship of the ECV with Flemish Roman Catholicism

In contrast with the relationship of the ECV with other Christian groups in Flanders, the ECV held less accommodating attitudes toward the Roman Catholic Church. The founders and shapers of the ECV most certainly saw the Roman Catholic Church as a Christian group which was neither conducting itself nor holding beliefs according to the Bible. In particular, the evangelical gospel taught and propagated by the ECV was distinctly different from the soteriology espoused by the Roman Catholic Church. This soteriology was not peculiar to the ECV, but was a mainstream evangelical view of the gospel held by groups both inside and outside of Flanders. The ECV taught an imputed grace by faith alone. This imputation was neither sacerdotal nor sacramental in nature. In contrast, Roman Catholic soteriology taught what could be termed an infused grace, grace through faith via the sacraments properly administered by a priest.[82] Thus, evangelical groups such as the ECV would have understood the mechanism by which soteriology was effected in a very different fashion than would have the Roman Catholic Church.

In addition to soteriological differences, the ECV and Roman Catholic Church had major ecclesiological differences. The ECV held to the autonomy of the local church as a representation of the universal Church and an apostolic succession of doctrine. Membership in the Church—the body of Christ—would have been through conversion to the evangelical faith. The Roman Catholic Church, in contrast, understood the Church "as a society [which] subsists in the catholic Church, governed by the successor of Peter and the Bishops in communion with him" whose people became members through the sacrament of water baptism properly administered.[83] *Dominus Iesus*, by Cardinal Ratzinger, clearly states,

> The Christian faithful are therefore not permitted to imagine that the Church of Christ is nothing more than a collection—divided,

---

82. *Code of Canon Law: In English Translation* (London: Collins Liturgical Publications, 1983), Canons 840–842.

83. *Code*, Canons 204, 849.

Development of the Evangelische Christengemeenten Vlaanderen

yet in some way one—of Churches and ecclesial communities; nor are they free to hold that today the Church of Christ nowhere really exists, and must be considered only as a goal which all Churches and ecclesial communities must strive to reach.[84]

Hence, Miroslav Volf could note of the Roman Catholics:

> Only those local fellowships "united to their pastors" [i.e. bishops] are, therefore, churches in the full sense of the word. This is why all other Christian fellowships. . . exhibit merely more or less significant ecclesial elements, but do not qualify as churches.[85]

When queried as to the status of "Christian Communities" born out of the Reformation, the *Congregatio Pro Doctrina Fidei* referenced the documents of Vatican 2 as well as *Dominus Iesus* and answered:

> According to Catholic doctrine, these Communities do not enjoy apostolic succession in the sacrament of Orders, and are, therefore, deprived of a constitutive element of the Church. These ecclesial Communities which, specifically because of the absence of the sacramental priesthood, have not preserved the genuine and integral substance of the Eucharistic Mystery cannot, according to Catholic doctrine, be called "Churches" in the proper sense.[86]

Thus, the Roman Catholic Church consistently held to its unicity. In the areas of soteriology and ecclesiology, the ECV and the Roman Catholic Church held decidedly different views. Accordingly, the goal of those within the ECV was to see Flemish Roman Catholics converted to evangelical Christianity.[87]

---

84. Joseph Cardinal Ratzinger, "Declaration *Dominus Iesus* on the Unicity and Salvific Universality of Jesus Christ and the Church," Vatican, http://212.77.1.247/roman_curia/congregations/cfaith/documents/rc_con_cfaith_doc_20000806_dominus-iesus_en.html (accessed 07 January 2007).

85. Miroslav Volf, "Community Formation as an Image of the Triune God," in *Community Formation in the Early Church and in the Church Today*," ed. Richard Longenecker (Peabody: Hendrickson, 2002), 215. For a further elaboration, cf. Miroslav Volf, *After Our Likeness: The Church as the Image of the Trinity* (Cambridge: Eerdmans, 1998), 259–263.

86. William Cardinal Levada, "Responses to some Questions Regarding Certain Aspects of the Doctrine on the Church" Congregation for the Doctrine of the Faith, Vatican, http://212.77.1.245/news_services/bulletin/news/20586.php?index=20586&lang=en#TESTO%20IN%20LINGUA%20INGLESE (accessed 07 January 2009).

87. For an apologetic from a Roman Catholic perspective aimed especially at "Bible

Not Weary of Well Doing

Opposition to the doctrine of the Roman Catholic Church did not mean that the ECV displayed a hostility toward its people or even its priests. During a door-to-door evangelistic effort in the early 1980s, for example, Gelling came face to face with the local Roman Catholic priest. Gelling and the priest talked after Gelling had explained the evangelical Gospel, and the priest asked if Gelling would like to speak at his parish church. Gelling agreed and a date later was set. As Gelling later looked back at this event, he noted two reasons why he accepted the invitation. First, he was given a "clean slate," he was allowed to preach anything he wanted. Second, he did not see this as something that would compromise his evangelical beliefs or set a bad example for the younger believers from the assembly. He had neither taught anything different than he would have at an ECV church, nor had he served or partaken of the eucharist during the mass and thus given some sort of affirmation to the Roman Catholic beliefs in this area. He likened this event to the examples of Peter and Paul in the book of Acts who were continually in the synagogues preaching the evangelical Gospel.[88]

Opposition to the official teachings of the Roman Catholic Church never changed among the founders or the shapers of the ECV. Indeed, in the official pronouncements of the Roman Catholic Church as noted above, neither did the Roman Catholic Church change in its view toward the ECV as well as others outside the Roman Catholic Church. However, toward the beginning of the twenty-first century, some practical softening was seen between the local Roman Catholic parish churches and the ECV assemblies in Flanders. This softening of attitudes came from both groups. Haverkamp noted that by the twenty-first century, however, he no longer preached against the Roman Catholic Church because their adherents really did not know what they believed any longer. The ECV often used the Roman Catholic chapels as places to conduct funerals and weddings. Usually the parish priest was present, and the priest's response often was something like, "You people still believe," commonly through "tear-filled eyes." In fact, Haverkamp believed that some evangelicals were to be found in the Roman Catholic Church by the early twenty-first century.[89]

The ECV looked for opportunities to build relationships with the local Roman Catholic leaders for the purpose of preaching the message of the

---

Christians," cf. Karl Keating, *Catholicism and Fundamentalism: The Attack on "Romanism" by "Bible Christians"* (San Francisco: Ignatius, 1988).

88. Henk Gelling, telephone interview by author, 04 January 2009.

89. Richard Haverkamp, telephone interview by author, 06 January 2009.

Development of the Evangelische Christengemeenten Vlaanderen

evangelical gospel in a Roman Catholic setting, yet the leaders also saw and maintained the difference between their soteriology and ecclesiology and the same within the Roman Catholic Church. That said, some among the second generation of those who grew up in the ECV assemblies looked to closer cooperation between evangelicals and Roman Catholics in Flanders as the necessary path of the future. At least one teacher of Bible and theology who grew up in the ECV assemblies held that even soteriological issues separating Flemish evangelicals and Roman Catholics were too much overplayed by the ECV.[90]

Concluding Thoughts

The founding and shaping of the ECV were remarkable for the shortness of time in which the churches were planted and a denomination was formed. Yet this remarkable record is perhaps less amazing when the ECV's attendant means and the circumstances which accompanied the Flemish evangelical revivals are considered. The functional ecclesiology as well as the providential timing and singular vision of the founders certainly assisted in this process. Though the vast majority of the new converts came from Roman Catholic backgrounds, only the future will show whether the Roman Catholic Church's centuries-long presence will be viewed by the ECV as more of an ally or opponent in the increasingly post-Christian, post-Christendom milieu of Flanders.

---

90. Creemers, interview, 06 September 2007; Jelle Creemers, discussions with author, Heverlee, Belgium, 02–03 September 2008.

Can a Christian Defend the Death Penalty Rationally?

PHILIP A. GOTTSCHALK

A famous politician said, "Never build a dungeon you wouldn't want be happy to spend the night in yourself." Perhaps you recognize this as a quote of the Patrician of Ankh-Morpork, from Terry Pratchett's Discworld novels.[1] He also said, "Never build a dungeon you can't get out of either."

All that has been written on the death penalty cannot be dealt with in one short article, so this chapter will be limited to three areas and three questions. The three areas are: 1) how Evangelical Christians in the U.S. defend the death penalty; 2) how a Christian might reject the death penalty; and 3) how some Muslims have defended the death penalty. In each area, three questions will be used to focus our thinking: 1) What does Scripture say? 2) What does tradition say? and 3) What does reason say? These questions represent three areas on which religious people rely when they defend the death penalty.

The former Iranian secretary of the Human Rights Commission of the Iranian Judiciary said, "*Shari'a*, whether *Shiite* or *Sunnite*, is not the *Shari'a* of the shame, because it is based on the Qur'an, the consensus of Islamic jurists and reason (*Aql*)."[2] In other words, he wanted to show that, far from

---

1. Terry Pratchett, *Guards! Guards!* (New York: HarperTorch, 2001), 286.

2. Ghassem Ghassemi, "Criminal Punishment in Islamic Societies: Empirical Study of Attitudes to Criminal Sentencing in Iran," in *European Journal on Criminal Policy and*

Can a Christian Defend the Death Penalty Rationally?

being a random and medieval code of law, *Shari' a* is based upon holy writ, tradition, and rational deliberation.

The threesome of the Qur'an, the consensus of Islamic jurists, and reason remind me of the famous Anglican three-legged stool of Scripture (the Bible), Tradition (Church Fathers, Reformers, classic Christian creeds, e.g. Nicene Creed) and reason. Interestingly, both faiths are able to and actually do reason in a similar way.

Let me state the conclusions before starting, so that the goal of this chapter is clear, and so that the argument is easier to follow. First, the traditional Reformed, Evangelical Christian defense is wrong on some points and inconclusive on others. Second, an Evangelical Christian, or a Christian from another tradition, can argue cogently against the death penalty. Finally, other faiths, specifically Islam, also argue for the death penalty using "scripture, tradition, and reason" (although Evangelical Christians might feel satisfied that they have the revelation of God on this point). Christians must work with people of other faiths who believe that they, too, have the unique command of God. Therefore, like it or not, evangelicals must make some appeal to "natural reason."

The Reformed, Evangelical Christian Defense of Capital Punishment from the Old Testament[3]

Evangelicals give pride of place to the Bible in any ethical discussion. Revelation from God trumps any and all other arguments. The main text used to defend capital punishment is found in Genesis 9:4–6:[4]

> But you shall not eat flesh with its life, that is, its blood. And for your lifeblood I will require a reckoning: from every beast I will require it and from man. From his fellow man I will require a

---

Research (2009) 15:159–180; 189 [ISNA, Iranian Students News Agency, Interview with the Chief Justice of Provincial Appeal Court of Tehran (2007)].

3. For the sake of this essay, I will use the position of Drs. John and Paul Feinberg, as found in their book *Ethics for a Brave New World*, to represent the Reformed, Evangelical view. The same view can also be found in *Evangelical Ethics* by John J. Davis. John S. Feinberg and Paul D. Feinberg, *Ethics for a Brave New World*, 2nd Kindle Edition (Wheaton: Crossway Books, 2010), 227–266. John J. Davis, *Evangelical Ethics,* 3rd ed. (Phillipsburg, NJ: Presbyterian and Reformed Press, 2004), 203–218.

4. All Scripture quotations are from the *English Standard Version*, unless otherwise noted.

reckoning for the life of man. Whoever sheds the blood of man, by man shall his blood be shed, for God made man in his own image.

These verses are a part of the Noahic Covenant, the covenant which God made with Noah after the Flood. Evangelicals see verse 9 as binding on all people, since it was given to Noah after the Flood as the progenitor of the renewed human race (father of all). They believe that this verse remains in force even after the Mosaic Law was abrogated (if it was abrogated), since it predates the Mosaic Law.

The main issue to which they appeal is the "life principle:" a life for a life. Though we typically think of "an eye for an eye and a tooth for a tooth (and a life for a life)" being part of the Mosaic Law (Exod. 21:23–25), Evangelicals also find it in Genesis 9:4–6. The main argument is the "image of God" principle: since man is made in God's image, it is making a sort of attack on God himself to kill another. Unlike the killing of animals, killing a human violates a special status of man relative to other creatures.[5]

שֹׁפֵךְ דַּם הָאָדָם בָּאָדָם דָּמוֹ יִשָּׁפֵךְ כִּי בְּצֶלֶם אֱלֹהִים עָשָׂה אֶת־הָאָדָם:[6]

In Hebrew, the text reads that the one who sheds the blood of (the) man, by a man shall his blood be shed (*yishshaphek*). The grammatical point at issue is whether the verb in this sentence (a niphal imperfect third person singular masculine verb) should be read as a simple future tense, "by a man his blood will be shed," or as a jussive (a command), "by a man shall (in the sense of must) or ought his blood be." This is a key point for those who rely upon and explain this biblical text for support of their argument. For example, H. C. Leupold in his commentary on Genesis promotes this view when he writes:

> There is a just retaliation about having life paid for life. No man can question the justice of the price demanded. Besides, we surely would not catch the purpose of the word if we were to take the imperfect *yishshaphek* as merely permissive or suggestive; it must be rendered as a strict imperative. Consequently, capital punishment is divinely ordained.[7]

5. Peter Singer, Princeton's Ira W. DeCamp Professor of Bioethics, would see this as "speciesism."

6. *Biblia Hebraica Stuttgartensia: with Westminster Hebrew Morphology*, Ge 9:6 (German Bible Society; Morphology published by Westminster Seminary, Glenside, PA, 1925).

7. Herbert Carl Leupold, *Exposition of Genesis* (Grand Rapids: Wartburg Press,

Can a Christian Defend the Death Penalty Rationally?

The Old Testament requires death for eighteen offenses: Murder, causing death of a child in a pregnant woman, killing by an animal which has killed before, kidnapping, rape of a married woman, fornication, adultery, bestiality, homosexuality, incest, striking a parent, cursing a parent or God, rebelling against parents, sorcery and witchcraft, leading people into false worship, vigilantism, and perjury in death penalty cases. No Evangelical Christian ethicists, to my knowledge, advocate the death penalty for fornication, adultery, homosexuality, incest, striking a parent, cursing a parent or God, rebelling against parents, sorcery and witchcraft, leading people into false worship, vigilantism, or perjury.[8]

Obviously, some principle exists by which they decide which of these biblical admonitions to follow. The principle invoked is the principle of continuity or discontinuity between the Old and New Testaments, or, in somewhat provocative terms: Moses or Jesus. The Feinbergs and Davis hold what is known as a Moderate Discontinuity View of the relationship between the Testaments. Basically, they believe that the ceremonial and civil aspects of the Mosaic Law are no longer in force because Christ abrogated it. Jesus said, "You have heard that it was said. . . but I say to you. . . ." (Matt. 5:21–22).[9] However, they believe that the moral law (or the part of the Mosaic Law that concerns our behavior) remains in place. Again they quote Jesus:

> Do not think that I have come to abolish the Law or the Prophets; I have not come to abolish them but to fulfill them. For truly, I say to you, until heaven and earth pass away, not an iota, not a dot, will pass from the Law until all is accomplished. (Matt. 5:17, 18).[10]

So they choose those principles which they believe continue to be in effect. Basically, they do this by appealing to some instances in the Gospels or

---

1942), 164, http://www.ccel.org/ccel/leupold/genesis.pdf (accessed Jan. 2, 2012). Other Evangelical interpreters of Genesis interpret this passage in the same basic way: Victor P. Hamilton. *The Book of Genesis : Chapters 1–17* [NICOT] (Grand Rapids: Eerdmans, 1990), 315; K. A. Mathews, *Genesis 1–11:26* (Nashville: Broadman & Holman, 1996), 402–407; Bruce K. Waltke and Cathi J. Fredricks, *Genesis: A Commentary* (Grand Rapids: Zondervan, 2001), 144, 145, 157, 158; Gordon J. Wenham, *Genesis 1–15*, vol 1 of *Word Biblical Commentary* (Waco, TX: Word, 1987), 193, 194.

8. Though some might speak as if they would; e.g., Greg Bahnsen, Marcellus Kik, and some theonomists.

9. J. Feinberg and P. Feinberg, *Ethics for a Brave New World*, 44.

10. J. Feinberg and P. Feinberg, *Ethics for a Brave New World*, 45, 46.

epistles of the New Testament, where they can invoke the explicit example or statements of Jesus or any of the Apostles (e.g. Paul, John).

The Reformed, Evangelical Christian Defense of Capital Punishment from the New Testament

Evangelicals appeal to three passages in the New Testament to justify their support of the death penalty: 1) John 7:53–8:11, the woman caught in adultery, 2) Romans 13:1–7, God's instituting the government, and 3) Acts 25, especially verse 11, where Paul is making his defense for his life before the Roman Governor Festus.

1. John 7:53–8:11

Davis would prefer to dismiss John 7:53–8:11, since it is not contained in the earliest manuscripts of the Gospel of John. His main argument is that the Greek New Testament text of this passage is not good. The earliest Greek manuscripts of the NT (P^{66} [Bodmer papyrus II from 200 AD], P^{75} *Papyrus* Bodmer XIV-XV, late 2nd, early 3rd c. AD, ℵ, A, B, C) omit it. However, he gives a brief defense of why Jesus' forgiveness of the woman caught in adultery does not mean that Jesus rejected the death penalty.

On the other hand, he does examine the meaning of ἀναμάρτητος [*anamartētos*] in John 8:7 "without sin," which is a *hapax legomenon* in the New Testament, a word used only once. He argues that Jesus' argument with the crowd who brought the woman "caught in adultery" is that they do not fulfill the legal requirements of the Mosaic Law to stone her, nor does Jesus. Obviously, they did not bring the man who was committing adultery with her. So, at the very least here, they fell short of the requirement of the Mosaic Law as witnesses. They affirmed that they saw her in the act, something which was required, but they did not bring the man.

Davis argues that, when Jesus let the woman go, he simply was saying, "I can't condemn you, since I wasn't an eyewitness of your sin." However, Jesus does say, "Go and sin no more," so he must have known that she was guilty.

Though Jesus let her go, he still could have taken the opportunity to overturn the sentence of death for adultery, but he did not. He set her free on a technicality. He did not change the law wholesale nor the penalty of the law.

2. Romans 13:1-7

Romans 13:1 Πᾶσα ψυχὴ ἐξουσίαις ὑπερεχούσαις ὑποτασσέσθω. οὐ γὰρ ἔστιν ἐξουσία εἰ μὴ ὑπὸ θεοῦ, αἱ δὲ οὖσαι ὑπὸ θεοῦ τεταγμέναι εἰσίν[11]

Evangelicals rely heavily on the beginning of the thirteenth chapter of Romans for their support of capital punishment (and the Just War Theory). They rely on two principles: God has ordained or instituted the current government, and the God-ordained government "does not bear the sword in vain" (Rom. 13:4).

Believers are to submit (obey) the (secular) government because it was τεταγμέναι [*tetagmenai*] (appointed, designated, or instituted) by God (Rom. 13:1). Since God has put the government in place, they argue, Christians are to submit to it if the command is not opposed to God's law. Many Evangelical Christians in the US have been sympathetic to the Republican Party and happy to defend the policies of Republican administrations, such as those of Ronald Reagan, George H. W. Bush, and George W. Bush, administrations which supported capital punishment. Since Evangelicals believe that no other biblical argument exists to overturn their idea of biblical support for capital punishment, they see no problem submitting to the ruling secular authority on this point.

They argue further from Romans 13:4 that "the ruler does not bear the sword in vain;" that is, this God-instituted government may use physical force to compel compliance to the law and to punish those who commit crimes. Since God has instituted or appointed the government, and the government has means of compulsion (including lethal means), capital punishment must be acceptable to God and Christians. They argue further that the word used for "sword" in this verse does not refer to a typical or ornamental sword, but specifically to a μάχαιρα [*machaira*], the sort of sword that a magistrate used to execute criminals. Paul, they claim, is saying that the government has been given the responsibility of protecting the order of society and of punishing criminals, up to and including the use of deadly force. So, obey.

H.C. Leupold goes so far as to connect the "command" to execute a murderer in Genesis 9:6 as the basis of God's instituting government:

---

11. Matthew Black, Carlo M. Martini, Bruce M. Metzger, and Allen Wikgren, *The Greek New Testament*, Romans 13:1 (Federal Republic of Germany: United Bible Societies, 1997).

This verse attaches itself directly to the preceding, particularly to that part which says: "from man will I demand the soul of man." This verse now shows how God does this demanding: He lets man be the avenger. As Luther already very clearly saw, by this word government is instituted, this basic institution for the welfare of man. For if man receives power over other men's lives under certain circumstances, then by virtue of having received power over the highest good that man has, power over the lesser things is naturally included, such as power over property to the extent of being able to exact taxes, over our persons to the extent of being able to demand various types of work and service, as need may arise. Government, then, being grounded on this word, is not by human contract, or by surrender of certain powers, or by encroachment of priestcraft. It is a divine institution.[12]

3. Paul's Defense before Festus

The third biblical passage to which Evangelicals refer is Acts 25:11. When Paul is being held captive by Roman Governor Porcius Festus, Paul says that his opponents have no evidence against him, and he is prepared to die (face the death penalty) if he has done something wrong. This statement, coupled with the statement in Romans 13:4, is used to support the idea that Paul recognized that a death penalty exists, and he was prepared to accept it, just as he was willing to affirm the Roman law behind it.

A Final Biblical Concern

Evangelical Christians have differed in their interpretations, and others outside of their camp have attacked them as presenting a schizophrenic God, one who is both a God of wrath (judgment) and love. How can God punish some people eternally on the one hand and, on the other hand, show amazing love by coming to earth in the person of Jesus to pay the price of sin and to reconcile some people to God? How can an Evangelical Christian maintain that the Christian God is a God of love and still say that God allows capital punishment? The Feinbergs affirm that God is both a God of justice and love. Being rather Calvinistic, they believe that God has the right to condemn all to hell; all have sinned and none can obtain forgiveness and

---

12. Leupold, *Exposition of Genesis*, 164.

salvation through his or her own efforts. However, they also believe that God, in grace and love, chose to do all that was necessary, even at his own expense, to save some. They believe that only a limited number of people are elect (chosen by God for salvation). They see no discontinuity between maintaining "original sin" and the lostness of all humankind, versus election and grace. They posit no contradiction if we understand the nature of God correctly. Therefore, they also see no contradiction between the love of God and temporal, capital punishment for specific offenses.[13]

Summary of the Evangelical, Reformed Christian View of Biblical Revelation

Though the Mosaic Law is no longer in effect, the Noahic Covenant which supports capital punishment *is* still in effect. Therefore, the Evangelical, Reformed view is that capital punishment is still valid. Neither Jesus, nor Paul, nor any other New Testament figure has rescinded capital punishment. Therefore, Evangelical Christians should accept it.

1. Evangelical, Reformed Christian use of "Tradition" in defense of the Death Penalty

In general, Evangelical, Reformed Christians do not rely heavily on Church tradition (for example, Church Fathers or Reformers). I think the Evangelical church should not turn to Church history for support of their view, since the practice was too often abused by "Christian" governments. Davis mentions the cautious support of Augustine for capital punishment, as well as of Thomas Aquinas, Martin Luther, and John Calvin.[14]

Calvin, for instance, was responsible for at least thirty-eight executions during his Geneva administration. Matthew Gross, a popular apologist for Calvin, feels that most of these executions were for adultery and murder, in both cases biblically sanctioned, and for other biblically punishable crimes except heresy, a crime which Gross does not believe merits capital punishment.[15]

---

13. J. Feinberg and P. Feinberg, *Ethics for a Brave New World*, 260–265.

14. Davis, *Evangelical Ethics*, 204, 205.

15. Michael Gross, "Calvin and Servetus," Reformed Answers, http://reformedanswers.org/answer.asp/file/99812.qna/category/ch/page/questions/site/ (accessed Jan. 2, 2012). The brevity of this appeal to "Tradition" is typical of Evangelicals, except that

2. Evangelical, Reformed Christian Use of "Reason" in Defense of Capital Punishment

There are also philosophical and pragmatic considerations regarding the death penalty. They are: a. retribution, b. deterrence, c. restoration, d. discrimination, and e. the possibility of executing the innocent.

Retribution: These days, people are scandalized by the idea of retribution and prefer restorative justice. However, Evangelicals argue that the biblical sacrificial system requires the idea of retribution. This is found in such ideas as penal substitutionary, vicarious atonement, or propitiation. Christ's death satisfies God's wrath and pays the price of our sins. Though the Bible opposes torture, the punishment must fit the crime. Accordingly, there is no reason to stop capital punishment.

Deterrence: Some believe that, regardless of whether a case can be made for retribution as an appropriate purpose for capital punishment, capital punishment serves as an effective deterrent to crime. Most often, this is a strong part of the Evangelical support for capital punishment from a "rational" standpoint.

The Feinbergs believe that the case for deterrence is inconclusive, so they continue to maintain support of capital punishment on other grounds, such as biblical evidence in favor of it.[16]

Restoration: Many opponents of the death penalty argue that the goal of punishment should be to restore the criminal to society. Prisons have been renamed as "correctional centers," and the "penal system" has been renamed the "correctional system." After much campaigning by reformers, the goal of punishment and imprisonment is seen to be restoring a reformed criminal into society. Obviously, an executed criminal cannot be reformed and rehabilitated. This is one reason that reformists have called for an end to the death penalty.

Evangelical ethicists think that reform and restoration are good goals where acceptable. However, they simply argue that not all punishment

---

they may appeal to their favorite Reformer's biblical commentaries to defend their views. Some Evangelical Anglicans and others have moved more towards "Tradition" and are turning out biblical commentaries which are compilations of the views of Church Fathers and other figures in church history. See *The Ancient Christian Commentary on Scripture* series, ed. Thomas C. Oden (Carol Stream, IL: IVP Academic).

16. "No one has figured out how to determine how many are deterred from homicide by the death penalty. However, if it cannot be shown that those who don't kill were deterred by fear of capital punishment, we must drop talk (pro or con) of capital punishment as a deterrent" (J. Feinberg and P. Feinberg, *Ethics for a Brave New World*, 236).

is restorative or rehabilitative. God determines which crimes are capital crimes. They deserve the sentence, and the sentence does not need to be restorative or rehabilitative in this life. In short, they again rely on their biblical evidence for support of capital punishment.

Discrimination: Briefly, more African-Americans are executed than whites. According to some Reformists, many American states with the death penalty do not have African-Americans on murder case juries, do not have African-American District Attorneys, do not have African-American judges (local or appellate), do not have adequate legal defense counsel (paid state public defenders underpaid). The rich, black and white, go free or only serve prison time.[17]

The Evangelical response is terse: If he is guilty, he deserves the punishment. The criminal justice system should be reformed, but that does not mean that murderers should not die.

Possibility of Executing the Innocent: Human courts make mistakes.[18] Innocent people may be and have been executed. Some condemned to die were found innocent later. Therefore, some argue that executions should stop.

The Evangelicals respond that it is terrible if this occurs. It may have occurred in the past, but DNA evidence now makes this unlikely. The fear of executing innocent people is not an argument against capital punishment *per se*, but for a more sure trial system such as in the case above.

Summary of Evangelical, Reformed Support of Capital Punishment

A. What does the Old and New Testament Say?

Genesis 9:6, John 7:53–8:11, Romans 13:1–7, and Acts 25:11 support capital punishment. God has determined that (at least) murder is worthy of the death penalty. Secular governments can use lethal force even against their own citizens (criminals) according to Romans 13:4.

---

17. See William R. Montross, Jr., "Go, Witness and Speak," in *Journal of the Society of Christian Ethics*, 28, 2 (2008): 3–21, esp. 7, 8.

18. "BILL DILLON: Fake Tracking Dog Sent Bill Dillon to Prison for 26 Years," CNN, Center on Wrongful Convictions, Northwestern University School of Law, http://www.law.northwestern.edu/wrongfulconvictions/exonerations/flDillonbsummary.html (accessed May 6, 2012).

Not Weary of Well Doing

B. What Does "Tradition" Say?

Augustine, Thomas Aquinas, Martin Luther, and John Calvin (among others) supported it or engaged in it.

C. What Does "Reason" Say?

Rational and pragmatic considerations do not count for much, or at least they are a far distant third to claims for support from revelation and tradition. Capital punishment does not have to be restorative. It legitimately (biblically) can be seen as a just punishment. It may or may not serve as a deterrent, but that doesn't matter, since there is biblical support. Discrimination and the possibility of executing innocent people may be a problem to reform, but they are not arguments against capital punishment *per se*. Therefore, capital punishment should continue to be carried out.

A Reformed, Evangelical Christian Opposition to Capital Punishment

In this section, I will answer some of the arguments used by Reformed, Evangelical Christians to support the death penalty. The arguments are mine, though I have been influenced by a variety of Roman Catholic, liberal Christian, and secular articles.[19]

A Reformed, Evangelical Christian Use of Scripture in Opposition to Capital Punishment

Genesis 9:6

Is "by man shall his blood be shed" a command as found in Genesis 9:6? No. There is no reason to take this as a jussive and not as a simple perfect. If you kill someone, you will more than likely be killed by someone.

Even if it were a command, why do we continue to say that this verse is in force, but not other verses? Why should the Noahic Covenant still remain in effect, when the Mosaic Law is not? The arguments that it is are not

---

19. See the footnotes citations for some of these.

persuasive to me, especially as I have reason to believe that it was abrogated later by Christ.

There is the problem, when one holds a Moderate Discontinuity View of the relationship between the Old and New Testaments, of having to figure out which verses (commands, prohibitions) remain in effect and which do not. Unless Jesus or the Apostles give a specific Scriptural affirmation or negation, it seems facile to say that we hold what is not abrogated as in force.

How do we decide which are still in force otherwise? There is the danger of "principlizing" (a term of Roy B. Zuck).[20] If we must find some principle in every O.T. text, we end up arbitrarily picking and choosing what we want and do not want. Why do we no longer advocate stoning adulterers and homosexuals? Calvin apparently executed quite a few adulterers. Should we as Evangelicals really only hold to execution of murderers, and if so how can we? Scriptural evidence suggests many more cases for capital punishment than we would accept, such as striking a parent.

There is a problem of determining which crimes are capital crimes, the distinctions between murder, being an accomplice to murder, and aiding and abetting a murderer. What about manslaughter charges, treason, espionage, armed rebellion? The problem of deciding which crimes were capital offenses finally caused the end of capital punishment in the U.K.[21] Consider this historical absurdity. According to the 1957 Homicide Act, a man who rapes a woman and then murders her by stabbing her to death cannot be punished for murder, since the murder did not involve a gun.

New Testament Passages

John 7:53–8:11

Jesus was omniscient. He knew whether the woman caught in adultery was innocent or guilty. He tells her, "Go and sin no more!" Yet he let her go and did not condemn her.

Reformed Evangelicals respond that Jesus did not fulfill the letter of the law to be an eyewitness of the crime; that is, he was not there when they

20. For an explanation of the practice and its difficulties, see David K. Clark, *To Know and Love God* (Wheaton, IL: Crossway, 2010), 92.

21. Liz Homans, "Swinging Sixties: the Abolition of Capital Punishment," in *History Today* 58, no. 12 (December 2008): 43–49. http://www.historytoday.com/liz-homans/swinging-sixties-abolition-capital-punishment (accessed May 11, 2012)

found her committing adultery and so could not accuse her formally. They also argue that, although he could have overturned the death penalty for adultery, he did not.

In response, it seems clear: he knew that she was guilty, but he let her go. Also, he does not explicitly reject the death penalty, but neither does he affirm it, and his action speaks loudly against it.

If we look at passages where Jesus explicitly interprets the Old Testament Law, he takes two tacks to it: 1. "You have heard it said. . ., but I say unto you. . . ; " and 2. "Do not think I have come to end the Law. . . rather I have come to fulfill it."

In dealing with adultery, Jesus actually upped the ante. He says in Matthew 5:27–28, "You have heard that it was said, 'You shall not commit adultery.' But I tell you that anyone who looks at a woman lustfully has already committed adultery with her in his heart. "

This means that every man has, at one time or another, been guilty of a capital crime! Will we execute them all? (Who would be left to execute whom?) Does Jesus expect us to? No, he expects us to seek forgiveness through his sacrifice.

I will argue it below under Retribution, but it seems to me that one death was sufficient. Jesus died for all. All who turn to him are forgiven.

Evangelicals will argue that forgiveness of sin and responsibility to "pay for one's crime" cannot be conflated. However, it seems that they almost always are. To me, it seems gruesome to think about ministers and priests giving final spiritual counsel or last rights to condemned people. Is this *Caritas* which saves?

With regards to rejecting the death penalty, the assumption of no punishment is not in view. Most people who reject the death penalty favor life imprisonment to capital punishment.

Romans 13:1–7

Of course, Christians are to obey the governing authorities as far as they can without disobeying God. That is a simple, clear statement.

However, the leap of logic from being ordained to rule and the means used to rule also being ordained seems incorrect. God ordained or instituted many kingdoms, such as those of Nebuchadnezzar and Cyrus, but he judged them later for cruelty. He ordained them as instruments of his judgment, but he did not approve of all they did.

If we used this sort of logic on all of Paul's epistles (whatever he supports, we should support), we would still be defending slavery with Robert L. Dabney.[22] Paul was a Jewish Roman citizen simply stating fact: If you rebel like Theudas (A.D. 45), you will be executed.[23]

Acts 25:11

Paul said that he was willing to die if he were shown to be guilty of a capital crime. Personally, I think that, in this case, it is best to see Paul as an orator. This statement is oratorical embellishment. It does not prove that he believed capital punishment to be just. It only shows that he did not believe he was guilty, and so had nothing to fear from this bold gesture.

Wrath or Love?

Marcion's theological stance—a "God of Wrath" in the Old Testament and a "God of Love" in the New—is indefensible; yet all the same, Jesus does introduce a New Kingdom with a new law. He gives explicit instructions about loving, about forgiveness and non-violence rather than hate and force: "Turn the other cheek!" (Mt. 5:38–40, 43), and "Love your enemies!" (44).

Reformed Evangelicals respond that Jesus' ethic was only meant for interpersonal affairs, not social order. Jesus' trial, however, was a public affair, and yet he did not use any power to defend himself.

Two Other Issues

Citizenship

Reformed Evangelicals, like traditional Roman Catholics and Eastern Orthodox Christians, see themselves having "dual citizenship," both to an earthly state and to a heavenly kingdom. Anabaptist Christians, however, believe they have only one ultimate citizenship: the heavenly one.[24]

---

22. Robert L. Dabney, *A Defence of Virginia. [and through her, of the south,] in recent and pending contests against the sectional party,* http://www.portagepub.com/dl/causouth/dabney.pdf? (accessed Jan. 2, 2012).

23. Flavius Josephus, *Jewish Antiquities* 20.97–98, http://www.josephus.org/ntparallels2.htm (accessed May 6, 2012).

24. "The disciple of Christ must be true to his new citizenship in the kingdom of

Not Weary of Well Doing

Such Anabaptist Christians do not rebel or oppose just laws, but neither do they believe that they can bring in the kingdom of God by political means. According to them, we first have to choose which kingdom gets our primary allegiance. Reformed Evangelicals often tend to identify themselves with the Republican Party and believe that they ought to be involved with policy making, etc. Trying to promote the political agenda of an earthly party compromises all who would advance that cause. Those who are citizens of the kingdom of heaven must focus their first efforts on Christ's explicit commands.

Continuity or Discontinuity of the Old and New Testaments

Reformed Evangelicals, like traditional Roman Catholics and Eastern Orthodox Christians, see a strong continuity between the Old and New Testaments. For example, they have a more church-state view of the situation. They may say that they hold a "moderate discontinuity view," but they hold views from the O.T. and defend them as if they are "givens." These "givens" come from a historical precedent (perhaps Augustine or Calvin, for example). There is a tendency to favor the interpretations of our forebears rather than to wrestle with the text alone and draw our conclusions from our exegesis alone.

These interpreters do not realize how compromised they are and how unbiblical these views are. Luther was a great man in some ways and not in others. His word is not Scripture. Neither is Calvin's nor Thomas Aquinas.'

The Guilty Evangelical Conscience

During the Reagan era, the Moral Majority was supposed to make a real difference morally in government. Instead, no legislation championed by Evangelicals was passed such as laws supporting prolife positions or allowing prayer in schools. Also, several of the politicians whom they supported were morally compromised, such as House Speaker Newt Gingrich. It may not be an argument against their views to say that they got virtually nothing they wanted, supported Saddam Hussein by default, and that some of

---

heaven, a kingdom of peace after the model of the Sermon on the Mount." Myron S. Augsburger, *Matthew*, vol 24 of *The Preacher's Commentary* (Nashville: Thomas Nelson, 2002), xcix. See also Myron S. Augsburger, "Christian pacifism" in *War: Four Christian Views*, ed. Robert G. Close (Winona Lake, IN: BMH Books, 1986), 82, 87ff.

the political leaders they supported had spectacular moral failures, but it makes one wonder whether the Evangelicals had the moral high ground as they claimed. Admittedly, some liberals and even Anabaptists have had similar moral failings, but the point is that merely being Evangelical does not equal having a moral high ground and, as a result, having the correct view on an issue, as some have insinuated.

A Reformed, Evangelical Christian Use of Tradition in Opposition to Capital Punishment

The Church Fathers and Reformers were divided on this issue, and some were compromised. Almost all held a strong Continuity view of the Old and New Testaments. Almost all held a strong commitment to an earthly governmental system, such as Luther with Fredrick the Elector.[25] Of the supposed unfitness of ideas in favor of the abolition of the death penalty because they were ideas of an Enlightenment or modern thinker, the obvious response is: Truth is truth wherever it is found. Finally, the Modern Age remains divided; some still prefer vengeance.

A Reformed, Evangelical Christian Use of Reason in Opposition to Capital Punishment

Philosophical and Pragmatic Considerations

Retribution

It is true that the biblical, sacrificial system depends on the concept of retribution. Penal substitutionary atonement (propitiation; vicarious atonement), that someone else should die in our place, is an absolutely central doctrine. But if that punishment has been paid, must it be paid twice? Releasing someone from the death penalty does not mean no punishment

---

25. If Frederik "the Wise," the Elector for Germany in the Holy Roman Empire, had not protected Luther, the Pope would have had him tried and burned for heresy. After Luther was in fact condemned by Pope Leo X, Frederik the Wise arranged for Luther to be "kidnapped" and protected him further. Douglas O. Linder, "The Trial of Martin Luther: An Account (Luther's Hearings Before the Diet at Worms on Charges of Heresy)," http://law2.umkc.edu/faculty/projects/ftrials/luther/lutheraccount.html (accessed May 11, 2012).

at all. Most people who reject the death penalty prefer a sentence of life imprisonment.

Restitution

It is true that the Bible opposes torture and says that the punishment must fit the crime. However, it seems best to see the allowance of a death penalty, a one-for-one restitution, to be only a limitation at the time in the ancient near East when vengeance was "I will kill two of yours for my one." In Albania and the former Yugoslavia, there is an idea that revenge (*inat, odmazda*) is a sacred Christian duty. My wife and I were missionaries in Yugoslavia from 1986–89 and then from 1992–94 during the Balkan War. A Serbian friend of mine was given the honor of being asked to come back to his home town in Bosnia to kill his father's murderer who had escaped justice in 1957 (when my friend was two). My friend did not kill him, and thus in 1994 ended the cycle of violence. Killing has to stop somewhere.

A current Albanian student of mine had to be taken to live with his grandparents because of a blood feud. He did not know why until he was 18. In a miracle of grace, he and the family of the murderer of his brother have reconciled. Someone must accept that they will not be satisfied or that someone else paid that price long ago. Again, such a stance does not say that there should be no justice. My student's assailant and murderer of his brother is sitting in prison for 35 years in Spain. He will likely die in prison. Someone, though, must stop the killing.

Consider the sorts of absurdities which follow from commitment to retributive justice. If the punishment must fit the crime, then the convicted murderer who killed two people with a pick ax should also be killed with a pick ax.[26] This brings us to the question of whether there is a humane way to execute criminals. There are problems associated with all methods. Those who administer execution through lethal injection are asking, "Are those being executed really unconscious before they are killed?" Some studies seem to suggest that those being executed were not unconscious when the killing drug was introduced, and thus they suffered.[27]

26. "Karla Faye Tucker: Born again on death row," http://articles.cnn.com/2007-03-21/us/larry.king.tucker_1_karla-faye-tucker-death-row-larry-king?_s=PM:US (accessed May 11, 2012).

27. Alison Motluk, "Execution by injection far from painless," The New Scientist, 14 April 2005, http://www.newscientist.com/article/dn7269-execution-by-injection-far-from-painless.html. (accessed May 11, 2012).

Can a Christian Defend the Death Penalty Rationally?

But why do we care? If we are correct that they deserve to die, then why care if they suffer? Yet we do. We recognize that it is barbaric to torture someone. Somehow we try to maintain that killing them if they are already unconscious is better than killing them when they are conscious. Is this distinction meaningful?

Homans mentions an absurdity of this sort. "A young man had shot and killed his 'girl' before turning the gun on himself. He only managed to destroy one of his own eyes. The man was then nursed in hospital and fitted with an artificial eye, only to be taken to the jail and hanged. Silverman (Conservative MP from Lancashire) remarked: 'I couldn't square this with any notion of civilized society.'"[28]

Deterrence

If there is no conclusive proof, deterrence seems like a good reason to stop capital punishment. We cannot raise the innocent dead whom we kill. The onus of proof would seem to be on those who continue to practice it. Henry Brooke, ex-Conservative Home Secretary, addressed Parliament in 1964: "The taking of a life is so grave a matter that the onus of proof must be on those who very sincerely believed that the death penalty should be retained."[29]

There is also the absurdity that, if the purpose of the execution is deterrence, then it does not matter who is killed so long as someone is killed, since the goal is deterrence and not retribution. Nazi executions spring to mind as effective deterrents. Davis mentions that C. S. Lewis rightly brought out this point.[30]

The evidence seems clearer that capital punishment is not a deterrent. For instance, those American states that ended capital punishment had lower murder rates: Michigan, Rhode Island, Wisconsin, Maine.[31] Most murders are not premeditated, such as in "crimes of passion" (a husband finds his wife in bed with another man and shoots them both). There is no "premeditation," but this is exactly why we make distinctions between

---

28. Homans, "Swinging Sixties."
29. Homans, "Swinging Sixties."
30. C. S. Lewis, *God in the Dock* (Grand Rapids, MI: Eerdmans, 1970), 291, as cited by Davis, *Evangelical Ethics*, 214, 215.
31. Davis, *Evangelical Ethics*, 215.

degrees of murder and manslaughter. We know instinctively that some murders are worse than others, but how do we decide?

We "reserve" the death penalty for "hardened killers," yet who decides which crimes deserve capital punishment and how to carry it out? Recall the British example above of the problem of deciding which were capital crimes and the absurdities it produced, resulting finally in the end of capital punishment in Britain.

Restoration

God's sacrifice of Christ was to restore us to a right relationship with him. I understand the argument that there must be punishment, or crime will abound. No one is arguing that there should be no punishment. However, many are arguing that punishment should be humane. Furthermore, nothing is wrong with making the goal of punishment to be somehow restorative. Even those who earlier argued for capital punishment allowed for ministers to "attend to" those to be executed, believing that even if their bodies were to die their souls could live. Because the chances of wrongful conviction are much higher than many assume, it seems best not to execute people and to spend the money necessary to keep them in prison for life (which is usually less than the cost of all appeals necessary to bring an accused criminal to the point of execution).[32]

Discrimination

The facts say clearly that there is discrimination. "The problem is particularly acute in 'the death belt,' which includes Texas, Oklahoma, Alabama, Mississippi, South Carolina, Missouri, and now (once again) Georgia, among others."[33] Holdridge and Hill, director and state strategy coordinator of the A.C.L.U.'s Capital Punishment Project, were speaking of the inadequate funding of court appointed public defenders, but the same is true of sentencing.

---

32. "To execute or not: A question of cost?" MSNBC 3/7/2009, http://www.msnbc.msn.com/id/29552692/ns/us_news-crime_and_courts/t/execute-or-not-question-cost/#.T6zfJeu_G6o (accessed May 11, 2012).

33. John Holdridge and Christopher Hill, "Rights to a Fair Trial (1 Letter)" NY Times, September 13, 2007, http://www.nytimes.com/2007/09/13/opinion/lweb13georgia.html (accessed Jan. 2, 2012).

Can a Christian Defend the Death Penalty Rationally?

It is true that a guilty person legally should bear the punishment, but if some people are more guilty than others before the court, there is a serious problem.[34] Evangelicals respond blithely that, if someone is guilty, then he is guilty and he should suffer the consequences.[35] However, when the rich white or black can hire lawyers and get off, isn't there a serious problem? When being a minority or poor results in unfair trials and more stringent sentencing, this would seem to be a serious argument for a moratorium on the death penalty. Reform is necessary and a moratorium, at least, is necessary until that reform is carried out, lest anyone be falsely tried and unfairly executed. Again, no one is arguing for exoneration of someone who is guilty, but rather for making sure that innocent people are not convicted wrongly.

Possibility of Executing the Innocent

It is true that no court system is perfect and some mistakes may take place, and even if there is now a sophisticated way to ensure almost certainly that the murderer is guilty (such as DNA), some innocent people might still be executed. Is it not better, therefore, to stop capital punishment and opt for life imprisonment without parole? The majority of people in the U.S. continue to favor the death penalty when polled (61 percent), yet their opinions shift significantly when they are given a choice between life imprisonment without parole and capital punishment. When presented with this option, the number of those supporting capital punishment falls to about half. With only half of the populace favoring capital punishment, it would seem presumptuous to ignore the opinion of so large a bulk of the populace.[36]

---

34. See William R. Montross, Jr., "Go, Witness and Speak," 7, 8.

35. "McDermott's argument jumps from the correct claim that capital punishment in the United States is fraught with racial discrimination to the notion that therefore U.S. courts have no legitimate power in capital cases." J. Feinberg and P. Feinberg. *Ethics for a Brave New World*, 246.

36. Frank Newport, "In U.S., Support for Death penalty Falls to 39-Year Low Fifty-two percent say the death penalty is applied fairly," Gallup.com October 13, 2011, http://www.deathpenaltyinfo.org/documents/death_penalty_poll_gallup_10_13_11.pdf (accessed May 11, 2012).

Not Weary of Well Doing

Response to the Feinbergs' Views on Grace

The Feinbergs argue that God is sovereign and can distribute grace as he sees fit. God forgave Moses and David, they argue. They were not executed for murder. That was God's choice and right.[37] The Feinbergs also feel that God has the right to execute all. No one deserves grace. God chooses to have mercy on whom he will have mercy. God is not obligated to forgive anyone or to show grace towards anyone. In the same way, a government official, such as a U.S. governor, can extend a pardon and does not need to give a reason.

Their opponents cannot see how it is logical to argue that those who receive no grace have no complaint. They clearly seem to have a complaint: someone else no more deserving was pardoned for no apparent reason. Thus, their opponents find their argument from grace less than cogent.

Summary

The Mosaic civil law is no longer valid, nor is the Noahic Covenant as regards murders.

I do not see that either Jesus or Paul (or other New Testament writers) support capital punishment. Arguments for capital punishment from the New Testament are arguments from silence. On the contrary, Jesus teaches the way of love, loving even one's enemies, which applies to all relationships. Therefore, Christians have no particular reasons to accept capital punishment. Regarding philosophical and pragmatic considerations, retributive justice has been satisfied in Christ. Deterrence is unproven. Therefore, capital punishment should be stopped. Discrimination is a real issue and a reason to stop (or at least have a moratorium on) capital punishment.

Vengeance belongs to God. We can't raise the dead whom we mistakenly send there. In the U.S., it is cheaper to keep condemned criminals in prison than to try them for murder seeking the death penalty, since the cost of appeals is more than lifetime imprisonment.[38] Most people would

---

37. See the section "Justice, Grace, and the Death penalty" in J. Feinberg and P. Feinberg, *Ethics for a Brave New World*, 261ff, esp. 263, 265.

38. "Save Lives, and Money Too," in *America*, March 16, 2009, 4, http://www.americamagazine.org/content/article.cfm?article_id=11509 (accessed May 6, 2012).

favor life imprisonment to capital punishment, if life imprisonment meant no possibility of parole.[39]

A final provocative question: If we as Christians rely on a Divine Command Theory (an argument "from Scripture") for our view on capital punishment, even if we have the true revelation and our interpretation is correct, how will we answer Muslims who say that they have a Divine Command to wage jihad on infidels?

A Muslim View of Capital Punishment

It is possible to generate *pro* and *contra* views on capital punishment among Muslim thinkers. However, as far as I have been able to divine, no Muslim sect (except perhaps Sufis) objects to capital punishment *per se*. The materials which I have examined do not suggest that capital punishment might be wrong, but rather tend to engage the question of *when* capital punishment should be administered, with a variety of answers. I have looked at materials which cover early Islamic legal judgments, Umayyad legal judgments, Ottoman legal judgments, and modern Iranian attitudes towards the death penalty.

Some of the writers were concerned with "legal" historical tradition. Others were concerned with current popular opinion in an Islamic republic. Some were clearly biased by modern or postmodern sensibilities, and others were "objective" and historical.

Interestingly, current Islamic judicial officials feel that they appeal to scripture (the Qur'an), tradition (the practices orally transmitted of Muhammad, *sunna, hadith, tafsir,* and "the consensus of Islamic jurists"), and reason (*Aql*). Since an Islamic jurist himself suggests this "three legged stool," I will continue to use my three question approach: What does the Qur'an say? What does tradition say? and What does reason say?

What does the Qur'an say?

Murderers

One verse in the Qur'an which most commentators turn to is 5:48:

---

39. Sarah Eekhoff Zylstra, "Capital Doubts: Supreme Court mulls lethal injections as Christian support for death penalty drops," in *Christianity Today*, March 2008, 20, 21.

> We ordained therein for them: "Life for life, eye for eye, nose for nose, ear for ear, tooth for tooth, and wounds equal for equal." But if any one remits the retaliation by way of charity, it is an act of atonement for himself. And if any fail to judge by (the light of) what Allah hath revealed, they are (no better than) wrongdoers.[40]

This *ayah* shows a close resemblance to the Mosaic Law in Leviticus 24:17–22:

> Anyone who takes the life of a human being is to be put to death. Anyone who takes the life of someone's animal must make restitution—life for life. Anyone who injures their neighbor is to be injured in the same manner: fracture for fracture, eye for eye, tooth for tooth. The one who has inflicted the injury must suffer the same injury. Whoever kills an animal must make restitution, but whoever kills a human being is to be put to death. You are to have the same law for the foreigner and the native-born. I am the Lord your God.'"

However, it seems that there is a concept of redemption for a murderer in Q 5:48. The aggrieved family member (who would execute the murderer) can elect to show mercy and require a cash payment. Thus, the aggrieved relative omits retaliation (*Qisas*), but receives money (*Diya*). This could be compared to a civil court judgment in place of a criminal sentence.

Though the Mosaic Law only allows this in the cases of killing an animal or an unborn child, there is the provision of "cities of refuge." In Deuteronomy 19, Moses mentions setting aside these cities for those who have committed manslaughter ("anyone who kills a neighbor unintentionally, without malice aforethought," vs. 4). An example follows of someone whose axehead flew off and killed someone nearby. Interestingly, Matthews notes in his commentary on Genesis 9:4–6, "Israelite tradition deemed

---

40. All references to the Qur'an from *The Holy Quran (Koran) English Translation of the Meanings* by Abdullah Yusuf Ali. From a version revised by the Presidency of Islamic Researches, IFTA, Call and Guidance. Published and Printed by the King Fahd Holy Qur'an Printing Complex in 1987. http://qurango.com/download/englishyusuf.pdf (accessed Jan. 2, 2012). Sura [chapters] and aya [verse] numbers do not match in different translations of the Qur'an. As Keith E. Swartley notes that "Qur'an versification is not standardized." He gives some direction which is useful for coping with the situation. "If the quote referenced does not match when reviewed in a Qur'an translation, refer to the adjacent verses to find the reference." Keith E. Swartley, *Encountering the World of Islam* (Downers Grove, IL: InterVarsity Press, 2005), xxxviii.

Can a Christian Defend the Death Penalty Rationally?

monetary compensation as an unacceptable penalty where malicious murder was involved (e.g. Lev 24:17; Num 35:31–34)."[41]

Building from this *ayah* 5:48, some commentators allow for such a payment. Some argue that Islam is more gracious than Judaism or Christianity. However, the situation is not so clear. Some verses of the Qur'an are unambiguous about execution for certain crimes. Consider the following from Qur'an 5:36–37:

> The punishment of those who wage war against Allah and His Apostle, and strive with might and main for mischief through the land is: Execution, or crucifixion, or the cutting off of hands and feet from opposite sides, or exile from the land: That is their disgrace in this world, and a heavy punishment is theirs in the Hereafter; Except for those who repent before they fall into your power: In that case, know that Allah is Oft-Forgiving, Most Merciful.

Those who fight against Islam deserve execution. Yet Muhammad did not consistently apply this sentence. Some he ransomed, some he released, and others he executed. Making sense of his behavior can be a case of exegesis of the pertinent *ayat* of the Qur'an. Sura 47:4 says:

> Therefore, when ye meet the Unbelievers [in fight], smite at their necks; At length, when ye have thoroughly subdued them, bind a bond firmly [on them]: thereafter [is the time for] either generosity or ransom: Until the war lays down its burdens. Thus [are ye commanded]: but if it had been Allah's Will, He could certainly have exacted retribution from them [Himself]; but [He lets you fight] in order to test you, some with others. But those who are slain in the Way of Allah, - He will never let their deeds be lost.

This passage would seem to fly in the face of 5:36.

Some focus on the relationship of 47:4 and 8:67 or 9:5. One possible explanation for the change is a verse abrogation scenario. Either 8:67 is later than 47:4, or 9:5 is earlier than 47:4. Sura 8:67 says:

> It is not fitting for a prophet that he should have prisoners of war until he hath thoroughly subdued the land. Ye look for the temporal goods of this world; but Allah looketh to the Hereafter: And Allah is Exalted in might, Wise.

If one interprets 8:67 as being later than 47:4, then Muhammad's view shifted from one of ransoming or releasing prisoners of war to executing

---

41. Mathews, *Genesis 1–11:26*, 403.

them. Presumably, earlier Muhammad had been collecting money for ransom. This was seen later to be unacceptable (it was seen as "greedy," perhaps like the ban in the O.T., according to Aken), and thus the death penalty was invoked without exception.[42]

It may be historically that this shift also came when Muhammad realized that "the people of the book" (Jews and Christians) would not support him, and some Jews went to war against him. *Ayat* in the Qur'an speak of the "people of the book"—equivocally sometimes calling them friends and saying that Muslims should befriend and protect them, and at other times calling for their extermination.

9:5 also seems to suggest a shift from the attitude of 47:4.

> But when the forbidden months are past, then fight and slay the Pagans wherever ye find them, and seize them, beleaguer them, and lie in wait for them in every stratagem [of war]; but if they repent, and establish regular prayers and practise regular charity, then open the way for them: for Allah is Oft-forgiving, Most Merciful.

It seems that again there is a shift from a more moderate position to a more harsh one.

The Qur'an assumes the death sentence for some murderers (if the victim's relatives would not accept payment). Discussions of when to apply the death sentence are more complicated. As we have seen, some prove that prisoners of war were not to have been killed, and others argue that they were.

Apostates

There is also a disagreement over whether apostates should or have ever been executed. Some argue that the punishment for apostasy is hell. Declan O'Sullivan attempts to show that many Muslim commentators deny that apostates should be executed.[43] His summary in his abstract pretty much covers what he has to say:

---

42. See Joshua 7:11ff.

43. Declan O'Sullivan, "The Interpretation of Qur'anic Text to Promote or Negate the Death penalty for Apostates and Blasphemers," in *Journal of Qur'anic Studies*, Volume 3, 63–93.

It can be argued that a clearer understanding of certain translations and interpretations of the sacred text underlying the *sharīca* can show that the established legal sentencing owes much to strong political undercurrents, as opposed to a single message revealed in only one, unequivocal interpretation of the Qur'an.[44]

The Qur'anic text at issue is 2:217:

> Nor will they cease fighting you until they turn you back from your faith if they can. And if any of you Turn back from their faith and die in unbelief, their works will bear no fruit in this life and in the Hereafter; they will be companions of the Fire and will abide therein.

O'Sullivan cites Mohammad Iqbal Siddiqi as interpreting that this verse "has recommended capital punishment for it" [apostasy].[45] This sage also says that *sunna* and the practice of the first four caliphs affirm this interpretation. Yet he also cites Mohammad Ali who says: "And neither here nor anywhere else in the Holy Qur'an is there even a hint at the infliction of capital punishment or any other punishment on the apostate."[46]

Those who say that the Qur'an does not call for the execution of the apostate say that their opponents have confused the Qur'an's call to execute those who turn in rebellion against Islam with a call to execute apostates. A first *ayah* which involves such a call is 5:36–37:

> The punishment of those who wage war against Allah and His Apostle, and strive with might and main for mischief through the land is: Execution, or crucifixion, or the cutting off of hands and feet from opposite sides, or exile from the land: That is their disgrace in this world, and a heavy punishment is theirs in the Hereafter; Except for those who repent before they fall into your power: In that case, know that Allah is Oft-Forgiving, Most Merciful.

Ayah 5:33 focuses on *hiraba* ("brigandage" or waging war). Muslims are allowed to fight and kill anyone who wages war against them. The idea is armed physical violence.

Verses 49:9–10 focus on *baghy* ("rebellion" or transgression).

---

44. http://www.euppublishing.com/doi/abs/10.3366/jqs.2001.3.2.63 (accessed Jan. 2, 2012).

45. O'Sullivan, "The Interpretation of Qur'anic Text," 64.

46. O'Sullivan, "The Interpretation of Qur'anic Text," 66.

Not Weary of Well Doing

> If two parties among the Believers fall into a quarrel, make ye peace between them: but if one of them transgresses beyond bounds against the other, then fight ye [all] against the one that transgresses until it complies with the command of Allah; but if it complies, then make peace between them with justice, and be fair: for Allah loves those who are fair [and just]. The Believers are but a single Brotherhood: So make peace and reconciliation between your two [contending] brothers; and fear Allah, that ye may receive Mercy.

The point is that Muslims are allowed to kill those who break their covenants with Muslims and thus with God. Covenant breakers give up their previous protection from attack or physical force, since they have dealt treacherously with Muslims. Marsham comments,

> What is more striking about most of the explanations in the *tafsīr*, is the emphasis placed on the dual factors of the *breaking of a covenant* and *the use of illegitimate violence* as the justification for the death penalty.[47]

At least initially, the execution of apostates was based on these ideas, though execution as a consequence of apostasy is not clearly demonstrated from the Qur'an. Later tradition, whether *hadith* or *sunna* or *tafsir*, of course, maintains the correctness of executing apostates.

Adulterers

There is no clear verse in the Qur'an to justify the execution of adulterers. The only Qur'anic text which directly speaks to the punishment of adulterers is 24:2, 3:

> The woman and the man guilty of adultery or fornication- flog each of them with a hundred stripes: Let not compassion move you in their case, in a matter prescribed by Allah, if ye believe in Allah and the Last Day: and let a party of the Believers witness their punishment. Let no man guilty of adultery or fornication marry any but a woman similarly guilty, or an Unbeliever: nor let any but such a man or an Unbeliever marry such a woman: to the Believers such a thing is forbidden.

---

47. Andrew Marsham, "Public Execution in the Umayyad period," in *Journal of Arabic and Islamic Studies* 11 (2011) 101–136, 108.

Can a Christian Defend the Death Penalty Rationally?

These *ayat* seem to suggest that only flogging is acceptable (though whether one would die from one hundred lashes might be an issue). Still it is clear that current practice allows, if not demands, the execution of adulteresses at least. This punishment cannot be based on Qur'anic text.

What Does Islamic Tradition Say?

Islamic tradition consists of stories about *hadith* (statements or actions of Muhammad not found in the Qur'an),[48] *sunna* (traditions about Muhammad and his actions handed down from the early elders),[49] and *tafsir* (commentary on the Qur'an). For the sake of clarity, I will continue to examine the same cases for which execution is demanded. Now, however, the focus will be on the role of Islamic tradition in adjudicating this dispute; i.e., when capital punishment is allowed or required.

Murderers

First, there is no doubt that the Qur'an allows capital punishment of murderers. It does allow for "retaliation" or for ransom or mercy (free release). Tradition supports this view. For our purposes, it is worth noting that there is no case for no executions, just what sort and under what conditions. There do not seem to be any Muslims who completely reject the death penalty. In a recent survey in Iran, 81 percent of respondents favored capital punishment.[50]

---

48. "*Hadith* implies the narration of a saying, or of an act, or of an approval (Taswib) of the Prophet (sws) [Muhammad – PAG], irrespective of whether the matter is authenticated or still disputed." Amin Ahsan Islahi, "Difference between *Hadith* and *Sunnah*," http://www.renaissance.com.pk/jafelif986.html (accessed Jan. 2, 2012).

49. "the *Sunnah* of the Prophet (sws)... means the way of life which the Prophet (sws) taught the people in theory and practice and for which, in his capacity as a teacher of *Shari'ah* (Islamic Law) he laid down ideal standards leading to a life which one should meet to earn Allah's approval through complete submission to His Commandments." Islahi, "Difference between *Hadith* and *Sunnah*."

50. Ghassemi, "Criminal Punishment in Islamic Societies," 171.

Not Weary of Well Doing

Apostates and Prisoners of War

I will treat these together, since they tend to be conflated in practice. As noted above, it is unclear whether the Qur'an is calling for the execution of apostates, but it is clear that Muslims may fight against and kill those who oppose or rebel against Islam and Allah. Apostates are seen as covenant breakers. They are considered to have renounced their earlier promises, and this is seen as rebellion. Usually, the tradition emphasizes that such apostates joined violent uprisings against Islam. Thus, they deserved to die in battle (the death sentence).

The *sunnah* gives mixed evidence on Muhammad's treatment of prisoners of war. After the Battle of Bakr, Muhammad apparently ransomed some of the Quraysh prisoners of war and released others. He supposedly accepted Abu Bakr's advice and rejected 'Umar's (to execute them). Yet there are two other reports that say he executed people.[51] Most modern Muslim states deny that anyone has ever been executed for apostasy. In fact, usually apostates are charged with some other crime which tradition deems worthy of death.

Mahmoud Mohammed Tasha, a Sudanese Muslim, was convicted of "heresy, opposing application of Islamic law, disturbing public security, provoking opposition against the government, and reestablishing a banned political party."[52] He had been opposing *Shari'ah* law and calling for its end. He was sentenced to death and executed, though he had done no violence. Those who would say that he did not die for being apostate or heresy say that he was guilty of disturbing the peace and inciting opposition to the government.

While some try to hide what has happened behind these terms, nothing seems worthy of a death penalty in this case. However, those who argued for his death believe that he was guilty of subverting the state, which they consider treason. Treason is still punishable by death in five American states: Arkansas California, Colorado, Georgia, and Lousiana.[53] From the Muslim point of view, opposing *Shari'a* is treason and worthy of death.

---

51. Lena Salaymeh, "Early Islamic Legal-Historical Precedents: Prisoners of War," *Law and History Review*, Fall 2008, vol. 26, no. 3, 521–544, esp. 524.

52. Robin Wright, *Sacred Rage*, 203 cited by Wikipedia, Mahmoud Mohammed Tasha, http://en.wikipedia.org/wiki/Mahmoud_Mohammed_Taha (accessed Jan. 2, 2012).

53. "Crimes Punishable by the Death Penalty," Death Penalty Information Center, http://www.deathpenaltyinfo.org/crimes-punishable-death-penalty (accessed Jan. 2, 2012).

Can a Christian Defend the Death Penalty Rationally?

(Islamic republics are theocratic states. They operate with the law of God (*Sharia*) as the law of the state.)

There are some Christians who advocate a similar view, Theonomists such as Greg Bahnsen and Rousas John Rushdoony. These people hold a strong Continuity view between the Old and New Testament and would have the "Kingdom of God" on earth use the Mosaic Law as civil law;" e.g., homosexuals should be executed.[54]

While to most Christians this is a ridiculous extreme, to many Muslims this sort of theocratic state is in fact the "Kingdom of God" on earth. Again, in the recent survey in Iran, most respondents agreed or strongly agreed that *Sharia* was preferable to Western type law systems.[55]

Muslims claim that no one is executed for apostasy, but in practice people are. Another man awaiting execution for apostasy is Pastor Youcef Nadarkhani in Iran. When Western activists opposed this Christian pastor's death sentence for apostasy, Islamic jurists announced a "clarification of his charges":

> After being convicted of apostasy — the crime of abandoning a religion — Iranian courts gave Pastor Nadarkhani five chances to repent. If he converted to Islam, authorities told Nadarkhani that he would be free. Nadarkhani refused all five times.[56]

---

54. Rousas John Rushdoony, *Institutes of Biblical Law* (Philipsburg, NJ: Presbyterian and Reformed, 1980). "Bahnsen declares, 'Jesus bound us. . . to every jot and tittle of the Old Testament legislation of God's will, not allowing us to subtract even the least commandment' (221). 'Jesus warned against dismissing even the least Old Testament commandment,. . . Not a single law, word, or stroke can be violated with impunity. . .' (99). 'Christ did not intend to have the slightest stroke of that law altered' (121). 'Matthew 5:17–19, for instance, teaches the abiding validity of every Old Testament precept. . .' (165)." All quotations taken from Greg L. Bahnsen, *By This Standard: The Authority of God's Law Today* (Tyler, TX: Institute for Christian Economics, 1985), as cited in John W. Robbins, "Will the Real Greg Bahnsen Please Stand Up?" in *The Trinity Review*, August 1992.

55. "The majority of the respondents, in spite of the significant difference between men and women, believe that Islam has the best rules for combating crimes. In the respondents' view Islam is something more than a religion which is to regulate the spiritual relationship between individuals and God. Islam, as a formal ideology of the state in Iran, is utilized as the legitimate base of public policy making." Ghassemi, "Criminal Punishment in Islamic Societies," 178.

56. Daniel Tovrov, "Youcef Nadarkhani Still in Danger: Ayatollah Khamenei to be his Final Judge," Monday, October 10, 2011 5:24 PM EDT, International Business Times.com, http://www.ibtimes.com/articles/228459/20111010/youcef-nadarkhani.htm (accessed Dec. 29, 2011).

Not Weary of Well Doing

In early October 2011, "Iran denied that Nadarkhani was ever convicted of apostasy, and claimed that he had been found guilty of rape, conspiracy and Zionism."[57]

This strategy is used by Islamic states to deny that anyone is executed for their faith or lack of it. However, the reality is that Islamic states see apostasy as seditious and treasonous, and particularly the actions that accompany it, such as opposing *Shari'a* law or spreading "anti-Islamic" propaganda.

As long as Islamic tradition, or *Shari'a*, is the deciding factor in whether an "apostate" dies or not, it seems that apostasy is in fact a capital offense. In effect, Islamic republics are similar (though much worse statistically to those who oppose them) to Calvin's Geneva or the Byzantine Empire. Wherever the conflation of the authority of church and state is practiced, such as in some Roman Catholic states [e.g. medieval papal states] and in Eastern Orthodox states [e.g. Stefan Nemanja's Serbian Grand Principality (*Rascia*)], religious dissent will result in persecution, if not execution.[58]

Adulterers

As we have seen, the Qur'an does not assign the death penalty to adulterers, and yet adulterers, and especially adulteresses, have been executed. Those who defend Shari'a law will say that the Qur'an is foundational, but the *hadith* and *sunna* allow for execution of adulterers of both sexes.

Marc Baer says in "Death in the Hippodrome" that "Mehmet IV was the only sultan to order an adulteress to be executed by stoning during 465 years of Ottoman rule in Istanbul."[59] Despite the popular, usual practice of monetary payments, Mehmet IV condemned this woman to stoning. He did it in contradiction to all common practice for hundreds of years.

---

57. Tovrov, "Youcef Nadarkhani Still in Danger."

58. Stephen Nemanja cut out the tongue of the leader of the Bogomils in the latter half of the twelfth century and his son, Sava, the founder of the Serbian Orthodox Church, also persecuted them in the thirteenth century. D. Obolensky, *The Bogomils* (Cambridge: Cambridge University Press), 1948, 284, as cited in Andrew P. Roach. "The competition for souls: Sava of Serbia and consumer choice in religion in the thirteenth century Balkans." Glasnik 50(1) 2006, http://eprints.gla.ac.uk/3786/1/Glasnik_article.pdf (accessed May 11, 2012).

59. Marc Baer, "Death in the Hippodrome: Sexual politics and legal culture in the reign of Mehmet IV," *Past and Present*, no. 210 (Feb. 2011): 61–91, esp. 61, http://past.oxfordjournals.org/content/210/1/61.short (accessed Nov. 24, 2011).

Can a Christian Defend the Death Penalty Rationally?

There was no reference to *Shari'a* at all in Mehmet's order. Baer cites several pragmatic factors that likely determined Mehmet's action, which we will deal with in the next section.

Sakineh Mohammadi Ashtiani, an Iranian woman, was accused of adultery and sentenced to death in 2009. She supposedly had sex with her husband's killer. She claims that she was raped. When Western pressure came to bear on Iran, her sentence was changed from adultery to conspiracy to murder; i.e., that she worked with the murderer to kill her husband.

> Iranian authorities originally accused Ashtiani of "illicit" affairs with two men and sentenced her to 99 lashings, a punishment that was later changed to stoning. After public pressure from the international community, new murder charges against Ashtiani emerged.[60]

Though there has been a temporary stay, she will still likely hang.

What Does Islamic Reason Say?

There are attempts to justify capital punishment in Islam via Islamic jurisprudence, which is a combination of legal and canon law. Qur'an, *hadith*, *sunna*, and *tafsir* are consulted. The historical precedents are considered. Reasons are given for decisions, condemnations, and legal sentences of death, but they probably will never be seen as "reasonable" to Westerners.

While Islam has a very glorious philosophical tradition, those who went too far afield from *Shari'a* had difficulties. For instance, Ghazali opposed Ibn Rushd or Averroes for his introduction of Aristotelian philosophy into Islamic thinking. Some Islamic states are attempting to "modernize." However, other Islamic states which modernized too fast, such as Iran and Northern Sudan, have undergone reversals with a more strict application of *Shari'a*.[61]

Any justification of a punishment in such a society must come from the Qur'an, *hadith*, *sunna*, or *tafsir*. The arguments and reasoning of Islamic jurists will seem at best arcane and irrelevant and strained, if not medieval, to Western critics.

---

60. Khristina Narizhnaya, "Iranian woman Sakineh Mohammadi Ashtiani charged with adultery, murder, will likely die by hanging," Wednesday, November 03, 2010 NY Daily News, http://articles.nydailynews.com/2010-11-03/news/27080171_1_murder-charges-iranian-woman-stoning (accessed Jan. 2, 2012).

61. Ghassemi, "Criminal Punishment in Islamic Societies," 174.

Murderers

Though the Qur'an and tradition allow for ransom or release, "philosophical and pragmatic considerations" have overruled Qur'anic text and tradition at various points in Muslim history and in various places. *Taazir*, punishments determined by Islamic judges and legislators, may involve the death penalty for instances other than those contained in the Qur'an or *sunna*. Recently, Iranian Islamic legislators "introduced the death penalty as *Taazir* of some crimes (especially drug offences)."[62] The majority of respondents in Ghassemi's survey of 810 Iranians felt that the death penalty was deserved for infractions of the Qur'an (*hudud*), that it was necessary for some crimes and some criminals. Eighty-one percent agreed that capital punishment was necessary. The majority felt as well that *Shari'a* was superior to other forms of law, including Western ones.

A place where "Western" reasoning might begin here is with the fact that the majority of respondents in Ghassemi's survey felt overall that *Shari'a* was good, *though they felt that it should respond to modern criticism and adapt to today's circumstances.* Such modern criticism is largely Western, although there are also Muslim dissidents who argue against *Shari'a*, such as Mahmoud Mohammed Tasha of Sudan. One must believe that those willing to answer Ghassemi's survey did so advisedly. They may not openly "criticize" *Shari'a*, but can they suggest that it be more flexible, more modern, maybe even more democratic?

We can only speculate what sort of changes such respondents hoped for, but women surveyed showed concern for adultery laws. Ghassemi notes, "According to the current Islamic Penal Code a man who finds his wife committing *Zina* (adultery) with another man may kill both (adulteress and adulterer) if he knows that his wife is willingly committing it."[63]

Apostates

We have touched on the plight of apostates above. It seems that there is no "reason" here. Those who reject Islam reject God's law and his covenant. Not only is this a religious act, it is a civil act. Since the state is theocratic, to reject the religion is to reject the state. To reject the state is treason.

---

62. Ghassemi, "Criminal Punishment in Islamic Societies," 164.
63. Ghassemi, "Criminal Punishment in Islamic Societies," 170.

Can a Christian Defend the Death Penalty Rationally?

Facing the criticism of the West, Islamic states have either changed the sentences or simply given sentences which are capital offenses apart from apostasy or heresy. While we in the West may be aghast at this, our own history is not so void of what we criticize in Islamic states. The Inquisition in Spain under Ferdinand and Isabella, the burning of Servetus in Calvin's Geneva, or Henry the VIII's burning of Thomas Cranmer, Thomas Ridley, and Hugh Latimer show that even Christian states can descend to similar behavior.

Freedom of religion or confession is a relatively modern notion. It exists in the Muslim mind only insofar as the notion that non-Muslims living in a Muslim state do not need to convert. However, there is no freedom to spread one's faith if one is not a Muslim, nor is there freedom for Muslims to convert to another faith.[64]

Prisoners of War

Islam teaches that the Qur'an and the *sunna* enjoin Muslim forces to be kind to captured warriors. *Sunna* has several stories of Muhammad's kindness towards prisoners of war, including ransom and release. Practice would appear to be a bit more complicated, however. Ivo Andric's novel, *The Bridge on the Drina*, and Ivan Vazov's novel, *Under the Yoke*, tell of the brutal treatment that the Ottoman Turks gave any Slavs who rebelled. Impaling and beheading were common.[65] Of course, violence by Christians against Muslims had been committed earlier during the Crusades.

Current day apologists for Islam argue that the Qur'anic teaching and the *sunna* are still followed; no foreign prisoners of war are mistreated or tortured or killed.[66] They cite sura 76:8: "And they feed, for the love of

---

64. Consider, for instance, Qatar. "Expatriate believers are allowed to practice their faith, but Qatari Christians risk arrest or worse. Government policy strictly limits Christian gatherings. Proselytism of Muslims is forbidden. Expatriates have been expelled in recent years for evangelizing Qataris. Criticism of the Muslim faith or the ruling family is a crime. There were no known Qatari believers before 1985, but several have come to the Lord outside the country and have suffered upon return to Qatar. Christians are treated as second-class citizens." "Qatar. Restricted Nations," Persecution.com, http://www.persecution.com/public/restrictednations.aspx?clickfrom=bWFpbl9tZW51 (accessed May 11, 2012).

65. Ivo Andrić, *The Bridge on the Drina* (New York: Macmillan, 1959) and Ivan Minchov Vazov, *Under the Yoke* (New York: Twayne Publishers, 1971).

66. "Treatment of prisoners of war in Islam," Arab News, Dec. 22, 2011, http://arab-news.com/lifestyle/islam/article552098.ece (accessed Jan. 2, 2012).

Allah, the indigent, the orphan, and the captive." They also cite Muhammad's gracious treatment of prisoners of war. However, they do admit that some prisoners warrant death, if guilty of serious crimes. The issue is who decides what such a crime is.

In the past, Muslim rulers have used capital punishment as a deterrent and as a factor to strike terror into both Muslim and non-Muslim constituencies. Violence, especially deadly violence, is a way to maintain control. Baer cites one of Sultan Mehmet IV's contemporaries, Chinese emperor K'ang-his, who wrote:

> Giving life to people and killing people—those are the powers that the emperor has. . . . He knows, too, that sometimes people have to be persuaded into morality by the example of an execution.[67]

Such pragmatic concerns are not merely for the seventeenth century in some rulers' views. Mehmet followed the policy of "better to be feared than loved." He made examples of many who opposed him by executing them.

Though the following example is not specifically one of execution, it shows how some Islamic rulers use violence as a deterrent to terrify the populace. Ismael Khalif Abdulle, a Somali man of 17, was cross amputated by al Shabaab in Somalia. He was arrested and held without explanation. Then he and three other boys were accused of stealing guns and cell phones. His protests of innocence were ignored. He and the other boys had no legal counsel. Ismael says that the judge "said we were guilty as spies and thieves, and that under sharia law a hand and a foot must be amputated."[68]

Ismael managed miraculously to escape after the cross amputation and made his way to Kenya, where he lives in a safe house. The writer of the story, Xan Rice, says, "His story offers a rare insight into how the Shabaab is using its extreme interpretation of Islam to establish order through fear—and to find recruits."[69]

---

67. Baer, "Death in the Hippodrome," 89.

68. Xan Rice, "Somali schoolboy tells of how Islamists cut off his leg and hand," *The Guardian*, Oct. 20, 2010, http://www.guardian.co.uk/world/2010/oct/20/somali-islamists-schoolboy-amputation-ordeal (accessed Dec 28, 2011).

69. Rice, "Somali schoolboy tells of how Islamists cut off his leg and hand."

Adulterers

Baer's article is a fascinating tale of how Mehmet IV ordered the execution of a supposed adulteress and her partner, a Jewish man, in 1680 in Istanbul during the Ottoman Empire. As we noted above, the usual Ottoman custom regarding enforcement of sexual mores was lax, allowing for monetary fines in place of corporal punishments, without insistence on capital punishment.

The woman's protests of innocence should have spared her. Her punishment, according to the Qur'an, was one hundred lashes. The Jewish man would normally have been able to pay his way out of the flogging at half the rate of a Muslim (since non-Muslims were not expected by the Turks to be virtuous in any event). However, Mehmet IV approved of and witnessed their executions.

There were many pragmatic factors affecting Mehmet's decision. Few of them had anything to do directly with strict interpretation of the Qur'an. First, Mehmet had ascended the throne at seven, only to be controlled by his grandmother and mother as regents. His father had been ineffectual and likewise controlled by royal women. In fact, women had controlled the Sultans for several decades. When he reached maturity, Mehmet had to demonstrate that he was powerful over women.

Being able to order the stoning of an adulteress allowed him to show any possible female contenders that he was serious about hanging onto his throne. He was the alpha male.

Second, being seen to uphold virtue allowed him to curry favor with the Kadızadeli, clerics who were in favor of reforming the lax standards in the Ottoman Empire and making them conform to Qur'an and *sunna*. These clerics were allies that he needed in his maintenance of power. They also gave him a lever to use against his opponents. He may also have been genuinely influenced by their teaching.

Third, he faced growing dislike of Jews and potential threat from the Jewish community. Shabbattai Zevi declared himself messiah in Smyrna in 1648. Zevi gathered many followers from all over Europe and into Ukraine. Finally, he was called before the Sultan in 1660 and given the choice of death or conversion, upon which he converted.

Mehmet, on one hand, could be seen as gracious; he allowed Zevi and others to convert. On the other hand, Mehmet needed to be able to maintain a new policy of driving Jews out of the center of Istanbul and driving them out of the Port itself. The head physician to the Sultan was a Jew who converted. Almost all doctors had been Jews. Baer notes:

> Whereas Jewish physicians had outnumbered Muslims by three to one, by 1680 Muslims (mainly converts to Islam) outnumbered Jews by five to one. The Jewish elite never regained the privileged political position at the Ottoman court that it had lost by that year.[70]

The Jews were getting too powerful and too wealthy. Mehmet's offers of conversion or death facilitated his task of conquering his own empire.

Mehmet was to be seen as "gracious," since he offered the Jewish man, caught in adultery, the opportunity to convert to Islam before his execution. In this way, the Jewish man would go to heaven and he would only be beheaded, rather than suffering a worse form of execution. Some of the other choices were the "cow" (a tub filled with molten lead in which one was thrown), immolation, or trampling by elephants.

Most forms of execution had been accepted as *Taazir*, but they have no Qur'anic foundation or even *sunna* support. Most had been inherited from the Ancient Near Eastern cultures, such as the Sumerians, the Hebrews, and the pre-Islamic Arab tribes and Iranians.

Finally Mehmet, as we mentioned above, simply needed to terrorize his populace. His reign had always been a struggle. He had to escape the Port to assert his Sultancy. He had to fight all over the known world to prove that he was Sultan material. He was losing his grip, and his defeat by Jan Sobeiski at the gates of Vienna was the last proverbial nail in his coffin. Capital punishment was a deterrent to rebellion. But draconian measures can only suffice so far.[71]

Conclusion

I have asked three questions throughout this essay: 1. What does Scripture say? What does tradition say? What does reason say? Both Christian and Muslim thinkers use these three questions, though of course they turn to different holy books and traditions, and they employ different sorts of reason.

On the one hand, it is clear that the sort of clerical or religious reasoning that is involved in interpreting the sacred text, comparing it with

---

70. Baer, "Death in the Hippodrome," 87.
71. Baer, "Death in the Hippodrome," 90, 91.

Can a Christian Defend the Death Penalty Rationally?

received tradition and making some attempt to apply more robust philosophical reasoning in the realm of faith, is not unique to Christians or Muslims. (I'm sure it is true also of Reform, Conservative, and Orthodox Jews.) In each faith, there are those who are conservative or orthodox and turn to their sacred writ and received tradition. There are also those who are broader than their mere received tradition, such as Aquinas and Averroes (Ibn Rushd).

My concern was to evaluate the Reformed, Evangelical Christian case for capital punishment. In my view, it fails, since it insists on a faulty or tenuous interpretation of the sacred text, Genesis 9:5, 6. It fails because it ignores or discounts reasonable criticisms. It fails because it is blind or at least inattentive to cries for justice and against discrimination. What is frightening is that believers from both Christian and Muslim faiths can fall into a sort of autopilot that simply accepts received tradition without much consideration. As long as we are among the favored, we will not likely care much about the minorities who suffer discrimination.

Most disturbing is the idea that neither deterrence nor discrimination matter much. These are merely areas for reform of the judicial system. No real concern or empathy seems to be evinced for the folks who will suffer just because they are black. It is true that the criminal deserves punishment, whatever his color, but it seems callous to believe that anything will change in the "Death Belt," those American states with the highest incidence of the execution of African Americans: Florida, Georgia, Alabama, Mississippi, Louisiana, and Texas.[72]

Even if deterrence is inconclusive, surely that is no reason to say that capital punishment should go ahead. Granted, Reformed, Evangelical Christians feel that they have biblical sanction for their view of capital punishment, but then Muslims in Islamic republics also believe that their holy book and tradition sanction capital punishment on their terms in their ways. Merely referring to one's holy book will not resolve this issue. We must ask the question of Wilhelm Gottfried Liebniz: Which holy book? It is an apologetic question and it will have to be answered irenically, but firmly and carefully.

So how can Christians answer the Muslim cleric who maintains that the death penalty is sanctioned by his holy book? I think we must work to understand his position and attempt to show him that we do understand

---

72. Sarah Oppenheim, "Capital Punishment in the United States," http://www.wcl.american.edu/hrbrief/spring98/html/death.html (accessed May 11, 2012).

him and his position. However, in the end, a battle of holy books and traditions and prophets will likely not end well.

On the one hand, Evangelical Christians and traditional Muslims may understand each other better than postmoderns will understand traditional Muslims. We understand the role of faith and holy books, prophets and tradition. However, we will need to appeal to "natural law" in our dealings with Muslims, other religionists, postmoderns, and nonbelievers. We must look for principles in Scripture (the Bible) which apply to all humankind.

We must appeal to "common sense," for terrorizing one's populace can only last so long before there will be a rebellion. We must focus on what being human essentially is. We may agree that being human is to be religious, but being human is also much more. Humanity has a day-to-day, pragmatic component as well. Appealing to religious sentiment and even religious duty will only go so far in coercing obedience before resentment sets in. We must focus on natural law, human rights and humanity: loving our families, caring for others, generosity, kindness, the arts; those things which make us other than beasts or worse.

Muslims emphasize that they are required to give alms and do good. Christians have similar obligations. Let us unite together to care for those who are dispossessed. We need to find a way to focus on the human rights of each person. While emphasizing that this term "human rights" may not be recognized by some, we have an innate sense that each person is unique and worthy of respect. We all love our children, unless we are mentally ill by any standard.

Support for capital punishment can be found among Christians, Jews, and Muslims. At the same time, it seems that there have always been dissenting voices in each tradition. If each person is created in the image of God, is that not more reason to preserve that life and seek its reformation? More often than not, capital punishment is an easy way out of a more expensive and difficult problem. No one should lose his life for pragmatic reasons.

While the heated debate about capital punishment will continue in the United States, at least one thing is sure: the cost of appeals to higher courts makes trying capital cases extremely expensive. As we have seen, it is less expensive to incarcerate convicted criminals for life than to try them on appellate levels in order to secure a death sentence. Many American states are accepting that this is an economic necessity. Thus, fewer executions are going forward.

Can a Christian Defend the Death Penalty Rationally?

Concerns about the humane character of various forms of execution also are under discussion, concerning whether they are painless or whether they are in fact a form of torture. We all realize that tormenting or torturing people, even convicted criminals, is wrong. All agree that justice must be served by legally constituted bodies and not by individuals or vigilantes.

What is not so clear is what our options are. Pragmatically, economically, incarceration for life is becoming the norm. Ethically this would seem to be a preferable alternative to capital punishment, especially when there is still evident discrimination in trials and sentencing and when there continues to be false evidence admitted in murder trials. The pressure to get a conviction and a death sentence for a high profile case is immense on law enforcement agencies and public prosecutors. This is not to be unkind. These are facts.

The story of the West Memphis Three is telling. Damien Echols, Jason Baldwin, and Jessie Misskelley Jr., were sentenced to prison—Echols to await execution following appeals, and Baldwin and Misskelley for life—when they were linked by investigators to a bizarre triple murder of young boys who were found naked and tied hand and foot. Public outcry demanded justice. Echols was a drifter and a "Goth," and he and the other two were accused of killing the three boys in a satanic ritual. A "confession" by Misskelley (later recanted and not officially used) led to their conviction along with hearsay evidence that people heard them plotting.

Finally, after many failed appeals, DNA evidence was found which showed that there was no genetic material from any of the three at the crime scene. Campbell Robertson of the New York Times reported:

> Over the years, appeals failed, as did post-conviction hearings, but the case got new life in 2007 when defense lawyers representing Mr. Echols reported that new forensic tests of evidence at the crime scene turned up no genetic material belonging to any of the men.[73]

A bizarre arrangement requiring so-called Alford pleas (admitting guilt while asserting one's innocence) were allowed. The judge then sentenced them to the time they had served in prison (18 years and 78 days) along with a suspended ten-year sentence. It is hard to believe that this was a way to lessen national pressure to release Echols. The facts seem clear:

---

73. Cambell Robertson, "Deal Frees 'West Memphis Three' in Arkansas," *New York Times*, August 19, 2011, http://www.nytimes.com/2011/08/20/us/20arkansas.html?pagewanted=2&_r=1 (accessed May 6, 2012).

investigators and prosecutors needed a quick conviction. Public outcry was rife. A conviction was obtained. However, it was wrong. These men wasted almost two decades in prison, not because DNA evidence convicted them, but because there was too much pressure on investigators and prosecutors to get justice.

While this may seem like a single case and one which would not likely be repeated, I challenge that idea. Mankind does not change. We are enraged by such crimes. We want justice, but we become blind to facts when we want justice quickly. We cannot resurrect those whom we execute. At least, if we have not executed them and they are later found innocent, we have not taken their lives, even if we have taken years of their lives (for which many are not even remunerated). These cases are not as rare as we might think. A brief glance at the website of the Center on Wrongful Convictions of the Northwestern University School of Law shows that it is not.

Even if we have a few verses from our holy book and the backing of our tradition, and our arguments seem persuasive to us, are we so sure that we have correctly assessed the situation that we are prepared to argue that "occasional miscarriages of justice" (people who die due to discrimination in trial and sentencing or who are convicted in a rush) are insignificant? If a person is created in the image of God, should we not be prepared to protect that life, even the life of a convicted criminal? Moses did not die. David did not die. Paul did not die.

Life imprisonment is favored by the majority of Americans. It is cheaper than the alternative of nearly endless appeals. Life imprisonment cannot take life that it cannot give back. Life imprisonment would seem, then, for all of these reasons, to be a better choice than capital punishment.

Contributors

Ellis R. Brotzman, PhD, New York University, New York, USA

Edward M. Curtis, PhD, University of Pennsylvania, Pennsylvania, USA

Gerald C. Ericson, DMin, Dallas Theological Seminary, Texas, USA

Philip A. Gottschalk, PhD, *Katholieke Universiteit Leuven (Louvain)*, Belgium

Peter J. Hays, PhD, Dallas Theological Seminary, Texas, USA

Thomas J. Marinello, PhD, *Evangelische Theologische Faculteit*, Belgium

Jordan M. Scheetz, Dr. theol., *Evangelisch-Theologische Fakultät der Universität Wien*, Austria.

H. H. Drake Williams III, PhD, University of Aberdeen, United Kingdom

www.ingramcontent.com/pod-product-compliance
Lightning Source LLC
Chambersburg PA
CBHW062000220426
43662CB00011B/1763